SANATANA DHARMA

THE PATHWAY TO A HAPPY LIFE

Edited by Jaganniwas Iyer
Preface by Sudesh K Verma

Vitasta
LET KNOWLEDGE SPREAD

Published by
Vitasta Publishing Pvt Ltd
2/15, Ansari Road, Daryaganj
New Delhi-110 002
info@vitastapublishing.com

ISBN 978-93-90961-99-3

First Edition 2022

Originally published as Sanatana Dharma: An Advanced Text Book Of Hindu Religion and Ethics Published by the Board of Trustees Central Hindu College, Benares, 1904.

MRP ₹599

Typeset & Cover Design by Somesh Kumar Mishra
Printed by Vikas Computer and Printers, New Delhi

सत्यमेव जयते नानृतम् ॥

उत्तिष्ठत जाग्रत प्राप्य वरान्निबोधत ॥

CONTENTS

PREFACE

The westernised educated youth in India today finds it difficult to identify himself or herself with the Sanatan Dharm. For him, being a Hindu is to chant those mantras that appear mumbo jumbos, worship in temples without being pious or keeping the temples clean. They are still guided by the stereotype that depicts worship, priests and temples. They find the humane aspects missing.

As society progresses from liberalism to neo-liberalism and various *-isms* come to dominate the thought process in the name of humanity, the essence of Sanatan Dharm or Hinduism is lost on them. It is only after some serious study of their culture and tradition that they would know that Sanatan Dharm encompasses the ideology of neo-humanism that seeks to value all animals and plants. Environmental consciousness and respect of all live forms has always been integral to Sanatan Dharm.

Sanatan in English means 'eternal or timeless' and *dharm* refers to 'duty, obligations, truth or righteousness'. Sanatan Dharm, in reality, is nothing but a way of existence that evolved with evolution of humans into higher consciousness. In the process of this evolution, from the hunting stage to a settled existence, humans were confronted with various difficulties. As the solutions came up, people started weaving moral narrative to make the act of living better and more meaningful.

Hence, Sanatan Dharm is an embodiment of this evolutionary process which makes it all the more necessary to understand the underlying principles behind every tenet of Sanatan Dharm. Sanatan Dharm is eternal; that means it has no end. But it also does not have an origin. No one is credited as originator unlike other religious orders where the messages from heaven came through a messenger. It is the constant evolution and revelations of human possibilities from Adi to Anant. Therefore, it is as old as the civilization itself.

We often end up confusing things when we try to equate dharm with religion. Religion is rituals and practices and ways to propitiate the Almighty God. Dharm is one's duty as a part of the cosmic order. Since Sanatan Dharm does not emanate from the Books, it is difficult for adherents of the Books to appreciate the finer points of the ever constant factor that is evolution. A Book is a final account of what civilization is and how people should behave. A Book has a beginning and historicity. And if any Book is considered as final, it would lead to an end of the evolutionary process of civilization.

Human existence and life are forever evolving. Sanatan Dharm justifies evolution and seeks to rationalize the responses. It does not debunk any path that tries to offer solution to the meaning of life and death but tries to find solution by any means available. Why one is born? Why one dies? What happens between death and birth? What is the meaning of human existence? How can one live fuller life? These are the questions that the philosophical aspects of Sanatan Dharm seek to address.

This explains why Sanatan Dharm is not opposed to any religion. It believes that all religious paths or rituals try to reach the Truth. Therefore, rituals should not become the reason for conflict in society. If religions are various paths to realize God with none in a position to claim, it has solutions to all issues facing mankind, any religious belief cannot claim to be Supremacist.

Sanatan Dharm is not supremacist and believes that man is always a seeker, a wanderer. One may stay in society but one is constantly trying to find meaning of their life. All the texts including the Vedas, the Smritis, the Puranas are repositories of knowledge and define human existence. What is considered religious texts such as *The Ramayana* and *The Mahabharata* actually talk about life and the values that should govern society. To those who are unaware of the Hindu tradition would take these to be morality plays where the protagonists try to establish dharm, which is righteousness.

Every religion tries to propound who made the universe. Who made lives and various creatures? There must be someone very powerful with infinite imagination and energy to have created different forms of lives. It cannot be automatic. There must be someone. Sanatan Dharm believes in the infallibility of the Vedas which have come directly from the mouth of God i.e., Brahma. The contents of the Vedas are supposed to be indisputable. When we talk of Vedic literature, we talk of all the texts that came up while explaining or adding to the Vedas.

In Sanatan Dharm, it is the Trinity that dominates the Universe. The Trinity in which Lord Brahma is the creator, Lord Vishnu is the preserver and Lord Shiva is the destroyer. The power that dominates the living—physical prowess, learning and wealth are respectively depicted by three Goddesses; Durga, Saraswati and Lakshmi. This denotes that the Sanatan Dharm conceptualized the primacy and powers of women. These are all functional Goddesses which guide human evolution.

Sanatan Dharm takes everyone, every life as embodiment of God, the ultimate Brahman, and takes the world as one family. This embodies the oft quoted expression "vasudhaiva kutumbakam" (the whole world is a family). It is this feeling that was used by Swami Vivekanand in his Chicago Address at the World's Parliament of Religion on 11 September 1893: "Sisters and brothers of America". This was the address that got him applause and standing ovation of world religious representatives for two full minutes. Those who claimed to speak of tolerance and brotherhood had not heard such an address before. The most used address has been 'ladies and gentleman'. But such non-committal address fails to define the link people have.

To quote further from his address, he said: "I am proud to belong to a religion which has taught the world both tolerance and universal acceptance....We believe not only in universal toleration, but we accept all religions as true. I am proud to belong to a nation which has sheltered the persecuted and the refugees of all religions and all nations of the earth."

While giving his concluding address he did not mince words to criticize those who talk of supremacist religion. "Much has been said of the common ground of religious unity. I am not going just now to venture my own theory. But if anyone here hopes that this unity will come by the triumph of any one of the religions and the destruction of the others, to him I say, "Brother, yours is an impossible hope." Do I wish that the Christian would become Hindu? God forbid. Do I wish that the Hindu or Buddhist would become Christian? God forbid."

He further added: "The seed is put in the ground, and earth and air and water are placed around it. Does the seed become the earth, or the air, or the water? No. It becomes a plant. It develops after the law of its own growth, assimilates the air, the earth, and the water, converts them into plant substance, and grows into a plant. Similar is the case with religion. The Christian is not to become a Hindu or a Buddhist, nor a Hindu or a Buddhist to become a Christian. But each must assimilate the spirit of the others and yet preserve his individuality and grow according to his own law of growth."

This, in essence sums up the beauty of the Sanatan Dharm that treats all religious beliefs as different paths to realize God. "Ekam Sat Vipra Bahudha Vadanti" which means Truth is One, and there are various ways to reach the Truth or There is One God and people have various ways to worship Him. And what is God? He is nothing but the Truth. The air we breathe, the water we drink, the Earth that makes our bodies are all embodiments of God. The sense of touch, taste, vision are all manifestations of human existence.

Sanatan tradition believes in soul and life after death. The karma theory is based on the concept of birth and rebirth. This keeps the relevance of Dharm alive. If one were to just take birth and die, there was no reason to follow the righteous path. But bad deeds in this life can destroy the next birth. The purpose of soul is to find salvation which is to ultimately merge with the Brahman. *Atma* into Brahman or *param atman* or *parmatma*. This keeps one involved in the constant process of seeking knowledge and improving existence. The concept of soul, rebirth, sin and pious deeds emanate from the philosophy that has tried to give answers to some of these questions.

The Bhagavad Gita is the philosophical text that tries to answer the concept of soul and human existence. Only after one knows and appreciates the temporariness of individual human lives and the relative permanence of society that one would be goaded to a life full of action. This book is, therefore, the philosophy of life and action.

Most scriptures or religious books that expound the theory of Sanatan Dharm have tried to define human sufferings and ways to overcome them. The Rishis were the ones who analyzed and explained the Vedas. Lord Krishna said in the "Bhagavad Gita" that all paths lead to God, the final truth.

Some people often try to equate Sanatan Dharm with rituals and religious beliefs. They confuse form with substance. They see uneducated priests performing puja in temples and start believing that this is Hinduism. The priests performing the religious duties may not actually know what Hinduism is. Often they chant mantras without knowing the meaning. Most mantras are ways to respect Nature because of their beneficial aspects for living beings.

Our youth should not lose sight of the fact that long before science could say anything, the Vedas had conceptualised that the Earth was round and that the Earth revolved around the Sun and that the Sun was a part of the galaxy. They must appreciate that our ancestors had better wisdom and knowledge and we can ridicule them at our own peril. We should never forget that Aryabhat who flourished during the Gupta period was an eminent mathematician and astronomer who calculated the circumference of the Earth. He excelled in Trigonometry.

Younger generation finds it difficult to identify with rituals or the way priests try to present religious worship to them. But rituals are not the essence of Sanatan Dharm. The beauty of Hinduism is liberalism, tolerance and love for humanity. If one is born into this Sanatan tradition and believes in being a seeker, one should not get confused with the rituals that priests indulge in without knowing the purpose or meaning of the rituals. It is most of the times abracadabra.

One may not go to temple or perform religious rituals, yet one would be Hindu if one is born in the Sanatan tradition and acquires those moral virtues that keep society moving. Parents are often equated with God because one has come into the world due to them. After the Creator who created life, the place of parents is important. But equally important is the position of Guru (the teacher) who gives awareness about the universe and ways to deal with it. We have often heard the famous quote from Kabir Das: "Guru Govind dono Khade, kake lagu paye; Balihari Guru apne Govind diyo batao" (If both the God, the creator, and the Guru are present at one place whose feet one should touch first. Kabir Das says it is the Guru because he is the one who taught who the God is). He represented the true Sanatan tradition and criticized organised religion while stressing on righteousness.

So while trying to understand or analyse Hinduism or Santan Dharm, one must not be guided by the narrative being peddled by those who confuse form with substance. Supremacist religions cannot comprehend the liberty and tolerance that Sanatan Dharm propagates for others. Like there are different flowers in a bouquet, various religious beliefs and practices are ways of humans to define existence and find salvation. There is no opposition or enmities.

Sanatan Dharm, one will find, is the most accommodative. This explains why many other religious faiths came to India and did not face any hostility. The philosophy that animated a true follower of Sanatan Dharm is *Datta, Dayadhvam, Damyata* (be self-controlled, be charitable and be compassionate to all mankind). No wonder the Supreme Court defined Hinduism as a way of life.

As we step into a new world, Sanatan Dharm will find increasing resonance with those who wish to understand religion and its purpose in life. This is because Sanatan Dharm is humanity in action: It is not prescriptive and gives individuals the liberty to be seekers and find their own enlightenment. It rather guides people to attain higher levels of spiritual discovery.

Sanatan Dharm falls under the realm of culture and tradition. With the changing times, we seem to be too engrossed in our silos of individual growth and achievements and tend to ignore or even ridicule the tradition. To be Western is the trend, without realising that the philosophical tradition of the West is trying to discover the beauty of Sanatan Dharm—an all-inclusive way of life that is not based on envy, mistrust or hatred.

We have started to ridicule the family way of existence, the various forms of Gods and Goddesses associated with the Sanatan tradition. It is now fashionable to laugh at the practices of our culture without trying to find out the reasons. For instance, people in ancient India worshipped trees and other aspects of nature because they were acutely aware of the importance of environmental balance and what the imbalance could lead to. In modern times, we have understood the importance of trees for human existence. Before ridiculing our ancestors for Totemism, we must learn to investigate and find out the purpose these served. It is not that they were less intelligent than us. The Vedas would reveal that.

Indifference or abhorrence to anything associated with Sanatan Dharm is because we often commit the mistake of looking at our own culture through the prism of the West. Empty knowledge is a dangerous thing. The more you try to know and discover, the more impressed you will get with the beauty of the intellectual pursuit that was associated with the Sanatan Tradition.

It all started with the British who concluded that unless mechanism was found to delink proud Indians from their Sanatan tradition, they would not be able to conquer India fully. Lord Macaulay introduced the English system of education to create people who would be Indians in colour but British in mannerism, tastes, and thinking.

Systematically, the English education led to collapse of the education system imparted in Sanskrit—a system that had created men of steel with high moral values who understood the way society runs and the finer purpose of their own existence. They could not be easily swayed by outside influence and stressed on learning and intellectual achievements. They could die easily for the motherland since they knew none was immortal. Amidst abundance, their needs were not too high. Sanskrit language, the language of Science was destroyed due to inferiority complex of the British. Now, Scientists at the NASA (National Aeronautics and Space Administration) have recognised the superiority of Sanskrit for use in computers.

At a time when India i.e., Bharat is celebrating 75 years of independence from the British Raj in the form or Amrit Mahotsava, it is essential to bring to Indian youth, in particular, the virtue of the Sanatan Dharm. The need is to make them understand what constitutes Sanatan Dharm and how their pursuit for excellence is going to be complimented by the syncretic nature of the culture they have inherited.

Yoga, meditation, concentration are other things that help seekers to evolve into better human beings through matured comprehension of the various principles that make the world go. Our Rishis had discovered Zero much before the world could think of this. We had discovered the planets and stars and their impact on existence. Astrology had evolved into a deeper and dependable science.

One would be wonderstruck while reading some lines of the Hanuman Chalisa that comprised forty verses. Goswami Tulsidas composed this in praise of Lord Hanuman. One verse goes thus: "Yug Sahasra Yojan per Bhanu, Leelyo taahi Madhur phal janu" (When Lord Hanuman sees the rising Sun, he decides to eat it, thinking it to be a delicious colour fruit). That this verse calculated the exact distance of Sun from the Earth should not surprise anyone who knew about India's advancement in astronomical sciences.

As one rises from a lower place of consciousness to higher ones, one rises from fake ritualism to higher order of self-awareness and its Union with God. One can work confidently in one's vocation only if they are sure that they are working to facilitate Dharm. Not crossing Red light due to the fear of being caught by the police and not crossing Red light because this may endanger lives are different levels of the same consciousness.

The same principles of Sanatan Dharm may be found to be pervading other denominations that came to exist on India soil such as Buddhism, Jainism or Sikhism. The beauty of Sanatan Dharm is, it is not rigid and keeps transforming with time to suit the need for existence. But the moral order underlying existence never changes. They guide the evolution of practices. When duty becomes a part of consciousness and gets the backing of impeccable philosophy of existence, life becomes much easier. Sanatan Dharm does just that.

The book has tried to explain the Sanatan Dharm and

the various texts associated with the great tradition and their meanings. I am sure that this would help younger generation to understand their culture and tradition, their evolution and the society to which they belong. Every generation must get their own revelations but the basics would remain the same.

Sudesh K Verma
Author and Columnist

FOREWORD

The Board of Trustees of the Central Hindu College has laid down the following principles on which religious and moral teaching is to be given in all institutions under its control. The object of the Central Hindu College being to combine Hindu religious and ethical training with Western education suited to the needs of the time, it is necessary that this religious and ethical training should be of a wide, liberal and un-sectarian character, while at the same time it shall be definitely and distinctively Hindu. It must be exclusive enough to unite the most divergent forms of Hindu thought, but exclusive enough to leave outside it forms of thought that are non-Hindu. It must avoid all doctrines that are the subject of controversy between schools recognised as orthodox; it must not enter into any of the social and political questions of the day; but it must lay a solid foundation of religion and ethics on which the student may build, in his adulthood, the more specialised principles suited to his intellectual and emotional temperament. It must be directed to the building up of a character-pious, dutiful, strong self-reliant, upright, righteous, gentle and well balanced—a character which will be that of a good human and a good citizen; the fundamental principles of religion, governing the general view of life and of life's obligations are alone sufficient to form such a character. That which unites Hindus in a common faith must be clearly and simply enunciated, while all that divides then must be ignored. Lastly, care must be taken to cultivate a wide spirit of tolerance, which not only respects the differences of thought and practice among Hindus, but which also respects the differences of religion among non-Hindus, regarding all faith with reverence, as roads whereby humans approach the Supreme. Therefore:

1. The religious and ethical instruction must be such as all Hindus can accept.
2. It must include the special teachings that mark out Hinduism from other religions.
3. It must not include the distinctive views of any special school or sect.

The textbook is intended to be studied by Hindu youths in colleges, after the elementary one and the catechism have been mastered in schooldays. It follows exactly the same general plan, filling in the broad outlines given in the elementary one, and supplying details that were not introduced before, lest they should confuse the minds of young learners.

It follows the same principle of expounding beliefs common to the vast majority of Hindus, avoiding special sectarian views. A very brief sketch of the great schools is given in the introduction, as every youth should know of their existence and of their distinguishing features.

The name to be given to this book was carefully discussed, and that of "Sanatana Dharma" was finally chosen, as connoting the ancient teachings, free from modern accretions. It should cover all sects, as it did in the ancient days.

May this book also aid in the great work of building up the national religion, and thereby pave the way to national happiness and prosperity.

Board of Trustees
Central Hindu College, Beneras, 1904

मंगल दिशतु नो विनायको
मंगलं दिशतु नः सरस्वती।
मंगलं दिशतु नः समुद्रजा
मंगलं दिशतु नो महेश्वरी॥

INTRODUCTION

श्रीगणेशायनमः। THE Religion based on the Vedas, the Sanatana Dharma, or Vaidika Dharma, is the oldest of living religions, and stands unrivalled in the depth and splendour of its philosophy, while it yields to none in the purity of its ethical teachings and in the flexibility and varied adaptation of its rites and ceremonies. "It is like a river, which has shallows that a child may play in, and depths which the strongest diver cannot fathom." It is thus adapted to every human need, and there is nothing which any religion can supply to add to its rounded perfection. The more it is studied, the more it illuminates the intellect and fulfils the heart. The youth who learns something of it ensures for himself a sure enhancer of happiness and certain consolation in trouble, for the rest of his life.

धारणाद्धर्ममित्याहुर्धर्म धारयति प्रजाः ।[1]

"That which supports, that which holds together the peoples (of the universe), that is Dharma."

Dharma is not merely a set of beliefs having no necessary connection with the daily life of humanity, but is the very (set of)

1 Mahabharata, Karna Parva. lxix, 59.

principles of a healthy and beneficent life. Therefore, to know those principles and act upon them is to be a true Āryan (or follower of Vaidika Dharma), and to tread the sure road to happiness, individual as well as general. The etymological meaning of religion is also the same, "That which binds together." "Vaidika" means "pertaining to the Veda or Perfect Knowledge." Hence Vaidika Dharma means "the Religion of Perfect Knowledge."

One of the most remarkable things in the Sanatana religion is the way in which it has laid down a complete scheme of knowledge, and has then crowned it with a philosophy composed of six faces, but governed by one idea and leading to one goal. No such comprehensive and orderly view of human knowledge is elsewhere to be found. This has been sketched in the Elementary Text-Book, but now requires some further elucidation.

THE BASIS OF SANATANA DHARMA

The श्रुतिः Shrutih, consisting of the Four Vedas is the final authority in the Aryan religion, and these four Vedas form in their entirety THE VEDA—THE PERFECT KNOWLEDGE—revealed by Brahma, the Rishis, and clothed in words by them for the benefit of the Åryan peoples.

युगान्तेऽन्तर्हितान्वेदान्सेतिहासान्महर्षयः ।
लेभिरे तपसा पूर्वम् अनुज्ञाताः स्वयम्भुवा ॥[2]

"The Vedas, together with the Itihasas, were withdrawn at the

2 Quoted by Shankaracharya, and attributed by him to Vyasa—Shārīraka Bhāṣhya. I. iii. 29.

end of the Yugas. The Maharshis, permitted by Svayambhu (Brahma), recovered them by Tapas."

It appears that modifications were introduced on such recoveries, which took place at the beginning of each cycle, so as to suit the again revealed Vedas to the special conditions of the age. For we read in the *Devi Bhagavata*:

वेदमेकंसबहुधाकुरुतेहितकाम्यया ।
अल्पायुषोऽल्पबुद्धींश्चविप्रान्ज्ञात्वाकलावथ ॥[3]

"Then, in the Kali age, He (Vishnu in the form of Vyasa) divides the one Veda into many parts, desiring benefit (to men), and knowing that the Brahmanas would be short-lived and of small intelligence," and hence unable to master the whole.

Thus the rishis are ever watching over the Religion they gave, withdrawing and again giving revelation according to the needs and the capacities of each age. If so much has disappeared from the sacred books—as may be seen by comparing the number of *shlokas* said to be contained in some of them, with the extant *shlokas*—this disappearance has been brought about by the rishis for men's benefit.

In Patanjali's *Mahabhashya* much higher figures, as regards the extent and content of the Vedas, are given than are found in the now extant books. He mentions 21 *shakhas* (branches) of the *Rigveda*, 100 of the *Yajurveda*, 1,000 of the *Sāmaveda* and 9 of the *Atharvaveda*. The *Muktikopaniṣhat* gives 21 *shakhas* of the *Rigveda*, 109 of the *Yajurveda*;1,000 of the *Sāmaveda*, and 50 of the *Atharvaveda*. Of these but few are now known.[4]

3 Loc. Cit., I. iii. 19.
4 Of. On this point Oharna-Vyūha

Each Veda has three generally recognised divisions:

(1) The संहिता Samhita, or Collection, consisting of सूक्तानि Suktani, Suktas, hymns used at sacrifices and offerings, the Mantras, on which the efficacy of the rite depends.

(2) The ब्राह्मणानि Brahmananani; Brahmanas, described by Āpastamba as containing precepts for sacrifice, reproof, praise, stories and traditions; they explain the connection between the Saktas and the ceremonies. They are treatises on rituals, but interspersed with the ritual directions are many illustrative stories, philosophical observations and profound ideas, especially in the *Tāṇdya Mahābrāhmaṇa* and the *Shatapatha Brāhmaṇa*. Treatises named अरण्यकानि Aranyakani, Aranyakas, or Books for the Forest, i.e., for study by recluses, are given at the end of the Brahmanas.

(3) The उपनिषदः: Upanishadah or *Upanishads*; philosophical treatises of a profound character, embodying the sunar Brahmavidya, on which the Six Darshanas (philosophies), or the great systems of philosophy are built up. They are many in number, 108 being the more important, and of these, 10 or 12 are called Major, and the rest Minor. The Major have been commented on by the founders of the leading schools of Vedanta, or by their early disciples.

The Samhita, or Collections of the Mantras of the *Rigveda*, contains 1,017 Suktas, arranged in 10 मण्डलानि Mandalani, or *Mandalas*, literally meaning circles. The *Sūktas* are for the most part prayers too, and invocations of the Devas, but we shall find later that the One Supreme Existence is also definitely taught in this ancient Āryan book. It is the book of the होता Hota, the priest who pours offerings into the fire, and, as its name implies, is the knowledge of *Richās*, or laudatory verses, to be recited aloud at the time of the sacrifice.

The Samhita of the *Yajurveda* consists of forty adhyāyas, or chapters, containing 1,886 shlokas, about half of which are also found in the *Rigveda*. There are two main versions of it, the *Krishna*, the black, or *Taittirīya*, in which the *Samhitā* and *Brāhmaṇa* are mixed up; and the *Shukla*, the white, or *Vājasaneya*, in which the *Samhitā* is separate from the *Brāhmaṇa*. There are other minor differences. The *Samhitā* consists of the invocations and prayers offered in sacrifices in the preparation of the materials, the altar, the bricks, the stakes, etc.

Details of the sacrifices often mentioned in histories—the *Rājasūya*, the *Ashvamedha*, etc.—may here be found as well as of domestic and other ceremonies. It is the book containing, as its name implies, the knowledge of sacrifices, and belongs especially to the अध्वर्युः *Adhvaryuh* (conductor), comprising his duties in a sacrifice.

The *Samhitā* of the *Sāmaveda* contains 15 books divided into 32 chapters, again subdivided into 460 hymns. Most of these are also found in the *Rigveda* mantras, only 75 being different. The *Sāmaveda* is the knowledge of song, and its hymns were chanted by the उद्गाता *Udgāta*, at sacrifices in which Soma was offered.[5]

The *Sāmhita* of the *Atharvaveda* is divided into 20 Kāṇdas, and these again are divided into 731 hymns. Its earthly compilation is ascribed to the descendants of Atharvaṇa, the Āngirasas and the

5 The Samhitā of the *Sāmaveda* comprises four different works, the ग्रामगेय the ऊहः, the ऊह्यं and the आरण्यगानं. All these four include the whole of the *Sāmaveda* as set to music. But as the hymns with their musical notations became wholly unintelligible, even in early days, they were rearranged into a distinct compilation, called the Archika. On this compilation Sāyaṇa wrote his Bhāṣhya (commentary). The figures used on the top of the mantras in the printed text indicate the notes of the gamut.

Bhrigus, to whom it was revealed. It is sometimes called *Brahmaveda*, probably because it was the special Veda used by the ब्रह्मा Brahmā, the chief priest at a sacrifice, who supervised the whole, and remedied any errors that might have been committed by the *Hotrī*, *Adhvaryu* and *Udgātri*. The name, however, may refer to the fact that in the *Atharvaveda* is also expounded the knowledge of Brahmaṇa which bestows *Moksha*, or liberation from rebirth, many of the more famous *Upanishads* forming part of it. Further, it throws much light on the daily life of the ancient middle class Āryan, the merchant and the agriculturist, as well as on that of the women of the same class, and thus has a special historical and sociological interest of its own.

There are two Brāhmaṇas attached to the *Rigveda*; the *Aitareya*, consisting of 40 *adhyāyas*, deals with the Soma sacrifices, the Agnihotra, and the ceremonies connected with the accession of a king. The Aitarya Aranyaka belongs to this Brahmana, in which the Aitareya Upanishad is included. The *Kaushītakī Brāhmaṇa*, sometimes also called *Shānkhāyana*, has 30 *adhyāyas* and deals with the Soma sacrifices. The Aranyaka of the same name belongs to it, and includes the *Kaushītakī Upanishad*. There are also 8 minor Upanishads attached to it.

In the *Krishna Yajurveda*, there are no separate Brāhmaṇas recognised by two schools, the prose portions mingled with the *Samhitā* taking this place; but a third school separates these as the *Taittirīya Brāhmaṇa* in 3 *adhyāyas*, with a *Taittirīya Aranyaka* containing the *Taittirīya Upanishad*. The *Kaṭha* and *Shvetāshvatara* Upanishads and 31 minor ones belong also to the *Krishna Yajurveda*.

The *Shukla Yajurveda* has the *Shatapatha Brāhmaṇa* in 100 *adhyayas*, the *Araṇyaka* of which contains the

Brihadāraṇyakopanishad, also called the *Vājasaneya*; the *Īshopaniṣhat* forms the last chapter of this Veda, together with 17 minor Upanishads.

The *Sāmaveda* has three generally known *Brāhmaṇas*; the *Talavakāra*, which includes the *Kenopanishad*; the *Panchavimsha*, containing 25 books; the *Chhāndogya Brāhmaṇa*, including the *Upanishad* of that name, and 14 minor ones.

The *Atharvaveda* has the *Gopatha Brāhmaṇa*, consisting of two books. Many Upanishads are attached to this Veda in different lists. The *Māndūkya*, *Muṇdaka* and *Prashna* are among those classed as the 12 chief Upanishads, and there are 31 minor ones attached to it in the *Muktikopaniṣhad*.

The 12 chief Upanishads are: the *Aitareya*, *Kaushītakī*, *Taittirīya*, *Katha*, *Shvetāshvatara*, *Brihadāraṇyaka*, *Īsha*, *Kena*, *Chhāndogya*, *Māndūkya*, *Muṇdaka* and *Prashna*. The student can find the complete list of all the 108 in the *Muktikopanishad*.

It is on these Shrutis that the entire fabric of Vaidika Dharma, the Religion of the Vedas, as it is truly named, is built. In modern times, much criticism has been directed against the Vedas, because the occult knowledge, on the possession of which depends the understanding of their inner meaning, has disappeared. They contain in their entirety a system by the mastery of which all the energies of nature may be controlled, for it is the system by which these energies were vitalised in our universe at its beginning, and are still directed by Īshvara. A true Vedavit could rule nature, and all her energies would be at his service.

It is therefore not wise to conclude hastily that passages in the Vedas are rubbish, or the babblings of a child-humanity, because they are not intelligible to the modern student, devoid of Yoga and of inner knowledge. The student should suspend his judgment whenever he feels inclined to see absurdity, remembering that some of the keenest intellects produced by humanity have seen wisdom where he sees none, and he should wait until riper years and increased purity of life have opened his eyes.

The Vedas are summed up in the Gāyatrī, the Gāyatrī in the Praṇava, and the Praṇava is the expression of the Absolute. This statement is repeatedly made in the Vedas themselves, and occurs again and again in Sanskrit literature. The real meaning or significance of this mysterious fact can only be discovered by prolonged study and meditation.

Next in order to the Shruti in authority comes the स्मृतिः Smritih, which explains and develops Dharma, laying down the laws which regulate Āryan national, social, family and individual obligations. They are the textbooks of law, and are very numerous[6], but four of them are regarded as the chief, and these are sometimes related to the four Yugas, Manu being said to be the authority for the Satya Yuga, Yājñavalkya for the Tretā, Shankha and Likhita for the Dvāpara, and Parāshara for the Kali.

कृतेतुमानवाःप्रोक्तासत्रेतायांयाज्ञवल्क्यजाः ।
द्वापरेशंखलिखिताःकलोपाराशराःस्मृताः ॥

"[The laws] of Manu are declared for the KritaYuga, those of Yājnavalkya for the Tretā; those of Shankha and Likhita are remembered for the Dvāpara, those of Parāshara are remembered for the Kali."

6 See the Introduction to Mandilik's translation of the *Vyavāhara Mayūkha* and *Yājnavalkaya Smriti.*

Thus we see that, as in the case of the Vedas, the Rishis with the necessary authority made alterations and adaptations to suit the needs of the time.

It was this characteristic of flexibility of Sanatana Dharma that preserved it through so many ages, when other ancient religions perished. The above saying, however, is in no way followed today.

Of the authority of the Shruti and Smriti, Manu says:

श्रुतिस्तु वेदो विज्ञेयो धर्मशास्त्रं तु वै स्मृतिः ।
ते सर्वार्थष्वमीमांस्ये ताभ्यां धर्मो हि निर्बभौ ॥[7]

The Veda is known as Shruti, the Dharmashastras as Smriti: these should not be doubted (but carefully consulted and considered) in all matters, for from them Dharma arose.

Of these Smritis, the two of Manu and Yajnavalkya are universally accepted at the present time as of chief authority all over India, and Yajnavalkya is chiefly consulted in all matters of Hindu law. The other Smritis are drawn upon when it is necessary to supplement these.

Manu, the original lawgiver of the Aryan race, is said in the *Nārada Smriti* to have composed a Dharmashāstra in 100,000 *shlokas*, arranged in 1,080 chapters: this was reduced by Nārada to12,000 *shlokas*, Mārkaṇḍeya to 8,000, and by Sumati, Bhrigu's son, to 4,000. The Laws now exist in 12 books, containing only 2,685 shlokas.

Manu expounds the origin of the universe, and then desires Bhrigu to recite the Institutes as taught by himself. Bhrigu,

7 Loc. cit. ii. Iv.

accordingly, sketches the work, and then expounds in detail the duties of the student (chap. ii.), the householder (chap. iii.), and of one who is a Snātaka (chap. iv.); he then deals with food, impurity and purification, and with women (chap. v.), and concludes the orderly life by describing the two last stages of the forest dweller and the Sannyāsī (chap. vi.). The duties of a king are then laid down (chap. vii.), and the administration of civil and criminal law (chap. Viii.). This is followed by the "eternal laws for a husband and his wife," the laws of inheritance, the punishments for some crimes, and some additional precepts as to royal duties (chap. ix.) The rules for the four castes, chiefly in times of distress, follow (chap. x.) and then laws on penances (chap. xi.). The 12th chapter deals with transmigration and declares that supreme bliss is to be gained by the knowledge of Atma, on whom "the universe rests".

The Yājnavalkya Smriti consists of 3 adhyāyas, or chapters, which contain 1,010 shlokas. They deal respectively with Āchāra (Conduct), Vyavahāra (Civil Law), and Prāyashchitta (Penances). In the first adhyāya the duties of the castes and āshramas are expounded, foods are dealt with, gifts, offerings, certain rites, and the duties of a king are explained. In the second, civil law and procedure and punishment for crimes are laid down. In the third, purifications are given, and these are followed by an explanation of duties in time of distress, and those of a forest dweller and an ascetic, and some physiological details; then follows a disquisition on the universal and the individual soul, the paths of liberation and of bondage, yoga, the siddhis, and transmigration, together with a number of penances.

Next in succession to the Smriti come the पुराणानि Purāṇāni, the Purāṇas, which, with the इतिहासाः Itihāsāḥ, the history, are sometimes said to form the पञ्चमोवेदः Panchamo Vedaḥ, the Fifth Veda. (Nārada, in telling Sanatkumāra what he has read[8], calls them the fifth, and Shankara says on this पञ्चमोवेदः ।) In the Vishṇu Bhāgavata occurs the phrase:

ऋग्यजुःसामाथाख्यवेदाश्चत्वारउद्धृताः ।
इतिहासपुराणंचपञ्चमोवेदउच्यते ॥[9]

Vyāsa "having recovered the four Vedas, named the Ṛig, Yajur, Sāma, and Atharva, completed the Itihāsa and Purāṇa, called the fifth Veda."

So also it is written:

प्रादुःकरोतिधर्मार्थीपुराणानियथाविधि ।
द्वापरेद्वापरेविष्णुव्यासरूपेणसर्वदा ॥[10]

"Always, in each Dvāpara age, Vishṇu, in the form of Vyāsa, reveals the Purāṇas, as is fitting, for the sake of Dharma."

Madhava says that like the six Angas, the Purāṇas, etc. are adapted to give a knowledge of the Vedas, and are therefore worthy objects of study.

So also Yājnavalkya:

पुराणन्यायमीमांसाधर्मशास्त्राङ्गमिश्रिताः ।
वेदाःस्थानानिविद्यानांधर्मस्यचचतुर्दश ।
इतिहासपुराणाभ्यांवेदंसमुपबृहयेत् ।इति । ।[11]

8 Chhāndogyop. VII. i. 2.
9 Loc. cit. I. iv, 20.
10 Devī Bhāg. I. jii. 18.
11 Loc. cit. I. i. 3.

"The Vedas, along with the Purāṇas, the Nyāyas, the Mīmānsās, the Dharmashāstras and the Angas, are the fourteen sources of knowledge and Dharma. (The student should) expound the Vedas with the help of the Itihāsas and Purāṇas."

Eighteen Purāṇas are reckoned the chief, and there are another eighteen, styled Upa-Purāṇas, or lesser Purāṇas. The 18 mukhya, or great Purāṇas are: Brahma, Padma, Viṣhṇu, Shiva, Bhāgavata, Nārada, Mārkaṇḍeya, Agni, Bhaviṣhya, Brahmavaivarta, Linga, Varāha, Skanda, Vāmana, Kūrma, Matsya, Suparṇa or Garuḍa, and Brahmāṇda. The 18 Upa-Purāṇas are: Sanatkumāra, Narasimha, Bṛihannāradīya, Shivarahasya, Durvāsas, Kapila, Vāmana (in addition to the Purāṇa thus named), Bhārgava, Varuṇa, Kālikā, Sāmba, Nandi, Sūrya, Parāshara, Vasiṣhṭha, Devī Bhâgavata, Gaṇesha, and Hamsa.

There has arisen a dispute as to which of the two, the Viṣhṇu Bhāgavata or the Devī Bhāgavata, is the Purāṇa and which the Upa-Purāṇa, and the point remains undecided: but it is certain that both are equally valuable and instructive. The Devī Bhāgavata is specially fitted for those who are inclined to metaphysics and science, while the Viṣhṇu Bhāgavata is most acceptable to the devotional temperament.

The Purāṇas contain the history of remote times when the conditions of existence were quite different from those which prevail in our days; they also describe regions of the universe not visible to the ordinary physical eye. Hence it is unfair to regard the conceptions of the Purāṇas as being of the same nature as those of modern science. When Yoga-*siddhis* are developed, the Paurāṇika pictures of the universe and its past history are seen to be infinitely more correct than those arrived at by the modern scientific use of our physical organs of perception, however much these may be aided by delicate scientific apparatus. Certain definite characteristics of a Purāṇa are given in the Viṣhṇu Purāṇa and in others:

सर्गश्चप्रतिसर्गश्चवंशोमन्वन्तराणिच।
वंशानुचरितंचैवपुराणंपञ्चलक्षणम्।।

"Creation, Secondary Creation [12], Genealogy, Manvantaras, and History, such are the five marks of a Purāṇa."

Vyāsa is the compiler of the Purāṇas from age to age, as we have seen, and for this age he is Kṛiṣhṇa Dvaipāyana, the son of Parāshara.

The other part of the Fifth Veda is the Itihāsa, the two great epics, the *Rāmāyaṇa* and the *Mahābhārata*. These are so well known that little needs to be said of them here.

The *Rāmāyaṇa* has for its author Vālmīki, and is the history of the family of the Solar Race, descended from Ikşhvāku, in which was born the avātara of Viṣhṇu, Rāmachandra and his three brothers. The story of their birth, education, and marriages, the exile of Rāmachandra, the abduction and recovery of Sītā, his wife, the destruction of Rāvaṇa, the Rākshasa, and the reign of Rāmachandra, are detailed at length. The whole gives a vivid picture of Indian life, as led towards the close of the Tretā Yuga, and is intended to provide, in the life of Rāmachandra and his brothers, a model of fraternal affection and mutual service, leading to prosperity and general welfare, that may serve as a lesson and inspiration in true Āryan living, and a model of kingship for all Āryan rulers. It is, perhaps, almost needless to

12 Some interpret the word as meaning 'reabsorption,' 'destruction.

add, that the life of Sita has always been, and is, regarded as the most perfect example of womanly fidelity, chastity and sweetness to be found in literature.

The *Mahābhārata* was compiled by Vyāsa, early in the Kali Yuga, but different recensions of it have been made.

The story is far more complicated and more modern than that of the Rāmāyana, and relates the varying fortunes of a family of the Lunar Race, which, rent by jealousies and rivalries, perished by internecine strife. Against this dark background stands out the figure of the avatara, Shrī Kṛiṣhṇa, dominating the whole, surrounded by the Pāṇḍava family, which triumphs by virtue of its righteous cause over the opposing Kurus; while, among the latter, shine forth the heroic Bhīṣhma, Droṇa, and Karṇa, the splendid but doomed defenders of wrongful sovereignty. The story fitly opens the Kali Yuga, in which good and evil contend with almost equal forces, and in which ethical problems and the complicated workings of karma baffle and bewilder the mind; in the destruction of the best and wisest of the Kshatriya caste it seems to presage the coming invasions of India, and in the gloom of its closing earthly scenes to forecast the darkness that was soon to settle down on Āryāvarta. The main thread of the story is constantly broken by interludes, consisting of instructive lessons and stories, among which are the immortal discourse of Bhīṣhma on dharma, and the most famous jewel of Āryan literature, the Shrīmad Bhagavad-Gītā. The whole forms an encyclopedia of history, morals and religion, not surpassed, or even rivalled, by any other epic in the world.

THE SCIENCE AND PHILOSOPHY OF SANĀTANA DHARMA

The science of ancient India was contained in the षडङ्गानि Ṣhaḍaṅgāni, Six Limbs, or Branches, of the Vedas. Its Philosophy was contained in the षड्दर्शनानि Ṣhaḍ-Darshanāni, the Six Views, or Systems, also called the षड्पांगानि Ṣhaḍ-upāṅgāni, Six Subsidiary Limbs. They are all designed to lead man to the One Science, the One Wisdom, which saw One Self as Real and all else as unreal. The Rishis, realising the unity of all knowledge, made no distinction between science, philosophy and religion. All alike were based on the Veda; the sciences were the Vedāṅgas, the limbs of the Veda, the philosophies were the Vedopāṅgas, other limbs of the Veda, all culminating in the Vedānta, the end of the Veda. And they were all summed up together as the Lesser Knowledge, the Knowledge of the One being alone supreme and indivisible; the revealed Veda was included in the former, in virtue of its being revealed, whereas in the latter the ātma knows Itself. Thus it is written:

द्वेविद्येवेदितव्येइतिहस्मयद्ब्रह्मविदोवदन्ति पराचैवाऽऽपराच।
तत्राऽऽपराऋग्वेदोयजुर्वेदः सामवेदोऽथर्ववेदःशिक्षाकल्पोव्याकरणंनिरुक्तंछन्दो
ज्योतिषमिति।अथपरायतदक्षरमधिगम्यते।[13]

"Two knowledges are to be known, thus say the knowers of Brahman – the supreme and the lower. The lower: Ṛigveda, Yajurveda, Sāmaveda, Atharvaveda, the Method of Study, the Method of Ritual, Grammar, Dictionary (Philology), Prosody, Astrology. The supreme, whereby, That Eternal is reached."

13 Muṇḍakop. 1. i. 4, 5.

The six Aṅgas are expounded in a vast mass of literature divided under six heads, it is composed of सूत्राणि Sūtrāṇi, Sūtras, with commentaries. A Sūtra is an exceedingly terse aphorism, literally a "thread," and it is easy to understand that where knowledge was orally transmitted, this style of composition would be exceedingly valuable. It appears to be certain that the Sūtras were the summing up of teachings contained in a vast mass of literature, long lost. These brief condensed aphorisms obviously contain the distilled essence of profound and abstruse teachings. These teachings being lost, the Sūtras needed to be again expanded and explained by the teacher, and hence a huge array of commentaries grew up, containing traditional explanations, with the comments of the immediate writer.

The six Aṅgas, as just mentioned, were:

1. Shikṣhā, Method of Study: This is a knowledge of phonetics, in which pronunciation and accent were fully dealt with in an extensive literature, the text of the Vedas being arranged in various forms of Pathas which guarded it from Alteration—the Pada-pāṭha, giving each word its separate form; the Krama-pāṭha, connecting the words in pairs, and other more complicated methods.
2. Kalpaḥ, Method of Ritual: To this belong the *Shrauta Sūtras*, explanatory of the ritual of sacrifices in the three fires; their supplement, the *Shulva Sūtras*, dealing with the measurements needed for laying out the sacrificial area, a subject that entailed full knowledge of geometry, which is consequently taught therein (the 47th proposition of Euclid, Bk. i., is the first subject dealt with in the *Shulva Sūtras*); the *Grihya Sūtras*, relating to domestic life; and the *Dharma Sūtras*, treating of customs and laws.
3. Vyākaraṇam, grammar; of which Panini is the latest great

representative, having summed up what went before him, and dominated all who followed him.

4. Niruktam, philology, etymology: Yāska represents this Aṅga, as Pāṇini represents the Vyākaraṇam, and has left a great commentary based on an earlier work.
5. Chhandaḥ, metre, dealing with prosody, a matter of vital importance in connection with the Vedas, of which the latest and best representative is Piṅgala.
6. Jyotiṣham, astronomy, including astrology, dealing not only with the movements of the heavenly bodies, but with their influence on human affairs.

The Six Darshanas are best understood by being seen in relation to each other rather than in opposition, for they form in their entirety, one great scheme of philosophic truth. They are arranged in pairs.

1) न्याय: Nyāyaḥ
2) वैशेषिकं Vaisheṣhikam
3) सान्ख्यं Sāṅkhyam
4) योगः Yogaḥ
5) मीमांसा Mīmānsā
6) वेदान्तः Vedāntaḥ.

The Prasthāna Bheda of Madhusūdana Sarasvatī, after summarising the Six Darshanas, lays stress on their unity. "In reality, all the Munis who have put forward these theories agree in wishing to prove the existence of the One Supreme Lord without a second...... These Munis cannot be in error, considering that they are omniscient: and these different views have only been propounded by them, in order to keep off all nihilistic theories, and because they were afraid that human beings, with their inclinations towards the objects of the world, could not be expected at once to know the true goal of man."[14]

As the Shruti says:

गवामनेकवर्णानांक्षीरस्याप्येकवर्णता ।
क्षीरवत्पश्यतेज्ञानंलिंगिनस्तुगवांयथा ॥[15]

"Cows are many-coloured; but the milk (of all) has but one colour. Look on knowledge as the milk, and on the teacher as the cows."

In each Darshana there is a Ṛiṣhi as teacher, who gives its principles in the form of aphorisms, Sūtras, and a भाष्यं Bhashyam, a commentary, regarded as authoritative.

The Darshanas are based on these Sūtras and commentaries. The object of all is the same—to rescue men from sufferings, and the way of rescue is the same— the removal of ignorance, which is बन्धः Bandhaḥ, bondage, and consequent union with the Supreme. Thus the Nyāya calls ignorance मिथ्याज्ञानं Mithyājnānam, false knowledge; the Sānkhya calls it अविवेकः Avivekaḥ, non-discrimination between the real and the unreal; the Vedānta calls it अविद्या Avidyā, nescience. Each philosophy aims at its removal by ज्ञान Jnānam, wisdom, whereupon आनन्दः Ānandaḥ, bliss, is enjoyed.

This Ānanda is the nature of the Self, and therefore cannot accurately be said to be obtained. The Self is Bliss, and it is only necessary to remove the illusion which causes suffering in order that Bliss may be enjoyed. The Nyāya hence speaks of its object as

14 Quoted in Max Muller's Six Systems. Pp. 107, 10S.
15 Brahmabindûp. 19.

अपवर्गः Apavargah, salvation or deliverance, and मोक्षः Mokşhaḥ, or मुक्तिः Muktiḥ, liberation, is the universally accepted goal.

The Ṛiṣhi of Nyāya, the system of Logic, is Gautama, and his Sūtras are divided into 5 Books. The authoritative commentary is that of Vātsyāyana. He lays down (by उद्देशः uddeshaḥ) 16 पदार्थः Padārthah or topics, into which he divides knowledge, and then proceeds to define them, (by at लक्षणा Lakṣhaṇa,) and finally to examine them, (by परीक्षा Parīkṣhā.) He begins with प्रमाणं Pramāṇam, measure, or proof of right perception, which comprises: प्रत्यक्षं Pratyaksham, sense perception अनुमानं Anumānam, inference उपमानं Upamānam, comparison, or analogy, and शब्दः Shabdaḥ, the word of an expert, testimony. By the means of objects of knowledge, प्रमेयं Prameyam, are established. After discussing the four succeeding Padārthas, he then defines syllogism, reasoning, conclusion, arguṃent, and then deals with various kinds of fallacies and sophisms. When man by right reason has freed himself from false knowledge, he attains liberation.

The Vaisheṣhika, the System of Particulars, literally, has for its Ṛiṣhi Kaṇāda, and for its Bhaşhyakāra, Prashastapāda. Kaṇāda laid down 6 Padārthas, under which all nameable things could be classified in categories, in fact. These are:

द्रव्यं Dravyam, substance; गुणः Guṇah, quality; कर्म Karma, action; सामान्यं Sāmānyam, what is common, i.e., makes a genus; विशेषः Visheşhah, particularity, what makes an individal; and समवायः Samavāyaḥ, inseparability. अभावः Abhāvaḥ, privation, non-being, a seventh Padārtha, was required by later philosophers of this School. Kaṇāda has 9 subdivisions under the head of substances –the 5 भूतानि Bhūtāni or elements; कालः Kālaḥ, Time; दिक् Dik, Space; आत्मा Ātmā, the Self; and मनः Manaḥ, mind. The universal form of the Self is God, the individual the जीवात्मा Jīvātmā; of the Bhūtas, आकाश Ākāshaḥ is eternal and infinite, whereas पृथिवी Prithivī, earth, आप: Āpaḥ, Water, तेज: Tejaḥ, fire, वायु Vāyuḥ, air, are atomic; the atom, अणु: Aṇuḥ, of each is eternal, but the aggregations that make our earth, water, light, and air, are temporary; creation is due to the conjunction of the atoms, the ceasing of a universe to their disjunction.

The Sāṅkhya, the system of Number, looks back to Kapila as the giver of its Sūtras, but their extant form is not regarded as that in which they were originally delivered. There are two Bhāṣhyas considered to be authoritative, those of Aniruddha and Vijnāna-bhikṣhu. There is also a third Bhāshya, by Vedānti Mahādeva. Another and older authority for the Sāṅkhya is the Sāṅkhya-kārika of Īshvara Kṛiṣhṇa with the Bhāṣhya of Gauḍapāda, and the much later Tīkā called the Sāṅkhya Tattva-Kaumudī of Vāchaspati Mishra. There is a higher authority mentioned by Vijnāna-bhikshu as the text book of the Sāṅkhya, and as older than the present Sūtras, ascribed to Kapila himself, the Tattva-Samāsa-Sūtras, on which several commentaries have been written.

The Sāṅkhya is an account, primarily, of the "How" of creation; it is often called Anīshvara, without a supreme Lord, but there is in it no denial of Īshvara, and the repeated appeals to the Shruti as the final authority, above perception and inference, are evidence to the contrary. But Kapila was engaged with the order of happening, not with the cause thereof. There are two primary roots of all we see around us, पुरुष: Puruṣhaḥ, Spirit, प्रकृति: Prakritiḥ, Matter. Puruṣha is many, as appears by the differences in happiness and misery, birth and death, etc., but all are of like essential nature; Puruṣha thus may be taken to represent a totality, the Subject side of existence. Prakriti is the Object side of the existence, and produces 23 substances, 7 of which share the name of Prakriti, and 16 are विकाराः Vikārāḥ, or विकृतयः Vikritayaḥ, modifications. Prakriti, as the opposite of Puruṣha, is अव्यक्तम् Avyaktam, the unmanifested, the producer of all, but itself unproduced. From this, in contact with Puruṣha, are produced in order: महत् Mahat or बुद्धिः Buddhiḥ, the Pure Reason; अहंकारः Ahamkārah, the "I"—making principle, the individualising or separative power; the 5 तन्मात्राणि Tanmātrāṇi, "measures of That," the essential powers that later form the senses. Then come the 16 Vikāras: 5 बुद्धीन्द्रियाणि Buddhīndryāṇi, the perceptive organs, or senses; the 5 कर्म्मेन्द्रियाणि Karmendriyāṇi, the organs of action: मनः Manaḥ, the mind, which is the unifying centre of the Indriyas; the 5 महाभूतानि Mahābhūtāni, great elements—ether, air, fire, water, earth. After this enumeration of the principles of the evolution of the universe, the Sāṅkhya alleges the त्रैगुण्यं Traiguṇyam, or the triple nature of Matter, its three Guṇas, or constituent factors: तमः Tamaḥ, रजः Rajaḥ, and सत्त्वं Sattvam. When these are in equilibrium there is no activity, no evolution; when they are out of equilibrium evolution begins. This evolution, संचरः Sancharaḥ, is next dealt with, and the succeeding dissolution, प्रतिसंचरः Pratisancharaḥ, and the meaning of अध्यात्मं Adhyātmam, with अधिभूतं Adhibhūtam, and अधिदैवतं Adhidaivatam, as applied to Buddhi, Manas and the 10 Indriyas. This is followed by an elaborate enumeration of activities, facts, and qualities, which must be studied in the books on the system, concluding with an explanation of the triple nature of Bandha, Mokṣha,.Pramāṇa and दुःखं Duhkham.

The Yoga, the system of Effort, or of Union, has, as the giver of its Sūtras, Patanjali, and the Vyāsa Bhāṣhya is its commentary. It is sometimes called the Seshvara Sāṅkhya, the Sāṅkhya with an Īshvara, because it accepts the Sāṅkhya as philosophy, and in adding to it a system of effort which should set the Puruṣha free, it makes one of the means of freedom ईश्वरप्रणिधानं[16] Īshvara-praṇidhānam, "Self-surrender to the Lord." Patanjali then defines Íshvara, as a special Puruṣha who has not been touched by pain, action, consequences of action, and desires, unlimited by time; तस्यवाचकःप्रणवः His name is Om. The Sūtras are 198 in number, arranged in 4 Padas, and have as their aim the exposition of the means of stopping the constant movements of the चित्तं Chittam, the thinking principle, and thus reaching समाधिः Samādhiḥ, the perfectly steady and balanced condition, from which कैवल्यं Kaivalyam, the isolation of the Puruṣha, i.e., the separation from Praktriti, can be gained.

One book out of the four is devoted to the description of the विभूतिः Vibhūtiḥ, the powers, obtained in the course of Yoga, but it is remarked that these सिद्धयः Siddhayaḥ, are obstacles in the way of Samādhi, and they are therefore not desirable.

The remaining pair of systems is called the Mīmānsā, for both deal primarily with the leading principles to be adopted in interpreting the text of the Vedas. But the Pūrva Mīmānsā generally bears the name, the Uttara Mīmānsā being usually known as the Vedānta.

The Pūrva, or Earlier, Mīmānsā has Jaimini as the giver of its Sūtras, Shabara's Bhāṣhya being the authoritative commentary. It is concerned with the कर्मकाण्डं Karmakāṇḍam of the Veda, that is with the sacrifices, offerings, and ceremonials generally; while the Uttara, or Later, Mīmānsā is concerned with the ब्रह्मज्ञानं Brahma-jnānam of the Veda, the knowledge of Brahman. The Mīmānsā

16 Sūtrāṇi, i, 93.

Sūtras are divided into 12 books, dealing with the Karmakāṇḍa in minute detail; they also contain a discussion of the Pramāṇas, which are regarded as five, Pratyaksham, Anumānam, Upamānam, Arthapatti (presumption), and Shabda. Authority is, in the Mīmānsā, vested only in the Veda, which, Jaimini devotes himself to proving, is of superhuman origin.

The Uttara Mīmānsā, or Vedānta is the Darshana which may be said to dominate Indian thought in the present day, in its three forms. Its Sūtras are the Brahma-Sūtras, given by Vyāsa, or Kṛiṣhṇa-Dvaipāyana, called also Bādarāyaṇa. The Vedānta has three great schools: the अद्वैतं Advaitam, non-duality, the authoritative Bhāṣhya of which is by Shaṅkara; the विशिष्टाद्वैतं Vishishtādvaitam, non-duality with a difference, with the Bhāṣhya of Rāmānuja; the द्वैतं Dvaitam, duality, with the Bhāṣhya of Madhva. Further, the student of the Vedānta being expected to travel through three stages, प्रस्थानत्रैयं Prasthāna-trayam, the study of the Bhagavad-Gītā, the Upanishads, and the Sūtras, each of the great commentators, or his early disciples, has written on each of these three. The Bhagavad-Gītā is the application of the philosophy to life, the explainer and the guide of conduct. The Upanishads contain the philosophy in an intellectual form, and on them the intelligence is exercised.

The Sūtras sum up the philosophy in terse aphorisms, intended to serve as the seeds for meditation, their deepest meanings being only attainable in Samādhi. For this reason no man was admitted to the study of the Vedanta until he possessed the Four Qualifications: वैराग्यं Vairāgyam, (freedom from selfish attachment to the things of the world), विवेकः Vivekaḥ, (a strong sense of the distinction between the permanent and the transient), षट्सम्पत्तिः Shat-sampattiḥ (the six mental and moral requirements, peacefulness, self-control, resignation, endurance, faith and collectedness) and मुमुक्षा Mumukshā, (the longing for liberation), and was thus fit for its reception.

The Dvaita Vedānta insists on the separateness of the Jivātmā and Paramātmā. It teaches that Viṣhṇu is the Supreme Deity, and formed the universe out of Prakriti, already existing; Viṣhṇu is the efficient cause of the universe, and matter is the material cause thereof, as the goldsmith and the gold are the double cause of the bracelet. Both Viṣhṇu and Prakriti are beginningless and endless, as also is Jīva, the individual soul; but Prakriti and Jīva are subordinate to, and dependent on, Viṣhṇu. Viṣhṇu is Sat, reality, Jnanām, wisdom, and Anantam, infinite.

He enters Prakṭiti—also called Jada-Prakriti—as Puruṣha, the animating universal soul, and thereupon follows the evolution of the universe, as given in the Sāṅkhya: Mahat, Ahamkāra, the Tanmātrās and the Indriyas. Then follow the Devatās and Avidyā in five aspects; these six, from Mahat to Avidyā, are called the प्राकृतसर्गः Prākrita-sargaḥ, the material manifestation.

It is followed by the वैकृतसर्गः Vaikrita-sargaḥ, the organised manifestation, in three divisions, the minerals and plants, the animals, and men. The manifestations of Viṣhṇu, guiding and ruling the preceding nine, are called the tenth creation. Jīva is immaterial, different from Viṣhṇu, and each Jīva is different from every other. The Jīva attains Moksha, in which it enjoys: भोगः Bhogaḥ, eternal bliss; this is fourfold and the Jīva reaches one or other of the four conditions, according to its deserts. These conditions are; सारूप्यं Sārūpyam, similarity to the Divine Form; सालोक्यं Sālokyam, vision of the divine Presence; सान्निध्यं Sānnidhyam, nearness to God; सायुज्यं Sāyujyam, union with God. This union must not be considered as one of identity of nature.

The Vishiṣhṭādvaita Vedānta is for those who, conscious of separation, and longing for union with the supreme, feel the necessity for an object of worship and devotion, and find it in the conception of the Saguṇa Brahman, the conditioned Brahman, Īshvara, the Supreme Lord. Brahman is the highest Reality, the One, but has attributes inseparable from Himself; from Brahman comes संकर्षणः Saṅkarṣhaṇaḥ, the separated soul, which produces प्रद्युम्नः Pradyumnaḥ, mind, which produces अनिरुद्धः Aniruddhaḥ, the I. These separated souls are व्यक्तः vyaktaḥ, manifested, during the period of activity, and when प्रलयः Pralayaḥ approaches they are drawn in, become अव्यक्तं avyaktam, unmanifested: Brahman is then in the कारणवस्था Kāraṇavasthā, the causal state, in which remain avyakta both soul and matter. Brahman is the Object of worship on whom the soul depends, the soul being not Brahman, but a part of Brahman. The separation is insisted on but union is sought.

The Advaita Vedānta is summed up in the words तत्त्वमसि, "Thou art That". Brahman is Nirguṇa, without attributes, and is Real, all else is unreal; Jīvātmā and Paramātmā are the same, there is no difference. The idea of difference arises from Avidyā, nescience, and when the Ātmā transcends nescience, it knows its own nature and is free.

The universe springs from Brahman, as hairs from a man's head; it is the work of Māyā. Cause and effect are one and the same, कार्यकारणाभेदः Kāryakāraṇabhedaḥ, not two different things, as an aggregate of threads is cloth, and there is no cloth apart from the threads that run lengthways and crossways. The unreality of the universe, having Reality as it were behind it has a kind of reality, like a shadow which could not exist without a substance, and this justifies and makes activity of all kinds essential. Hence also there is an अपराविद्या Aparāvidyā, the knowledge of the phenomenal, as well as a पराविद्या Parāvidyā, the knowledge of the Noumenon. Having established the fundamental truth of unity, the Vedānta explains the conditions which surround the Ātmā, enveloped in Āvidyā, the उपाधिः Upādhiḥ, which makes its illusory separateness, their grouping as the स्थूल Sthūla, सूक्ष्म Sūkṣhma and कारणशरीराणि Kāraṇa-Sharīrāṇi and the states of consciousness belonging to these. When the Ātmā identifies Itself with the Upādhis, it is bound; when It knows Itself as Itself, it is free. For those who are not yet ready for this effort after Self-knowledge, ritual is not only desirable but necessary; but for those who have reached the point where only the Ātmā attracts, Jnānam is enough, Brahman is the goal.

It must not be supposed from this that the Jnānī is an abstainer from action. On the contrary, he best understands action, and has the best reason for engaging in it.

तस्मादसक्तःसततंकार्यकर्मसमाचर।
असक्तोह्याचरन्कर्मपरमाप्नोतिपूरुषः॥
सक्ताःकर्मण्यविद्वांसोयथाकुर्वतिभारत।
कुर्याद्विद्वांस्तथाऽसक्तश्चिकीर्षुलोकसंग्रहम्॥[17]

"Therefore, without attachment, constantly perform action which is duty, for in performing action without attachment, man verily reacheth the Supreme.

"As the ignorant act from attachment to action, O Bharata, so should the wise act without attachment, desiring the maintenance of mankind."

---

17 Bhagavad-Gītā. iii. 19. 25.

And so Shankara himself: "If I had not walked without remission in the path of works, others would not have followed in my steps, O Lord."[18] The Jnānī recognises his duties to all around him, plants, animals, men, gods, Īshvara, and performs them the better, because he acts with opened eyes, and without personal object to confuse his judgment. But he performs actions as free, and, being without desire, is not bound by them.

The Six Darshanas may now be seen as parts of a whole. In the Nyāya and Vaisheshika, a man learns to use his intellectual powers rightly, to detect fallacies and to understand the material constitution of the universe. In the Sāṅkhya, he learns the course of evolution, and in the Yoga how to hasten his own growth. In the Mimamsa he is trained to use invisible world for the helping of the visible, and in the three schools of the Vedānta he learns to climb from the idea of himself as separate from Brahman to the thought that he is a part of Brahman that can unite with Him, and finally that he is and ever has been Brahman veiled from Himself by Āvidyā.

Further, a coherent view of the whole vast school of Āryan teachings, as an ascending path of evolution for the Jīvātmā, may now be gained. The literal meaning of the Veda, with its ritual and daily obligations, developed the Manas, the mind, of the Āryan, disciplined his Kāma, his passions and desires, and evolved and directed his emotions. It is said in *Amṛitabindūpanishat*:

मनोहिद्विविधंप्रोक्तंशुद्धंचाशुद्धमेवच ।
अशुद्धंकामसंकल्पंशुद्धकामविवर्जितम् ॥[19]

18 Quoted in Max Muller's Six Systems. P 217.

19 Loc, cit. I.

"Manas is said to be of two kinds, pure and impure: moved by Kāma it is impure; free of Kāma, it is pure."

Manas, joined to Kāma, was gradually purified by a life led according to Vaidika rules. Such a Manas, becomes pure, was further developed in capacity by the study of the Angas, was trained and developed, and thus became capable of the strain of philosophic thought. To a mind thus trained to see and to understand the many, the Veda would unfold its deeper occult meanings, such as intellect could master and apply. The end of all this study was to make possible the evolution of Pure Reason, Buddhi, which cannot unfold unless Manas is developed, any more than Manas can unfold without the development of the senses.

It thus led up to the Darshanas, which develop the Pure Reason, which sees the One in the many, and then realises its unity with all, which therefore hates and despises none, but loves all. To the Buddhi, thus unfolded to see the One, the Veda would unveil its spiritual meaning, its true end, Vedanta, intelligible only to the pure compassionate Reason. Then, and then only, is man ready to reach the goal, the Parā-vidyā is attained, Ātmā beholds Itself.

Thus utterly rational, orderly, and complete is the Sanātana Dharma, the Āryan Religion.

PART I

BASIC HINDU RELIGIOUS IDEAS

THE ONE EXISTENCE

एकमेवाद्वितीयम् ।[1]

"One only, without a second."
Thus all the Shrutis proclaim.

INFINITE, Absolute; Eternal, Changeless, the All, is THAT, without attributes, without qualities, beyond name and form, निर्गुणब्रह्म, Nirguṇa-Brahman.

नासदासीन्नोसदासीत् आनीदवातंस्वधयातदेकंतस्माद्धान्यन्नपर: किंञ्चनास ॥[2]

"Then was not non-existence nor existence...THAT Only breathed by its own nature: apart from THAT was naught."

It contains all; therefore can no particular thing be said of IT. It is all, therefore can no one thing be ascribed to IT. It is not Being only, for that would exclude Non-Being; but being arises in IT, and Non-Being is also there.

यदाऽतमस्तन्नदिवानरात्रिर्नसन्नचासच्छिवएवकेवल: ।[3]

1 Chhāndogyop. VI. ii. I.
2 Ṛigveda. X. cxxix. I. 2.
3 *Shvetāshvatarop*. iv. 18.

"When no darkness (was), then (there was) not day nor night, nor being nor not being, (but) the Blessed alone."

The same Upanishad says:

द्वेअक्षरेब्रह्मपरेत्वनन्तेविद्याऽविद्येनिहितेयत्नगूढ़े ।[4]

"In the imperishable, infinite, supreme Brahman knowledge and ignorance are hidden."

अस्तीति, "It is,"[5] such is all that can be said:

One mysterious sound alone denotes THAT which is beyond number and beyond name: it is the Praṇava. When Nachiketā presses Yama, Lord of Death, to reveal to him the supreme secret, and when Yama has admitted that he is worthy, Nachiketā prays:

अन्यत्नधर्मादन्यत्नाधर्मादन्यत्नास्मात्कृताकृतात् ।
अन्यत्नभूताच्चभव्याच्चयत्तत्पश्यासितद्वद ॥[6]

"Other than dharma and adharma, other than action and inaction, other than past and present, THAT which thou seest, THAT declare."

And Yama answers:

सर्वेवेदायत्पदमामनन्तीतपांसिसर्वाणिचयद्वदन्ति ।
यदिच्छन्तोब्रह्मचर्यचरन्तितत्तेपदंसंग्रहेणब्रवीमि, ओं
इत्येतत् ॥एतद्ह्येवाक्षरंब्रह्मएतद्ध्यवाक्षरंपरम् ॥[7]

"THAT which all the Vedas declare, THAT which all austerities utter, THAT, desiring which they lead the life of Brahmacharya, THAT WORD I tell thee briefly: it is AUM. That Word is even Brahman; that Word is even the Supreme."

---

4 *Kaṭhop*. II. vi. 12.
5 Ibid.v.I.
6 Ibid.I.ii.14
7 Ibid. I.ii. 15-16.

This Unity, which never appears but which is, is implied in the very existence of universes, and systems, and worlds, and individuals. It is not only recognised in all religion, but also in all philosophy and in all science as a fundamental *necessity*. Endless disputes and controversies have arisen about It, but none has denied it. Many names have been used to describe It, and It has been left unnamed; but all rest upon IT. It has been called the All and the Nothing, the Fullness and the Void, Absolute Motion and Absolute Rest, the Real, the Essence. All are true, yet none is fully true. And ever the words of the Sages remain as best conclusion:

नेतिनेति," Not this, not this"

Words seem to put far off and to veil in mystery THAT which is in truth nearest and closest, nay, which is more than close, is our very Self. One name, perhaps, speaks most clearly, the परमात्मा, Paramātmā, the Supreme Self.

अयमात्माब्रह्म[8]

"This Ātmā (is) Brahman."

Such is the truth declared over and over again, insisted on in various forms, lest it should not be grasped. As by knowing one clod of clay all clay is known, as by knowing one piece of gold all gold is known, as by knowing one piece of iron all iron is known, no matter by what number of names men may call the objects made of clay, or gold, or iron; so, to know one Self is to know THE Self, and knowing It, all is known.[9]

8 Māndūkyop. 2.

9 Chhāndogyop. VI. i. 4, 5, 6.

Moreover, as is said in the *Chhāndogyopanishat*:

सर्वेखल्विदंब्रह्म[10]

"All this verily (is) Brahman."

"This is the technical word for the universe, and the universe is Brahman, because तज्जलानिति, therefrom it is born, thereinto it is merged, thereby it is maintained."[11] All that we see around us comes forth from that Fullness and is as the shadow of that Substance. And yet, as the Upanishad declares, we need not go far to seek:

एष म आत्मान्त र्हृदय एतद् ब्रह्म[12]

"This, my Self within the heart, this (is) Brahman."

It is not necessary for a youth to try to metaphysically grasp this great truth, nor to grapple with the questions that spring up in the thoughtful mind when it is stated. It is enough that he should know that this truth is recognised in some shape or another by all thoughtful men, that it is the foundation of all right thought, and later may be known to himself by deeper study. Enough for the present—in the case of most, at least -if he tries to feel the Unity as a centre of peace and a bond of fellowship with all, IT is the Heart of the universe, equally in all and therefore in himself; and this may be felt before it is understood intellectually.

This knowledge is the Parā-vidyā, the Supreme Wisdom, and it is to be gained by purity, devotion, self-sacrifice and knowledge.

10 Ibid. iii. xiv. 1.

11 तज्जलात् is equal to तज्ञजायते, लीयते, आनिति।

12 Chhāndogyop. III. xiv. 4.

नविरतोदुश्चरितान्नाशान्तोनासमाहितः ।
नाशान्तमानसोवापिप्रज्ञानेनैनमाप्नुयात् ॥[13]

"(He who) has not renounced evil ways, nor (is) subdued, nor concentrated, nor (of) subdued mind, even by knowledge he may not obtain it."

नाऽयमात्माबलहीनेनलक्ष्यो
नचप्रमादात्तपसोवाप्यलिङ्गात् ।
पतैरुपायैर्यततेयस्तुविद्वां-
स्तस्यैषआत्माविशतेब्रह्मधाम ॥[14]

"Nor is the Ātmā obtained by the strengthless nor by the careless, nor without marks of austerity: the wise, who strives by these means, of him the Ātmā enters the abode of Brahman."

Here is the Supreme Peace, the Nirvāṇa of Brahman:

लभन्तेब्रह्मनिर्वाणमृषयःक्षीणकल्मषाः ।
छिन्नद्वैधायतात्मानःसर्वभूतहितेरताः ॥[15]

"The Ṛiṣhis, their sins destroyed, their doubts removed, their selves controlled, intent upon the welfare of all beings, obtain the Brahma Nirvāṇa."

Of such a one says Shrī Kṛiṣhṇa, शांतिमृच्छति ,[16] "he goeth to Peace."

But now we read:

---

13 Kaṭhop. I. ii. 24.

14 Muṇḍakop. III. ii 4.

15 Bhagavad-Gītā. V.25.

16 Ibid. 29.

एतद्वैसत्यकामपरञ्चापरञ्चब्रह्मयदोङ्कारः ।[17]

"Verily, O Satyakāma, this Omkāra (is) the Supreme and lower Brahman."

And again:

द्वेवावब्रह्मणोरूपेमूर्त्तञ्चैवामूर्त्तञ्च ।
मत्तर्यञ्चामृतञ्चस्थितञ्चयच्चसच्चत्यच्च ।।[18]

"There are two states of Brahman, formfull and formless, changing and unchanging, finite and infinite,[19] existent and beyond (existence)."

This, second, lower, formfull, changing, finite, existent Brahman is not "another," but is Brahman conditioned—and therefore limited, manifesting—and therefore सगुण saguṇa, with attributes.

The Ṛigveda, in the hymn before quoted, gives this appearing:

तपसस्तन्माहमाजायतेकम् ।[20]

"By the great power of Tapas uprose THE ONE."

Again, the Wise are asked:

वियस्तस्तम्भषडिमारजांस्यजस्यरूपेकिमपिस्विदेकम् ॥[21]

"What was that ONE, who, in the form of the Unborn, hath established these six regions?"

THE ONE: that is His Name, for THAT wherein He arises is

---

17 Prashnop. V.2.

18 Brihadāraṇyakop. II. iii, I.

19 Shankara gives thus the meaning of स्थितञ्चयच्च.

20 Loc. cit. X. cxxix.3.

21 Ibid, I. elxiv.6.

Numberless, beyond Number, and being THE ALL is neither One nor Many.

Manu describes that uprising in stately shlokas:

आसीदिदंतमोभूतमप्रज्ञातमलक्षणम् ।
अप्रतक्र्यमविज्ञेयंप्रसुप्तमिवसर्वतः ॥
ततःस्वयंभूर्भगवानव्यक्तोव्यञ्जयन्निदम् ।
महाभूतादिवृत्तौजाःप्रादुरासीत्तमोनुदः
योऽसावतीन्द्रियग्राह्यःसूक्ष्मोऽव्यक्तःसनातनः ।
सर्वभूतमयोऽचिन्त्यःसएवस्वयमुद्बभौ ॥
यत्तत्कारणमव्यक्तंनित्यंसदसदात्मकम् ।
तद्विसृष्टःसपुरुषोलोकेब्रह्मोतिकीर्त्यते ॥[22]

"This was in the form of Darkness, unknown, without marks (or homogeneous), unattainable by reasoning, unknowable, wholly, as it were, in sleep.

"Then the Self-Existent, the Lord, unmanifest, (but) making manifest This—the great elements and the rest-appeared with mighty power, Dispeller of Darkness."

"He who can be grasped by that which is beyond the senses, subtle, unmanifest, ancient, containing all beings, inconceivable, even He Himself shone forth."

"That unmanifest Cause, everlasting, in nature Sat and Asat, that produced the Purusha famed in the world as Brahma."

"This" is the universe, but here in Darkness, i. e., in the unmanifested condition, as मूलप्रकृति: Mūla-prakritih, the Root of Matter, "unknowable."

This becomes manifest only when Svayambhū shines forth.

22 *Manusmriti*. i. 5, 6, 7, 11

The emergence is simultaneous; for He cannot become manifest save by clothing Himself in This, and This cannot become manifest save as illumined, ensouled, by Him. This Two-in-One, by nature Sat and Asat[23], the Self and the Not-Self, Purușha and Prakriti, everlasting but appearing and disappearing, is the Cause of all things.

तमेवभान्तमनुभातिसर्वतस्यभासासर्वमिदंविभाति ।[24]

"When He hath shone forth, all shines forthafter (Him); (by) the shining forth of Him all This shines forth."

We have seen that He is the Saguṇa Brahman, and He is declared to be in His own nature सत्, चित्, आनन्द Sat, Chit, Ānanda, Pure Being, Pure Intelligence, Pure Bliss. He is called अक्षर Akṣhara, the Indestructible One, on whom the other—Prakriti-— is woven;[25] He is the आत्माऽन्तर्याम्यमृतः, Ātmā-ntryāmyāmritaḥ, the Self, the Inner Ruler, Immortal, who dwells in the earth, the waters, the fire, the atmosphere, the wind, the heavens, in all that is, in the Devas, in the elements, in the bodies of all beings, the all-prevading.

अदृष्टोद्रष्टाऽश्रुतः श्रोताऽमतोमन्ताऽविज्ञातोविज्ञाता नान्योऽतोऽस्तिद्रष्टानान्योऽतोऽस्तिश्रोतानान्योऽतोऽस्ति मन्तानान्योऽतोऽस्तिविज्ञातैषतआत्मान्तयाम्यमृतोऽतोऽन्यदार्तं ॥[26]

"Unseen He sees, unheard He hears, unthought of He thinks, unknown He knows. None other than He is the Seer, none other than he is the Hearer, none other than He is the Thinker, none

23 सदसच्चाहमर्जुन" Sat and Asat am I, O Arjuna!" Bhagavad-Gītā. ix. 19.

24 Kaṭhop. II. v. 15.

25 Brihadāraṇyakop III. vii. 8.

26 Ibid. 23.

other than He is the Knower. He is the Self, the Inner Ruler, Immortal. That which is other perishes."

He is the आत्मा, सर्वभुताष्यस्थितः,[27] "the Self, seated in the heart of all beings." This is the clearest idea to grasp.The conditioned Brahman is the Self-conscious Universal Ego as against the Non Ego, Spirit as against Matter, the "I" everywhere, always, and in all things, identical in nature with the Nirguṇa Brahman, but manifested, with qualities, and always united to Mūlaprakriti.

In the language of symbols, so largely employed by the Sanātana Dharma, Īshvara is represented by a triangle pointing upwards, the triangle symbolising His triple nature, Sat, Chit, Ānanda.

We see this, especially when interlaced with a second downward-pointing triangle which will presently be explained – in many temples.

This idea of the eternal Subject, the Spirit, the Self, the "I" being firmly grasped, the student must next seek to grasp the eternal Object, Matter, Mūlaprakriti, the Not Self, the Not-I.

We have already seen in *Manusmriti* that, in the unmanifested state, this is homogeneous and unknowable; it is therefore often compared with the ether, formless but the root of all forms, intangible but the root of all resistances. Its inherent nature is divisibility, as that of the eternal Subject is inseparateness; it is multiplicity, as He is unity. While He is the Father, the Life Giver, she is the Mother, the Nourisher. Matter is the womb in which the germ is placed.

ममयोनिर्महद्ब्रह्मतस्मिन्गर्भदधाम्यहम् ।[28]

27 Bhagavad Gītā. X. 20.

28 Bhagavad-Gītā. xiv. 3, and Shankara's Commentary.

"My womb is the Mahat-Brahma in that I place the germ"—explained by Shankara as त्रिगुणात्मिकाप्रकृतिः, the Prakṛiti of three Guṇas.

We must pause for a moment on the three guṇas, for an understanding of them is necessary to any clear conception of the working of nature.

The guṇas are not qualities, nor attributes of matter, though both terms are often used in translation; they are the very materiality of matter, that which causes it to be matter. Matter cannot be thought of without these, and wherever there is matter, there are these, inseparable, existing in the ultimate particle as much as in the hugest system.

When these are in equilibrium, balancing each other, there is Pralaya, sleep, inactivity, and to matter in this state the term प्रधानं Pradhānam is usually applied. These guṇas are named:

तमः Tamah, or Tamas; रजः Rajah, or Rajas; सत्त्वम् Sattvam, or Sattva. Tamas—often translated darkness or foulness, the effect of tamasic predominance being taken as the guna itself—is resistance, stability, what is called in science the inertia of matter. All matter is fundamentally and always resistant, it resists. Its capacity for taking form is due to this constituent. Rajas is motion, the capacity of every particle to change its place, and the necessity of so changing it unless prevented, in scientific phrase, this is motion, inherent in matter. Sattva is rhythm, the limiting of movement to an equal distance in an equal time on each side a fixed point, the power and necessity of what is, scientific phrase, vibration. Hence every particle matter has resistance, motion, and rhythm. When the equilibrium of the three is disturbed by the breath of Ishvara, these three gunas at once manifest: tamas appearing as inertia, resistance; rajas throwing every particle of the resistant mass into active movement, thus producing what is called Chaos; and sattva imposing rhythm on the movement of each particle, each thus becoming a vibrating, i.e, a regularly moving particle, capable of entering into relations with the surrounding particles. All the qualities found in matter arise from the interaction of these three gunas, their endless permutations and combinations producing the endless variety of attributes found in the universe. The predominance of tamas in a body made up of countless particles gives rigidity, immovability such as is seen in stones and other things that do not move of themselves. The predominance of rajas in a body gives unregulated hasty movements, restlessness, excess of activity. The predominance of sattva gives harmony, controlled rhythmical movements, order, beauty. But in the most immovable stone, the minute particles are in a state of unceasing vibration, from the presence of rajas and sattva in the most restless animal there is stability of material and vibration of particles from the presence of tamas and sattva; and in the most harmonious and controlled man there is stability of material and movement from the presence of tamas and rajas.

As the triple nature of Īshvara, Sat-Chit-Ānanda was symbolically represented by a triangle pointing upwards, like a flame, so is the triple nature of Mūlaprakriti symbolised as a triangle, but now it points downwards, like a drop of water.

From these two triangles is formed the symbol of Īshvara and his universe, often seen in Temples, the two interlaced, and a point in the centre, the symbol of the ONE, the whole giving the Great Septenary, the Supreme Brahman and the Universe.

Thus we have before us the second member of the Duality which, as we saw above in *Manusmrti*, is the Cause of all things.

The Divine Power, or शक्तिः Shaktih, the will of Īshvara, His light sent forth and making "This" manifest, as says the Smriti, is called Māyā. Māyā is inseparable from Īshvara; "Their unity is like that of the moon and the moonlight, or that of the fire and its power to burn," says Nīlakaṇṭha, commenting on Devī Bhāgavata. VI. xv. 49.

Thus we read:

तस्यचेच्छास्म्यहंदैत्यसृजामिसकलंजगत् ।
समांपश्यतिविश्वात्मातस्याहंप्रकृतिःशिवा ॥[29]

"The Will am I, O Daitya, of Him (the Supreme Puruṣha); I send forth the whole universe. He beholds me, He the Universal Self, I His benign nature."

Nīlakaṇṭha, commenting on above, quotes one of the Shiva Sūtras:

इच्छाशक्तिःउमाकुमारी

"Will-power (is) Umā, the Virgin."

While inseparable from the Lord, when turned towards Him She is called महाविद्या Mahāvidyā, Supreme Knowledge. She is also called, when turned away from Him, अविद्या Avidyā, Nescience, and emphatically महामाया, Mahāmāyā, the Great Illusion, as she permeates Mūlaprakriti and becomes inseparable from it.

These are Her two forms:

राममायाद्विधाभातिविद्याऽविद्यतितेसदा ।[30]

"O Rāma! Māyā manifests as a duality; these (are) ever Vidyā and Avidyā."

---

29 Devī Bhāgavata. V. xvi. 36.
30 Adhyātama-Rāmāyaṇa III. iii. 32.

This identification of the Shakti of the Lord with Mūlaprakriti often causes Māyā to be called Mūlaprakriti and Prakriti. So, Shrī Kṛishna-having defined Prakriti as generally understood:

भूमिरापोऽनलोवायुःखंमनोबुद्धिरेवच।
अहङ्कार इतीयं मे भिन्ना प्रकृतिरष्टधा ॥
अपरेयम.................

Earth, water, fire, air, ether, Manas, and Buddhi also, and Ahamkāra, these are the eight-fold division of My Prakriti. This the inferior –goes on:

..........अन्यां प्रकृतिं विद्धि मे पराम्।
जीवभूतां महाबाहो ययेदं धार्यते जगत् ॥[31]

"Know my other Prakriti, the higher, the life element, O mighty-armed, by which the universe is upheld."

This "other Prakriti" is also spoken of by Him under the name of "ममदैवी प्रकृतिः" "My divine Prakriti,"[32] "His own Power, his योगमाया Yoga-Māyā, by which truly the universe is upheld."

As says the Shruti:

मायां तु प्रकृतिं विद्यान्मायिनं तु महेश्वरम्।[33]

"Let (the student) know Māyā as Prakriti; the Possessor of Maya as the Great Lord." In the Devī Bhāgavata some very beautiful descriptions are given of this Matter side of Nature, regarded as Māyā. Thus:

एषा भगवती देवी सर्वेषां कारणं हि नः।
महाविद्या महामाया पूर्णा प्रकृतिरव्यया।
इच्छापरात्मनःकामं नित्यानित्यस्वरूपिणी ॥

31 Bhagavad-Gītā. vii. 4, 5.
32 Ibid. ix. 13.
33 Shvetāshvatarop. iv. 10.

वेदगर्भा विशालाक्षी सर्वेषामादिरीश्वरी ॥
एषा संहृत्य सकलं विश्वं क्रीडति संक्षये।
लिङ्गानि सर्वजीवानां स्वशरीरेनिवेश्यच ॥
मूलप्रकृतिरेवैषा सदा पुरुषसंगता।
ब्रम्हाण्डं दर्शयत्येषा कृत्वा वै परमात्मने।
तस्यैषा कारणं सर्वा माया सर्वेश्वरी शिवा ॥[34]

She (is) Bhagavatī, the Goddess, the cause of us all, Mahāvidyā, Mahāmāyā, the fullness, the imperishable Prakriti.......

"The will of the Supreme Self verily (is She), in Her nature (uniting) the ever-lasting and the ever passing........."

"(Her) embryo the Veda, the long-eyed, the primal Goddess of all."

"At the Pralaya, having rolled up the universe, She sports, hiding within Her own body the types of all living beings..."

"Mūlaprakriti is she indeed, ever united with Purușha. Having made the world-systems, she shows them to the Supreme Self."

"The cause of it (is) She, the All, Māyā, the benignant All-Ruler."

This Māyā is inseparable from Īshvara, the Saguṇa Brahman, as said below:

सा च माया परे तत्त्वे संविद्रूपेऽस्ति सर्वदा।
तदधीना प्रेरिता च तेन जीवेषु सर्वदा ॥
ततो मायाविशिष्टां तां संविदं परमेश्वरीम्।
मायेश्वरीं भगवतीं सच्चिदानन्दरूपिणीम्।
ध्यायेतू[35]

"She, Māyā, is ever in the Supreme Essence, whose nature is

34 Loc. cit. III. iii. 51.61
35 Ibid.VI. xxxi. 48, 49

Consciousness, subordinate to Him, and by Him ever sent forth among Jīvas."

"Therefore, should be worshipped that Consciousness, whose nature is Sat, Chit and Ānanda, Lord of Māyā, the Divine, with Māyā, the Supreme Lady."

Being thus seen as the illusion-producing Power of the Lord, She is known as the cause of bondage and also as the path to liberation. As Avidyā she deludes; as Vidyā she leads to Her Lord, and as She vanishes in Him, the Ātmā knows itself as free.

भेदबुद्धिस्तु संसारे वर्तमाना प्रवर्तते ॥
अविद्येयं महाभाग विद्या च तन्निवर्तनम् ।
विद्याऽविद्ये च विज्ञेये सर्वदैव विचक्षणैः ॥
विनाऽऽतपं हि छायाया जायते च कथं सुखम् ।
अविद्यया विना तद्वत्कथं विद्यां च वेत्ति वै ॥[36]

"This notion of separateness being present sends (the jīva) forth into Samsāra. This is Avidyā. O fortunate one! Vidyā is the turning away from this. Vidyā and Avidyā should be always known by the wise. Without sunshine how (should) the pleasure of shade be known? Without Avidyā how should Vidyā be known?"

प्रवृत्तिमार्गनिरता अविद्यावशवर्तिनः ।
निवृत्तिमार्गनिरता वेदान्तार्थविचारकाः ॥[37]

"The travellers on the Pravritti Mārga (the forth-going path) are under the power of Avidyā.

The travellers on the Nivritti Mārga (the returning path)

---

36 Devī Bhāgavata. I. xviii, 42, 43, 44.
37 Adhyātma-Rāmāyaṇa. III. iii. 32.

ponder the teaching of the Vedānta."

When the Jīva goes forth, facing Prakriti and looking at it, Māyā envelopes him as Avidyā. When he turns his back on Prakriti, turns towards the Lord then she turns with him and becomes Vidyā, and he is free. As Nilakantha says, quoting the Shaivāgama, अन्तमुखा शक्तिरेव विद्या[38] "The inward-facing Shakti is Vidyā."

Then he realises the mighty power of Māyā. Her divine nature, and Her identity with the Supreme, and hymns Īshvara and Māyā as One:

अनन्तकोटिब्रह्माण्डनायिके ते नमोनमः ॥
नमः कूटस्थ रूपायै चिद्रूपायै नमोनमः ।
नमो वेदान्तवेद्यायै भुवनेश्वर्यै नमोनमः ॥
नेति नेतीति वाक्यैर्या बोध्यते सकलागमैः ।
तां सर्वकारणां देवी सर्वभावेन सन्नताः ॥[39]

Thou Sovereign of endless crores of world systems, we bow to Thee !

Hail! (Thou that art) in the Form of the Rock-seated (the changeless and motionless Eternal), the Form of Consciousness, we bow to thee!

Hail! (Thou that) mayest be known by the Vedānta, the Ruler of the universe, we bow to Thee!

"Thou whom all the Sacred Books only describe by the words 'Not thus, not thus.'

"Goddess! The Cause of all, with our whole nature we bow to thee!"

The Supreme Īshvara, by His Māyā, creates preserves and

38 Commentary on Devī Bhāg. VI. xv. 47, 48.
39 Devī Bhāgavata. VII. xxviii, 31, 32.

destroys the innumerable world systems that form the ocean of Samsāra.

He produces The Many.

तदैक्षत बहु स्यां प्रजायेय ।[40]

"That willed: May I be Many, may I be born."

Then, He is given many names:

एकं सद्विप्रा बहुधा वदन्ति ।[41]

"To what is One, the Wise give many names." But whatever the names given, Īshavara is One. Thus has it ever been taught in the Shruti and Smriti, as we have seen, and this is repeated in the more popular teaching of which the Viṣhṇu Purāṇa may serve as example.

सृष्टिस्थित्यंतकरणाद्ब्रह्मविष्णुशिवात्मिकाम् ।
स संज्ञां याति भगवान् एक एव जनार्दनः ॥[42]

"Thus, the One Only God, Janārdana, takes the designation of Brahmā, Viṣhṇu and Shiva, accordingly as He creates, preserves or destroys... He is the Cause of creation, preservation, and destruction."

To sum up, the student must remember,

UNMANIFESTED

1. The Absolute, the All, Paramātma, Nirguṇa Brahman.

MANIFESTED

40 Chhāndogyop. VI. ii. 3

41 Ṛigveda. 1. cxiv, 46.

42 Loc. cit. I. ii, 62.

1. The One, Īshvara, the Self, the Subject, Sat, Saguṇa Brahman.
2. Mūlaprakriti, the Not-Self, the Object, Asat.
3. Māyā, the Shakti, the power, the Will, of Īshvara.
4. The Many, arising from Mūlaprakriti by the Māyā of Īshvara.

As to the precise definition of the nature of these Five, and of Their mutual inter-relations, there is much discussion, and more less difference of opinion, in the Six Darshanas and their subdivisions, as now taught. But the fact of these Five under whatever names, is recognised by all, and the student who studies deeply enough will come to the conclusion that the differences between the Darshana arise from each great Teacher emphasising one aspect of the relations and that all the six Darshanas, rightly understood, from one organic whole.

THE MANY

अव्यक्ताद्व्यक्तयः सर्वाः प्रभंवत्यहरागमे।
रात्र्यागमे प्रलीयन्ते तत्रैवाव्यक्तसंज्ञके ॥
भूतग्रामः स एवायं भूत्वा भूत्वा प्रलीयते।
रात्र्यागमेऽवशः पार्थ प्रभवत्यहरागमे ॥
परस्तस्मात्तुभावोऽन्योऽव्यक्तोऽव्यक्तात्सनातनः।
यः स सर्वेषु भुतेषु नश्यत्सु न विनश्याति ॥
अव्यक्तोऽक्षर इत्युक्तस्तमाहुः परमां गतिम्।[1]

FROM the unmanifested all the manifested stream forth at the coming of day; at the coming of night they dissolve, even in That called the Unmanifested.

"This multitude of beings, going forth again and again, is dissolved at the coming of night; by law, O Pārtha, it streams forth at the coming of day.

"Therefore, verily there existeth, higher than that unmanifested, another Unmanifested, which, in the destroying of all beings, is not destroyed.

---

1 Bhagavad-Gītā. viii. 18, -21.

"Unmanifested, the Indestructible, It is called; It is named the highest goal."

Here, in a few shlokas, the coming forth of the Many is stated. At the beginning of the Day of manifestation, all beings stream forth from the unmanifested Root of matter, Mūlaprakriti, from "This" in darkness, as *Manusmriti* has it. When the Day is over, and the Night of Pralaya comes, then all these separated existences again dissolve into Mūlaprakriti. Over and over again this occurs, for universes succeed universes, in endless succession. Behind this, then, there must be another Unmanifested, Īshvara, the Saguṇa Brahman, other than Mūlaprakriti, the Indestructible Lord.

......भूतपृथग्भावमेकस्थमनुपश्यति।
ततएवचविस्तारं ....[2]

The wise man "seeth the diversified existence of beings as rooted in One and proceeding from it."

Now, we have to study the nature of this procession from, or production of the Sarga, the sending forth, or evolving. The Sanātana Dharma does not recognise an unscientific creation, a making of something out of nothing. The supreme Īshvara evolves all beings out of Himself.

यथोर्णनाभिः सृजते गृह्णते च
यथा पृथिव्यामोषधयः सम्भवन्ति।
यथा सतः पुरुषात्केशलोमानि
तथाऽऽक्षरात्सम्भवतीह विश्वम्॥[3]

---

2 Ibid. xiii. 30.

3 Muṇḍakop, 1.i.7.

"As the spider sends forth and retracts (its web), as in the earth herbs grow, as from a living man the hairs of the head and body, so from the Indestructible the universe becomes."

यथा सुदीप्तात्पावकाद्विस्फुलिङ्गाः
सहस्रशः प्रभवन्ते सरूपाः ।
तथाऽऽक्षराद्विविधाः सोम्य भावाः
प्रजायन्ते तत्र चैवापि यन्ति ॥
एतस्माज्जायते प्राणो मनः सर्वेन्द्रियाणि च ।
खं वायुर्ज्योतिरापः पृथिवी विश्वस्य धारिणी ॥
तस्माच्च देवा बहुधा सम्प्रसूताः
साध्या मनुष्याः पशवो वयांसि ।[4]

As from a blazing fire in a thousand ways similar sparks spring forth, so from the Indestructible, O beloved, various types of beings are born, and also return thither.......

"From That are born Breath, Mind, and all the Senses, Ether, Air, Fire, Water, and Earth, the support of all.........

"From that in various ways are born the Gods, Sādhyas, Men, Beasts, Birds."

In the *Manusmriti*, more details are given as to the order of evolution, and here again it is said that the immediate Creator, Brahmā, created all beings from Himself and from the elements previously produced from Himself, as we shall immediately see.

ब्रह्माण्डान, Brahmāṇḍāni, literally Eggs of Brahmā, or as we should say, world-systems, are numberless, we are told.

अस्यब्रह्माण्डस्यसमन्ततःस्थितान्यताद्दृशान्यनन्तकोटिब्रह्माण्डानिसावरणानि ज्वलन्ति। चतुर्मुखपञ्चमुख-षण्मुख-सप्तमुखा-ष्टमुखादिसंख्याक्रमेण सहसावधिमुखान्तैर्नारायणांशै रजो

4 Ibid. II. i. 1, 3,7

गुणप्रधानैरेकैकसृष्टिकर्तृभिरधिष्ठितानि विष्णुमहेश्वराख्यैर्नारायणांशैः सत्त्वतमोगुणप्रधानैरेकैकस्थितिसंहारकर्तृभिरधिष्ठितानि महाजलौघमत्स्यबुद्बुदानन्तसंघवद्भ्रमन्ति ॥[5]

"All around this Brahmāṇḍa, there blaze infinite crores of other similar Brahmāṇḍas, with their envelopes. Four-faced, five-faced, six-faced, seven-faced, eight-faced, successively, up to the number of a thousand-faced portions of Nārāyaṇa, in whom the Rajoguṇa is predominant, Creators of each of one world-system, preside in them. Portions of Nārāyaṇa, called Viṣhṇu and Maheshvara, in whom the Sattva and Tamas Guṇas predominate, also preside in them, performing the work of preservation and destruction in each. They wander about, these Brahmāṇḍas, like shoals of fishes and bubbles in a vast mass of water."

संख्याचेद्रजसामस्तिविश्वानांनकदाचन ॥
ब्रह्मविष्णुशिवादीनामतथासंख्यानविद्यते ।
प्रतिविश्वेषुसन्त्येवब्रह्मविष्णुशिवादयः ।[6]

"Grains of sand are perhaps numerable, but of universes (there is) not any (numbering.)

"So, there is no numbering of Brahmās, Viṣhṇus, Shivas and the rest. In each of these universes there are Brahmā, Viṣhṇu, Shiva, and other (Devas)."

This we could have imagined, even had we not been told it, for since, as we saw in the *Viṣhṇu Purāṇa*, the one and only God, Janārdana, takes the designation of Brahmā, Viṣhṇu and Shiva accordingly as He creates, preserves, or destroys, and creation, preservation and destruction must go on in every world-system, God must manifest in each in these three Forms.

---

5 Atharvaṇa (or Tripād-Vibhūti) Māyānārāyaṇop. vi.

6 Devī Bhāg. IX, iii. 7. 8.

This is the Trimūrti, the reflection as it were in Space and time of that Supreme Triple Unity, the Source of beings –the Nirguṇa Brahman, the Saguṇa Brahman and Mūlaprakriti, out of Space and Time, Eternal.

The Trimūrti is the manifestation, then, of Īshvara in a world system, or Brahmāṇḍa, and is therefore the Supreme Will, Wisdom and Activity in a concrete form.

Brahmā is the Creator, and His Shakti is Sarasvatī, the Goddess of Wisdom, without whom Activity could not be wisely guided. He is pictured with four heads, one looking towards each quarter, as the Maker of the four quarters and their contents, and riding on the हंसः, Hamsah, the Swan. The name हंसः, a re-arrangement of सःअहंसाऽहं, is an allusion to His relation with Ahamkara, the divider, the maker of atoms.

Viṣhṇu is the Preserver and Sustainer, the principle underlying and sustaining the universe in order, and preserving forms, holding them together by His attracting force. His Shakti is Lakṣhmī, the Goddess of Happiness, of Prosperity, of all desirable objects. He is pictured with four arms, as sustaining the four quarters, and rides on Garuḍa, the emblem of speed and of intelligence, He is the source of Avatāras, and in Them, or in His own Person, is perhaps the most generally worshipped manifestation of Īshvara. Indeed, as Narāyaṇa, He whose dwelling is in the waters. He is worshipped as Saguṇa Brahman, dwelling in Matter.

Shiva, or Mahādeva, or Maheshvara, is the Destroyer, He who frees Ātmā from imprisoning forms, who destroys Avidyā and so gives Vidyā, and who, finally rolling up the universe, brings the peace of liberation. His Shakti is Umā, इच्छा Ichchhā,

Will, also called ब्रह्मविद्या, Brahmavidyā, who reveals Brahman[7], He is pictured ever as an Ascetic, it being He who is the Object of worship for Yogis, who have renounced the world. He rides on the Bull, the emblem of the mind (and sometimes of physical nature), as having subdued it, and wears the tiger-skin, the emblem of the slain desire-nature. Hence he is, as the name Shiva implies, Ānanda, the peace and bliss of Ātmā, freed from desire and master of mind.

These Supreme Forms of Īshvara, separated by their functions, but One in Essence, stand as the central Life of the Brahmāṇḍa, and from and by Them it proceeds, is maintained, and is indrawn. Their functions should not be confused, but their Unity should never be forgotten.

Brahmā, as the creative God, is spoken of as appearing first, born in the Golden Egg, which grows out of the seed of the One in the waters of Matter.

सोऽभिध्याय शरीरात्स्वातिससृक्षुर्विविधाः प्रजाः ।
अप एव ससर्जादौ तासु बीजमवासृजत् ॥
तदण्डमभवद्धैमं सहस्रांशुसमप्रभम् ।
तस्मिञ्जज्ञे स्वयं ब्रह्मा सर्वलोकपितामहः ॥[8]

"He, having meditated, desiring to produce various beings from His own body, first put forth the waters; in these He placed the seed."

"That became a Golden Egg, equal in radiance to the thousand-rayed (the Sun). In that was born Brahmā Himself, the Grandsire of all worlds."

---

7 See *Kenop*, iii, iv.

8 *Manusmriti*, i. 8, 9.

Here the Waters, Matter, Mūlaprakṭiti, receive the seed of Life, and this becomes the Hiraṇyagarbha, the Golden Egg, in which the Creator is born, in order to form his world-system. Hence a world-system is called a Brahmāṇḍa, a Brahmā Egg, a very significant epithet, as world-systems are oval, like an egg, and seen from outside, present exactly an egg-like form, each planet following an egg-like orbit. Of this Egg we read in the Viṣhṇu Purāṇa that within it Brahmā and the world-system were contained, while it was invested externally by seven envelopes, water, fire, air, ether, the origin of the elements (Ahamkāra), Mahat and Primal homogeneous Matter, which surrounds the whole.[9]

Every world system is thus surrounded by the great cosmic elements, as described in the First Chapter of *Manusmriti* by Manu himself (shl. 5 to 59). The account of the later creation is given over to Bhrigu, who explains briefly the repetition of the process within the World-Egg. A similar and fuller account is given in the Mahābhārata, and in the Viṣhṇu and other Purāṇas.

It will be enough if the student grasp the general principles, and he can fill up the complicated details later from the many accounts given in the sacred books. He should remember that the process in the universe containing many Brahmāṇḍas, and in the separate Brahmāṇḍas, is similar. A very fine and instructive description of the general principle of emanation-which will also be found illuminative when the student comes to the bodies in which the Jīvātmā dwells –is given in The Devī Bhāgavata.

स पुनः कामकर्मादियुक्तया स्वीयमायया।
पूर्वानुभूतसंस्कारात्कालकर्मविपाकतः ॥

9 Loc. cit. I. ii.

आववेकाच्च तत्त्वस्य सिसृक्षावान्प्रजायते ।
अबुद्धिपूर्वः सर्गोऽयं कथितस्ते नगाधिप ॥
एतद्धि यन्मया प्रोक्तं मम रूपमलौकिकम् ।
अव्याकृतं तदव्यक्तं मायाशवलमित्यपि ॥
प्रोच्यते सर्वशास्त्रेषु सर्वकारणकारणम् ।
तत्त्वानामादिभूतं च सच्चिदानन्दविग्रहम् ॥
सर्वकर्मघनीभूतमिच्छाज्ञानक्रियाश्रयम् ।
ह्रींकारमन्त्रवाच्यं तद् आदितत्त्वंतदुच्यते ॥
तस्मादाकाश उत्पन्नः शब्दतन्मात्ररूपकः ।
भवेत्स्पर्शात्मको वायुस्तेजोरूपात्मकंपुनः ॥
जलं रसात्मकं पश्चात्ततो गन्धात्मिका धरा ।
तेभ्योऽभवन्महत्सूत्रं यल्लिङ्गं परिचक्षते ॥
सर्वात्मकं तत्संप्रोक्तं सूक्ष्मदेहोऽयमात्मनः ।
अव्यक्तं कारणो देहः सचोक्तः पूर्वमेवहि ॥
यस्मिञ्जगद्बीजरूपं स्थितं लिङ्गोद्भवो यतः ।
ततः स्थूलानि भूतानि पञ्चीकरणमार्गतः ॥
तत्कार्यं च विराड्देहः स्थूलदेहोऽयमात्मनः ॥[10]

"He by His Māyā, conjoined with Kāma and Karma, because of the Samskāra of past experience, and the ripeness of time and Karma, and cause of non-discrimination of the Tattva, becomes desirous of creation. This emanation, O King of mountains, is not preceded by Buddhi.

This transcendental form of mine that I have described to thee, is the undifferentiated Avyakta, and the Māyā-coloured; in all the Shāstras it is described as the Cause of all causes, and the first Element of all the elements, the embodiment of Sat-Chit-

10 Loc. cit. VII. xxxii. 22, 28

Ānanda, compacted of all Karma, the base of Ichchhā, Jnāna and Kriyā. It is declared by the mantra Hrīm, and is called the Ādi-Tattva."

"From it was born Ākāsha, in the form of the Tanmātrā of sound. Thereafter arises Vāyu, of the nature of touch. Then Tejas, of the nature of vision. Then Water, of the nature of taste. And then Earth, of the nature of smell....... From them arose the great Thread, which is called the Liṅga.

It is declared to possess the nature of all. It is the Sūkṣhma Deha of the Ātmā. The Avyakta is the Kāraṇa Deha, declared before, in which the world exists as a seed, from which the Liṅga arises, wherefrom (arise) the gross elements in the way of Paṅchīkāraṇa....The result of that is the VirāṭDeha, which is the Sthūla Deha of the Ātmā."

The first emanation is here the Ādi-Tattva; then the Buddhi Tattva, sometimes called Mahat-Tattva, said to follow the first; then the five Tattvas in order. The terms used, denoting the first two, vary in different accounts; they are sometimes represented as mahat and Ahamkāra, or as Ādi-Bhūta and Mahat. In any case, the materials from which the worlds are made are seven, and these seven are spoken of in Manu as the source of all:

तेषामिदं तु सप्तानां पुरुषाणां महौजसाम् ।
सूक्ष्माभ्यो मूर्तिमात्राभ्यः सम्भवति..[11]

"Verily, this becomes from the subtile formative particles of these seven very mighty Beings."

We shall now see that the creative process within a Brahmāṇḍa follows on the same lines.

11 Loc. cit. I.19.

Brahmā is surrounded by homogeneous matter, called Pradhāna, in the Vishṇu Purāṇa—in which the Guṇas are in equilibrium; His energy disturbing this tamasic condition, Rajoguṇa prevails and there is rapid motion. Then He puts forth the principle of Mahat-Buddhi, Pure Reason—which, entering matter, being invested by it, and causing the predominance of the Sattva-guṇa, the motion becomes rhythmical, harmonious. Then follows Ahamkāra, the individualising principle, separating the homogeneous matter into particles, Aṇus, atoms. Ahamkāra, causing the Tamo-guṇa to prevail in Prakṛiti, forms successively the five Tanmātrās, or subtle elements, and the senses: hearing, touch, sight, taste, smell, with their appropriate gross elements: ākāsha, vāyu, agni, apa, prithivī—ether, air, fire, water, earth. Causing Rajo-guṇa to prevail, Ahamkāra gives rise to the ten Indriyas: the 5 ideal types of sense-organs and the 5 ideal types of action organs.

Causing Sattva-guna to prevail, Ahamkāra calls out the ten Deities connected with the sense-and-action-organs, and Manas, the centralising organ of the Indriyas.

These three creations are called respectively the भूतादि Bhūtādi, that of the elements; तैजस, Taijasa, that of the fiery, the active energies; and वैकारिक, Vaikärika, the directing, administrative, powers.

The points to remember here are: in what is usually called matter, Tamo-guṇa predominates; in the Indriyas, Rajo-guṇa predominates; in the presiding Deities, Sattva-guṇa predominates.

The work of creation proceeded by calling into existence the Suras or Devas, described by Manu as कर्मात्मान: "whose nature is action," that vast multitude of intelligent Beings, of very varying power and authority, who guide the whole course of nature, and direct all its activities.

It is of course, clearly understood by all Hindus that this vast host of Devas no more obscures the Unity of Īshvara, in His triple form as Brahmā, Viṣhṇu and Shiva, than do the vast hosts of men animals, plants, and minerals. As said in the Shruti:

इन्द्रं मित्रं वरुणमग्निमाहु-रथोदिव्यः स सुपर्णो गरुत्मान् ।
एकं सद्विप्रा बहुधा वदन्ति अग्निंयमंमातरिश्वानमाहुः ॥[12]

"Indra, Mitra, Varuṇa, Agni, they call him and He is golden-feathered Garutmān. Or what is One, sages speak as manifold; they call Him Agni, Yama, Mātarishva."

So also, the Smriti:

आत्मैव देवताः सर्वाः सर्वमात्मन्यवस्थितम् ।[13]

"All the Gods (are) even the Self: all rests on the Self."

एतमेकेवदन्त्यग्निंमनुमन्येप्रजापतिम् ।
इन्द्रमेकेऽपरंप्राणमपरेब्रह्मशाश्वतम् ॥[14]

"Some call Him Agni, others Manu, (others) Prajāpati, some Indra, others Life-Breath, others the eternal Brahman."

But the Devas have their own place in nature, as the ministers of the will of Īshvara, ruling, protecting, adjusting, guiding, with intelligence and power far greater than human, but still limited. The name, Deva, Shining or Radiant, very well describes their resplendent appearance, their bodies being formed of a subtle luminous matter, and hence flashing out light. They are concerned with the matter-side of nature, and the guidance of its evolution,

---

12 Ṛigveda. clxiv. 46.

13 Manu. xii. 119.

14 Ibid, -123

and all the constructive energies studied by science are the energies of the Devas.

On their work depend the fruits of all human activities concerned with production, in all its branches. Those who seek material prosperity need their continual co-operation, and this co-operation is granted under quite definite laws. It may be obtained by a scientific knowledge of their methods of working, humans falling in with their activities and thus sharing the result. Or it may be obtained from them by what is literally exchange, humans supplying them with objects which facilitate their work, or which they enjoy, and they, in return, directing their energies, the energies of "nature," to suit his ends—as a strong human may help a weak one in the performance of a task. Or their increased co-operation may be won by prayers, accompanied by such acts as they approve, such as feeding the hungry, clothing the naked, etc. Or their services may be commanded by great Ṛishis and Yogis, who, by purity, knowledge, and austerity, have risen above them in the scale of being. Sometimes a human wins the favour of a Deva by some service done in this or a previous birth, and then all his efforts prosper, and he succeeds where others fail, and he is called "lucky."

"Good luck" is the result of the working of Devas, and as their working is invisible, men think the result is a chance, or accident. But it must be remembered that all Devas work within law, and not by arbitrary fancies. The sacrifices and offerings prescribed in the Vedas form a great occult system for obtaining and regulating this co-operation between Devas and men, whereby the work of both was carried on with the largest results.

देवान्भावयतानेन ते देवा भावयन्तुवः।
परस्परं भावयन्तः श्रेयः परमवाप्स्यथ।

इष्टान्भागान्हि वो देवा दास्यन्ते यज्ञभाविताः ।[15]

"With this nourish ye the Devas, (and) may the Devas nourish you: thus nourishing each other ye shall obtain the greatest good."

"Nourished by sacrifice, the Devas shall give you (all) desired enjoyments."

And the reason is given:

अन्नाद्भवन्ति भूतानि पर्जन्यादन्नसम्भवः ।
यज्ञाद्भवति पर्जन्यः[16]

"From food creatures become; from rain is the production of food; from sacrifice rain proceedeth."

कांक्षंतः कर्मणां सिद्धि यजन्त इह देवताः ।[17]

"They who desire success in action here worship the Devas."

But the benefits obtained from them are transient:

अन्तवत्तु फलं ।[18]

"Transient indeed the fruit."

Hence the worship of the Devas is not practised by men whose hearts are set on spiritual things. They worship Īshivara, rather than His ministers, either as Brahman, or as revealed in the Trimūrti, or in the Shaktis, or in such a Deva as Gaṇesha for learning, or in the Avatāras. But this will be further dealt with in Part 11, Chapter V.

The Devas of the Elements—Ether, Air, Fire, Water and

15 Bhagavad-Gītā. iii. 11, 12.
16 Ibid. 14
17 Ibid. IV. 12.
18 Ibid. vii. 23.

Earth—Indra, Vāyu, Agni, Varuṇa and Kubera, are the Five Devarājas, Deva Kings, of these great departments of nature, Indra being the Chief Ruler. Under them are divided the great hosts of Devas. Thus the Sādhyas, Vasus, Ādityas, and Apsarās are specially connected with Indra; the Maruts with Vāyu; the Yakṣhas, Gandharvas, Vidyādharas, and Kinnaras with Kubera. Some have charge of the animal kingdom, as the Nāgas and Sarpas of snakes, the Suparṇas of birds, etc.

Four great Gods rule the four quarters: Indra, Yama, Varuṇa and Kubera, as the protectors of mankind. Yama is the Lord of Death, the wise and gracious Deva who instructed Nachiketā.

The Asuras, the beings who are opposed to the Suras, or Devas, in their activity, embody the destructive energies of nature; they are as necessary and as useful as the constructive, though on the surface opposed to them. They hinder and obstruct evolution, embodying the very essence of matter, Tamas-guṇa, inertia, resistance, and by that very resistance make progress steady and durable.

These creations belong to the invisible worlds, although, in their activities, they were to be closely connected with the visible--the worlds visible and invisible, indeed, forming the field of a vast evolutionary process—Samsāra, the World Process.

The order of the process in the physical world at its origination was: minerals, plants, animals, men. In the *Vishṇu Purāṇa* it is stated that while Brahmā was meditating on creation—the three primary Prakrita creations of Mahat, the elements and the indriyas, bring over—the immovable creation, minerals and plants, appeared. Then followed the animal kingdom, called Tiryaksrotas. The creation of some Devas followed here, according to the Purāṇa, but they do not belong to the physical world, with which we are dealing here. Then came the creation of men. It must be remembered that while this is the fundamental order of evolution, many varieties occur in different *kalpas*, and accounts in the different books vary, within certain broad limits, since these great classes of beings overlap each other, so that new kinds of animals and plants appear long after man. The world in fact is ever-becoming along the four great lines, however much we may separate them for purposes of exposition.

The stages of evolution are very plainly given in the Aitareya Brāhmaṇa.

तस्य य आत्मानमाविस्तरां वेदाश्नुते हाविर्भूयः ।
ओषधिवनस्पतयो यच्च किञ्च प्राणभृत्सआत्मानमाविस्तरांवेद ।
ओषधिवनस्पतिषु हि रसो दृश्यते ।
चित्तं प्राणभृत्सु ।प्राणभृत्सु त्वेवाविस्तरामात्मा ।
तेषु हि रसोऽपि दृश्यते । न चित्त मितरेषु । पुरुषे त्वेवा
विस्तरामात्मा ।स हि प्रज्ञानेन सम्पन्नतमः । विज्ञातं वदति ।
विज्ञातं पश्यति । वेद श्वस्तनम् । वेद लोकालोकौ ।
मतर्येनामृतम् ईप्सति । एवंसम्पन्नः । अथेतरेषां पशूनामशनापिपासे एवाभिविज्ञानम् । न
विज्ञातं वदन्ति । न विज्ञातं पश्यन्ति ।
न विदुः श्वस्तनम् । न लोकालोकौ ।
त एतावन्तो भवन्ति । यथाप्रज्ञं हि सम्भवाः ॥[19]

"He who knows the Ātmā as Him (the Puruṣha) in manifestation, he most enjoys that manifestation. Herbs and trees and all that bears life, he knows as the Self in manifestation. In herbs and trees, Rasa (sap, life,) is seen, and mind in them that have Prāṇa. In them that have Prāṇa, the Ātmā is (more) manifest. In them, Rasa also is seen, while mind is not seen in the others.

19 Aitareyāraṇyaka. II. iii. 2.

In man, the Ātmā is (most) manifest; he is most supplied with knowledge. He speaks that which he knows; he sees that which he knows; he knows what occurred yesterday; he knows the visible and the invisible; by the mortal he desires the immortal. Thus supplied is he. But of the others, animals, hunger and thirst are the only knowledge. They speak not the known; they see not the known; they know not what belongs to yesterday, nor the visible and the invisible. Only this much they have. According to the knowledge are the births."

On this Sāyaṇa comments as follows:

"सच्चिदानन्दरूपस्य जगत्कारणस्य परमात्मनः
कार्यभूताः सर्वेऽपि पदार्था आविर्भावोपाधयः। तत्राचेतनेषु
मृत् पाषाणादिषु सत्तामात्रमाविर्भवति न चात्मनो जीवरूपत्वम्।
ये तु ओषधिवनस्पतयो जीवरूपाः स्थावराः ये च श्वासरूपप्राणधारिणो जीवरूपा जङ्गमाः ते उभये अतिशयेन आविर्भावस्थानम् इति...... ।।"

"All objects whatsoever, being of the nature of effects, are Upādhis for this manifestation of the Supreme Self, Sat, Chit, Ānanda, the cause of the universe. In the unconscious, earth, stones, etc., only Sat is manifest, and the Ātmā has not yet attained the form of Jīva. The unmoving Jīvas, namely the herbs and trees, and also the moving Jīvas, which have Prāṇa as breath; both these are stages of manifestation in a higher degree."

The student should note these passages, as it is currently supposed that the idea of evolution is of modern birth.

The work of Brahmā consisted in producing all the materials, as we have seen, and by His tapas, or meditation, he formed the archetypes of all living things. But we learn from the *Shiva Purāṇa* and the *Viṣhṇu Bhāgavata* that He needed the help of Viṣhṇu in order to endow these forms with life, Viṣhṇu being that aspect of

Īshvara from whom the sustaining life, प्राणः, Práṇah, that is the life that holds forms together and preserves them as forms, together with चित्, Chit, consciousness, comes forth.

Moreover, it is further stated in the *Shiva Purāṇa* that when these forms had been fully developed, Mahādeva was appealed to, and He gave immortality; that is, He linked to the forms the Jīvātmās evolved in previous *kalpas*. This is generally referred to in the ascription of Ahamkāra to Rudra. These three great stages in the building of worlds—the work of Brahmā, creative of materials and of the ideal forms of all living beings; the work of Viṣhṇu, in breathing Prāṇa and Chit into these forms, and maintaining them in life; the work of Shiva in giving the eternal Jīvātmās—should be clearly understood.

In the *Manusmriti* nothing but hints of these details are given, only the name Brahmā being used; but it is indicated that He changed His form, divided Himself and produced Virāt, who produced Svāyambhuva Manu, who then called forth the ten Maharṣhis, they in turn producing seven Manus.

After that, these became the active and direct agents in creation, Brahmā Himself disappearing after creating the worlds, a class of Devas (those connected with the great elements), and some other general fundamental principles and beings. The account is very brief, and from its brevity somewhat difficult, but this summary of the World-Process is only introductory to the main object of the book.

The *Shiva* Purāṇa, as mentioned, gives the following details:

He (Brahmā) emanated water first and therein sowed a handful of the seed which was His. The same grew up as an Egg, made up of the 24 *tattvas*. Brahmā, who appeared as Virāt, perceived the Egg becoming hard. This caused doubt in His mind and He gave Himself up to *tapas*. Thus He spent twelve years, concentrating His thought on Viṣhṇu. Then Viṣhṇu appeared and said: "I am pleased with Thee; ask what boon Thou desirest." Brahmā said: "O Lord! It is just as it should be, for I have been placed by Shiva in your charge. The world which Shiva commanded me to create is here, but I see it is motionless (*jaḍa-rūpa*) and material. So be thou, O Lord, as Life (Prāṇa) unto it, and make it conscious (*chetanā*)." Thus Brahmā spoke, and Viṣhṇu, following the directions Shiva gave, entered the Egg—His form being one of a thousand heads, a thousand ears, a thousand feet and hands—the Universal Puruṣha who touched heaven and earth and pervaded the Egg.

As Viṣhṇu entered it, that Egg of 24 *tattvas* became full of life and consciousness (*sa-chetanā*) from Pātāla to Satya Loka.

Hari, the best of all Puruṣhas adorned the seat that is Satya, which He occupied. Brahmā stood in the world of *Tapas*, while other Puruṣhas occupied the other worlds as became them. Brahmā first created a number of sons born of the mind.

But they all became ascetics. He created more again, but they also renounced the world. So He began to cry, out of annoyance. As He cried, Mahādeva appeared. Because He came forth from Brahmā's cry, He is called Rudra. Immediately on His appearance, He addressed Brahmā, saying:

"What aileth Thee? Tell that to Me and I will remove it."

"O Deva," answered Brahmā, "There are obstacles in the way of further manifestation. Do thou therefore so ordain it, as may make it free from Impediments." When he heard this, Mahādeva, the destroyer of all trouble, resolved to do what Brahmā desired and said: "This creation of yours, I will make it everlasting."

So saying, Mahādeva, the Lord who is Bliss, although known

as Rudra, disappeared to Kailāsa with His gaṇas. Then (with Shiva's help) Brahmā created Bhṛigu and six other Ṛiṣhis. From His lap, He also caused Nārada to be born, from His shadow (*chhāyā*) Kardama, and from His thumb Dakṣha He made. Thus there appeared ten Ṛiṣhis. And after Bhṛigu came Marīchi, whose son was Kashyapa. It is this Kashyapa who with his progeny filled the world.[20]

In the *Viṣhṇu Bhāgavata* the mention is in connection with the making of the World-Egg as an organised form, but, as said before, the process is similar on the large scale or the small. The point to be recognised is that Viṣhṇu is the Organiser.

यदैतेऽसङ्गता भावा भूतेन्द्रियमनोगुणाः ।
यदायतननिर्माणे न शेकुर्ब्रह्मवित्तम ॥
तदा संहत्य चान्योन्यं भगवच्छक्तिचोदिताः ।
सदसत्त्वमुपादाय चोभयं ससृजुर्ह्यदः ॥[21]

"When these separated existences, the Bhūtas, Indriyas, Manas and Guṇas, were unable to create organisms (literally a dwelling-place, an Upādhi), O best of Brahma-knowers, then, mixing with each other, they were impelled by the power of Bhagavān (Viṣhṇu), and, becoming both Sat and Asat, existent and non-existent evolved this."

The ten Maharṣhis, Marīchi, Atri, Aṅgiras, Pulastya, Pulaha, Kratu, Prachetas, Vasiṣhṭha, Bhṛigu and Nārada, were superhuman beings, who having obtained liberation in former *kalpas*, were called forth to aid in the direction of the World Process, and who remain, superintending the destinies of the

20 Shiva Purana. I. vi. 1-20
21 Loc. cit. II. v. 32, 33.

worlds, and will remain until Pralaya. Sometimes only seven are given this rank, Prachetas, Bhṛigu and Nārada not being included in the list. Sometimes others are added, as Dakṣha and Kardama.

The Kumāras, variously given as four, five, six and seven, are, as their name implies, Virgin Beings, ascetics, and they watch over the world. Shiva Himself took the form of one—Rudra or Nīla-lohita. Sanatkumāra, Sanandana, Sanaka and Sanātana are the four most often referred to. Ṛibhu, Kapila and Sana are also mentioned.

To this brief sketch of the World-process it should be added that the early human races preceding the Āryan are often referred to under the names of Dānavas and Daityas, huge beings of enormous strength and energy, who carried on many a struggle with the Devas themselves. The Rākṣhasas were another race, more brutal in nature, usually malformed, huge, cruel, powerful, cannibals, the terror of milder races. They possessed, moreover, many magical secrets of a dark kind, which they used for terrorising and oppressing. All these have entirely disappeared from the earth.

Such is the vast field of Samsāra, in which the pilgrim Jīvātmās wander, until, in some human form, they reach the knowledge of the Self, and obtain liberation.

The points to be remembered are:

1. The coming forth of the Many from Saguṇa Brahman and Mūlaprakriti by the power of Māyā, and their return at the close of the Day of manifestation.
2. The manifestation of Īshvara as the Trimūrti, in the forms of Creation, Preservation, and Destruction, Brahmā, Viṣhṇu and Shiva, with their Shaktis, Sarasvatī, Lakṣhmī and Umā.
3. The work of Brahmā, forming the materials of the universe and the

ideal types of all beings, Suras, Asuras, minerals, plants, animals and men.

4. The work of Viṣhṇu, giving Prāṇa and Chit, and hence making living organised forms possible, all such forms being preserved and maintained by Him.
5. The work of Shiva, breathing into these forms, when they arrive at the human stage, Jīvātmās that have reached in previous *kalpas* a stage at which such highly organised bodies can be utilised by them, bodies in which Avidyā can be destroyed, and they can attain Vidyā.
6. The existence throughout the World-Process of lofty superhuman intelligences, such as Ṛiṣhis and Kumāras, intent on human welfare.
7. The past races on the earth, Dānavas, Daityas, Rākṣhasas.

REBIRTH

सर्वाजीवे सर्वसंस्थे बृहन्ते
तस्मिन्हंसो भ्राम्यते ब्रह्मचक्रे।
पृथगात्मानं प्रेरितारं च मत्वा
जुष्टस्ततस्तेनामृतत्वमेति ॥[1]

"IN the vast Brahman-wheel, the source and support of all Jīvas, the Hamsa (the individual) is made to wander, thinking himself and the Ruler different. United with Him, he obtains immortality."

Here, in a single shloka, we are given the reason of rebirth and its ending. Man wanders about in the universe so long as he thinks of himself as different from Ishvara; knowing himself to be one with Him, he obtains liberation. In Shruti and Smriti, in Purāṇa and Itihāsa, the Self in man is declared to be of the nature of Brahman.

ततःपरं ब्रह्म परं बृहन्तं
यथा निकायं सर्वभूतेषु गूढम्।
विश्वस्यैकं परिवेष्टितारम्

1 Svetashvatarop. i. 6.

ईशं तं ज्ञात्वाऽमृता भवन्ति ॥
अङ्गुष्ठमात्रः पुरुषोऽन्तरात्मा
सदाजनानां हृदये सन्निविष्टः ।[2]

"Then, having known the Supreme Brahman, the Supreme Immensity, as the Essence hidden in all creatures, the one Pervader of the universe, the Lord, they become immortal."

"The measure of a thumb, the Puruṣha, the inner Self, ever dwelling in the heart of men."

स वा अयमात्मा ब्रह्म ।[3]

"He, this Self, is Brahman."

स वा एष महानज आत्मा योऽयं विज्ञानमयः प्राणेषु य एषोऽन्तर्हृदय आकाशः ।[4]

"He, this great unborn Self, (is) He who (is) this intelligence in living creatures, He who (is) this Ākāsha in the heart."

स वा एष महानज आत्माऽजरोऽमरोऽमृतोऽभयो ब्रह्माभयं ।[5]

"He, this great, unborn, undecaying, deathless, immortal, fearless Self, (is) the fearless Brahman." It is this nature, identical with Brahman as the sparks from a fire are identical with the fire, which evolves, unfolds itself as the Jīvātmā in all living beings. As a seed grows to be a tree like its parent, so the Jīvātmic seed grows into self-conscious Deity. Samsāra exists that the Jīvātmā may learn to realise himself. The Jīvātmā differs from Brahman only as the seed from the tree that bears it.

---

2 Ibid. iii.7.13.
3 Brihadāraṇyakop. IV. iv. 5.
4 Ibid. 22.
5 Ibid. 25.

ज्ञाऽज्ञौ द्वावजावीशानीशौ । ।[6]

"Wise and unwise, both unborn, powerful and powerless."

Therefore, although unwise and powerless, the Jīvātmā can become wise and powerful; to this end he must evolve, and his evolution is on the wheel of births and deaths.

Transmigration is the word usually given to this journey, for the Jīvātmā transmigrates from one body to another; as one grows old and wastes away, he takes another.

वासांसि जीर्णानि यथा विहाय
नवानि गृह्णाति नरोऽपराणि ।
तथा शरीराणि विहाय
जीर्णान्यन्यानि संयाति नवानि देही ॥[7]

"As a man throws away old garments and takes others (that are) new, so the Embodied casts away old bodies and puts on new ones."

The word "re-incarnation" is also very generally used in modern days, the stress being here laid on the body rather than on the Jīvātmā; it again takes a fleshly covering.

This truth of the evolution of the Jivatma from ignorance to wisdom, from feebleness to power, is definitely revealed in the Shruti, and knowledge of it is necessary as a basis for good conduct and for the wise shaping of life. Man is not a creature of a day, here to-day and gone to-morrow, but an unborn immortal being, growing into a knowledge of his true nature and powers. Everything is within him, the fulness of divine wisdom and power, but this capacity has to be unfolded, and that is the object

6 Shvetāshratarop. i. 9.
7 Bhagavad-Gītā. ii. 22.

of living and dying. Such a view of man's nature gives dignity and strength and sobriety to life. It has been belived in by wise men in all ages, and has been a part of every ancient religion. For the best proof of this great truth by pure reasoning as distinguished from direct experience with Yoga-developed superphysical faculties, the student should consult Vātsyāyana's *Bhāṣhya* on the *Nyāya Sūtras* of Gautama.

Only in modern times, during a period of great ignorance, was this truth lost sight of in the West, and very irrational and fantastic notions have in consequence grown up there as to the human soul, its nature and destiny, undermining belief in the just and loving rule of Īshvara.[8]

The Jīvātmā contains within himself infinite possibilities, but when first thrown down into Prakriti, embodied in a Rūpa made up of the five elements. all these are inherent, not manifest. He passes through the diversified existences of the mineral kingdom, and of the plant and of the animal realms—the उद्भिज्जा Udbhijjāḥ (born by fission in the minerals and plants); the स्वेदज: Swedajah (born by exudation or gemmation, in certain low forms of plants and animals); the अण्डजा: Aṇḍajāh (born first as eggs, the oviparous animals)—before coming into the जरायुजा: Jarāyujāḥ (the viviparous higher animals and the human kingdom).

In these many of his lower powers are developed, and his consciousness passes from the latent to the active condition. A double evolution goes on; there is the continued life of the Jivatma

8 But even in the West such great scientific thinkers as Professor Huxley have begun to recognise the continued existence of the Jīvātmā from life to life. "Like the doctrine of evolution itself," he says, "that of transmigration has its roots in the world of reality, and it may claim such support as the great argument from analogy is capable of supplying." *Evolution and Ethics*) P. 16).

himself, continually increasing in richness and complexity; and there is a corresponding, Continuity in the forms he occupies, as each physical form is directly derived from a preceding physical form. Each form, however independent it may seem, was once part of another form, whose characteristics it shared, and from which it has been separated off for an independent career. While part of the parent form it shared all the advantages and improvements, or the reverse, due to the developing Jīvātmā within that parent form, and thus starts on its separate life on a little higher level than its parent if the Jīvātmā has progressed, or on a little lower level if it has retrograded. For while the general movement is one of progress, there are little ebbs and flows, like the waves that run on and fall back in a rising tide. This unbroken physical inheritance from form to form causes what science calls heredity, the passing on of characteristics from parents to offspring. But it has been observed by scientific men that mental and mortal characteristics do not pass from form to form, and they are puzzled in accounting for the evolution of consciousness. Their theory needs to be completed by the acceptance of transmigration. For just as physical continuity is necessary for physical evolution, so is the continuity of consciousness necessary for the evolution of mental and moral characteristics. This continuity is the consciousness of the Jīvātmā, which takes a form suitable to his condition—as we shall see presently in Chapter IV—enlarges his own powers by using the form, and thereby improves the form too; the bodies of the children of the body share these improvements of the form, are improved again by other Jīvātmās, and pass on still more improved bodies. When the old body is worn out, the Jīvātmā throws it off, and takes another form, as said above.

When the animal stage has been fully experienced, and the Jīvātmā is ready to pass on into the human form, his triune nature, reflection of the triune nature of Īshvara, begins to manifest. The human Jīvātmā—as we may now call him—manifests the three aspects of Jnāna, Ichchhā and Kriyā which have ever been in him, and these begin to evolve as self-consciousness; ahamkara appears, and the recognition of the "I"as opposed to the "Not- I" rapidly develops. The desire-nature, developed in the animal kingdom, now becomes much more powerful, by seizing on the evolving mind as its slave, and using its growing powers for the satisfaction of its own cravings. As the mind grows stronger, and the Jīvātmā by experience learns the pains that result from unbridled desires, he begins to exert his strength in checking and directing the desires, and the long struggle commences between the Jīvātmā, dimly beginning to feel his own divinity, and the kamic elements of his upadhis. As is written in the Kaṭhopanishat:

आत्मानं रथिनं विद्धि शरीरं रथमेवतु ।
बुद्धिं तु सारथिं विद्धि मनः प्रग्रहमेवच ॥
इन्द्रियाणि हयानाहुर्विषयांस्तेषु गोचरान् ।
आत्मेन्द्रिय मनोयुक्तं भोक्तत्याहुर्मनीषिणः ॥
यस्त्वविज्ञानवान्भवत्ययुक्तेनमनसासदा ।
तस्येन्द्रियाण्यवश्यानि दुष्टाश्वाइवसारथेः ॥
यस्तु विज्ञानवान्भवति युक्तेन मनसासदा ।
तस्यन्द्रियाणिवश्यानिसदश्वाइवसारथेः ॥
यस्त्वविज्ञानवान्भवत्यमनस्कःसदाऽशुचिः ।
नसतत्पदमाप्नोतिसंसारंचाधिगच्छति ॥[9]

---

9 Kaṭhop, I. iii. 3.7.

"Know the Self the chariot-owner, the body the chariot; know Reason the charioteer, and the mind as the reins; they call the senses - the horses, the sense objects their province. The Self, joined to the senses and mind, (is) the enjoyer; thus say the wise. Whoever is ignorant, always with mind loose, his senses (are) uncontrolled, like bad horses of the charioteer. Whoever is wise, always with mind tightened, his senses (are) controlled, like good horses of the charioteer. Whoever is indeed ignorant, thoughtless, always impure, he does not obtain that goal, (but) comes again into Samsāra."

When a term of earth-life is over, the Jīvātmā withdraws from the physical body, and in a subtle vehicle passes into the invisible worlds. He carries thither the results of the earth-life, to be enjoyed and suffered as fruits, going to the worlds in which these fruits can be consumed.

A description of this is given in the *Brihadāraṇyakopanishat* . The Jīvātmā leaves the body, taking with him the knowledge he has gained and the result of his work; then:

तद्यथा पेशस्कारी पेशसो मात्रामुपादायान्यन्नवतरं कल्याणतरं रूपं तनुत एवमेवायमात्मेदं शरीरं निहत्याविद्यां गमयित्वान्यन्नवतरं कल्याणतरं रूपं कुरुते ॥[10]

"As a goldsmith, having taken a piece of gold, makes another form, new and more beautiful, so verily the Ātmā, having cast off this body and having put away Avidyā, makes another new and more beautiful form."

In this he goes to the invisible world for which he is fitted-a matter to be dealt with in Chapter VI—and then the Upanishad goes on to say what happens: when his fruit in that invisible world is consumed.

10 Loc. cit. IV. iv. 4.

प्राप्यान्तं कर्मणस्तस्य यत्किञ्चेह करोत्ययं।
तस्माल्लोकात्पुनरेत्यस्मै लोकाय कर्मण इति नु कामयमानः ॥[11]

"Having arrived at the end of (the fruit of) that work—(of) whatsoever he here does—this one returns again from that world to this world of action; thus verily (the story of) him who desires."

This process is repeated over and over again as long as he has desires, for these desires bind him to the wheel of transmigration. It is truly "the story of him who desires." So also in the Devī Bhāgavata the same idea is expressed:

पूर्वदेहं परित्यज्य जीवः कर्मवशानुगः।
स्वर्गं वा नरकं वापि प्राप्नोति स्वकृतेन वै ॥
दिव्यं देहञ्च संप्राप्य यातनादेहमर्थजम्।
भुनक्ति विविधान्भोगान्स्वर्गे वा नरकेऽथवा ॥
भोगान्ते च यदोत्पत्तेः समयस्तस्य जायते।
तदैव सञ्चितेभ्यश्च कर्मभ्यः कर्मभिः पुनः।
योजयत्येव तं कालः.......[12]

"Having abandoned the former body, the Jīva, following Karma's rule, obtains either Svarga or Naraka according to his deeds.

"And having obtained a celestial body, or a body of suffering born of objects of desire, experiences varied fruit in Svarga or Naraka.

"At the end of the fruits, when the time for his rebirth arrives......then Time unites him again with Karmas (selected out) of the Sañchita karmas."

---

11 Ibid, 6.

12 Loc. eit. IV.xxi. 22-25.

The development of the Chit aspect of the Jīvātmā, and the purification of the Ichchhā aspect, being the main work of the human stage of evolution, the growth of Manas, and later of Buddhi, marks out the steps of the journey.

The constitution of the human being is very clearly outlined in the *Mahābhārata*,[13] from which we give the following summary:

The Self in man, the Jīvātmā, is identical in nature with the Supreme Self, Brahman. From this comes forth the understanding (Buddhi) and from the understanding, the mind (Manas); then to these, the Senses (Indriyas) are added, the man, the Dweller in the Body, is complete; the Body, his dwelling, is made up of the five elements. The senses, through the body, come into touch with the outer world; the senses hand on to the mind the results of the contact, giving the attributes or properties of the objects contacted—the way in which the objects affect them. The mind receives these reports, and groups them into mental images, and presents these to the understanding; the understanding pierces to the reality in which these mental images, made up of attributes, inhere. This is the outgoing of the Jīvātmā, and his gathering of experience, the प्रवृत्तिमार्गः the Pravṛitti Mārgaḥ, the path of going forth.

The first step, or stage, of this evolution is the experiencing of varied sensations; and therefore Manas is regarded as the sixth sense, which receives and organises the impressions conveyed to it by the five senses, affected by their contact with the outer world through the sense-organs.

मनःषष्ठानीन्द्रियाणि ।[14]

---

13 Loc. cit, Shānti Parva, ccii.

14 Bhagavad-Gītā xv. 7.

"The senses, Manas the sixth."

Or, when the senses and sense organs are taken together

इन्द्रियाणि दशैकं च ।[15]

"The ten senses and the one."

Manas, at this stage, is the slave of Kāma, and develops its capacities by directing the search for objects of enjoyment. Evolution is quickened by the instruction of the Ṛiṣhis, who teach man to sacrifice the objects of enjoyment to the Devas, first to gain increased worldly prosperity, and then to gain the delights of Svarga.

The second stage of evolution is one of continual conflict between Manas and Kāma, Manas being now sufficiently developed to recognise that the pleasures longed for by Kāma usually, in the long run, bring more pain than pleasure.

येहिसंस्पर्शजा भोगा दुःखयोनय एव ते ।[16]

"The delights that (are) contact-born, these verily (are) only wombs of pain."

Manas, therefore, begins to resist the searching for objects of enjoyment, instead of directing it, and hence conflict, in which Manas grows more rapidly. The thwarting of the *kāmic* longings. purifies Kāma, and the higher aspect of Ichchā begins to show itself—Ichchhā that is Will, the Shakti of Shiva, who is the

15 Ibid xiii. 5.
16 Ibid v. 22.

destroyer of Kāma, the son of Vishṇu and Lakshmī; and also the lower aspect of Ichchhā.[17]

The third stage of the evolution of Manas consists in the development of the higher intellectual powers; Manas no longer enslaved by, nor even struggling with Kāma, has become free, is the pure Manas, engaged with ideas, wrought out by his own labour, not with sense-born images. The Jīvātmā ceases to delight in sense-contacts, or in their mental reproductions, and engages himself in pure thought, in the endeavour to understand the Self and the Not Self. This stage leads up to the evolution of Buddhi, the Pure Reason or the Higher Understanding, of which the expression is Wisdom, the result of the union of knowledge and love, Wisdom which sees and loves the Self alone.

श्रेयान्द्रव्यमयाद्यज्ञाज्ज्ञानयज्ञः परन्तप ।
सर्वं कर्माखिलं पार्थ ज्ञाने परिसमाप्यते ॥
येन भूतान्यशेषेण द्रक्ष्यस्यात्मन्यथो मयि ॥[18]

"Better than the sacrifice of objects is the sacrifice of Wisdom, O Parantapa! All actions in their entirety, O Pārtha, culminate in wisdom. By this thou shalt see all beings without exception in the Self, and thus in Me." When the Jīvātmā reaches this stage, he is on the threshold of liberation. He has long विरतादुश्चरितात् "ceased from wicked ways," is शान्तः subdued समाहितः "concentrated," शान्तमानसः "of pacified mind."[19]

यस्तु विज्ञावान्भवति समनस्कः सदाशुचिः ।
स तु तत्पदमाप्नोति यस्माद्भूयोनजायते । ।[20]

17 Dharma is born from the Wisdom of Vishṇu, Kāma from His Love, which must be developed in man first by desire for material objects; therefore Dharma, Kāma and Artha are enjoined together on the Pravṛitti Mārga.

18 Bhagavad-Gītā, iv. 33, 35.

19 Kaṭhop. 1. ii. 23.

20 Ibid. iii. 8.

"Whoever verily is wise, thoughtful, always pure, he obtains that goal whence he is not born again."

For this round of births and deaths is not ever lasting for the Jīvātmā; bound to it by his own desires, with the ceasing of those desires he becomes free; bound to it by his ignorance of his own nature, with the ceasing of that ignorance he knows himself free. Only

मृत्योः स मृत्युमाप्नोति य इह नानेव पश्यति ।[21]

"He goes from death to death who here sees manyness."

यदा सर्वे प्रमुच्यन्ते कामा येऽस्य हृदिश्रिताः ।
अथमर्त्योऽमृतो भवत्यत्र ब्रह्म समश्नुत इति ॥[22]

"When all the desires hiding in his heart are loosed, then the mortal becomes immortal; here he enjoys Brahman."

तस्मादेवंविच्छान्तो दान्त उपरतस्तितिक्षुः समाहितो भूतात्मन्येवात्मानं पश्यति सर्वमात्मानं पश्यति नैनं पाप्मा तरति संर्व पाप्मानं तरति नैनं पाप्मा तपति संर्व पाप्मानं तपति विपापो विरजोऽविचिकित्सो ब्राह्मणो भवत्येष ब्रह्मलोकः[23]

"Therefore having thus becomes wise, calm, subdued, dispassionate, enduring, collected, he sees the Self in the Self, he sees the Self as all; nor does sin overcome him, he overcomes all sin; nor does sin consume him, he consumes all sin. Free from sin, free from passion, he becomes a Brāhmaṇa (of the nature of Brahman); this the Brahman-world."

The return is the reversal of the process of outgoing, as is very clearly outlined in the *Mahābhārata*, from which we can summarise the return as we summarised the outgoing.

21 Brihadarāṇyakop. IV. iv. 19.
22 Ibid. 7.
23 Ibid.23.

The senses are withdrawn from contact with the outer world through the body, and become tranquil, शान्त. The mind is withdrawn from its study of the images obtained by the senses, and thus also becomes tranquil. The understanding withdraws from the study of the concepts presented by the mind, and, thus tranquil, reflects the Self. So long as the mind turns to the senses, it finds misery. When it turns to the understanding, it finds bliss.

Along this road, the निवृत्तिमार्गः the Nivṛitti Mārgah, or returning path, the Jīvātmā returns from his wanderings in Samsāra and reaches his true home, the Eternal, paying, while he treads this path, all the debts contracted on the Pravṛitti Mārga.

To see the Self is Jnāna, wisdom; to love the Self is Bhakti, devotion; to serve the Self is Karma, action. Such Jnāna, Bhakti, Karma, are the three Mārgas, ways, to Mokṣha, liberation. The Jnāna Mārga is for those in whom Chit predominates; the Bhakti Mārga for those in whom Ichchhā predominates; the Karma Mārga for those in whom Kriyā predominates. But in each path, as each Jīvātmā is triune, the evolution of all of its three aspects must be carried on. The Jnāni as he gains wisdom, will find devotion and right activity appear; the Bhakta, as devotion is perfected, will find himself possessed of activity and wisdom. The Karmaṇya, as his activity becomes wholly selfless, will achieve wisdom and devotion. The three Mārgas are, in fact, one, in which three different temperaments emphasise one on other of its inseparable constituents. Yoga supplies the method by which the Self can be seen and loved and served.

The words spoken by Shrī Kṛiṣhṇa, as to the Sāṅkhya and Yoga Darshanas, may well be applied here:

सांख्ययोगौपृथग्बालाः प्रवदन्तिन पण्डिताः ।
एकमप्यास्थितः सम्यगुभयोर्विन्दते फलम् ॥

यत्सांख्यैः प्राप्यते स्थानं तद्योगैरपिगम्यते ।[24]

"Children, not Paṇḍits, speak of the Sāṅkhya and Yoga as different. (He who is) duly established in one obtaineth the fruit of both.

"The place obtained through the Sāṅkhyas is gained also through the Yogas."

The Mukta, the man who has reached liberation, may or may not remain active in the three worlds. The Ṛiṣhis are Muktas, and are employed in the maintenance and guidance of the worlds. Janaka was a Mukta, and was a king, ruling his realm. Tuladhāra was a Mukta, and was a merchant, weighing out his goods. Many a Mukta is spoken of in the Itihasa who is surrounded by physical conditions. For Mukti is not a change of conditions, but a change of condition; not an alteration of the circumstances surrounding the Jīvātmā, but the attitude of the Jivatma to the Self and the Not-Self.

It was said above that while the general sweep of evolution is upward and onward, temporary retrogression might occur, and in some of the very ancient Aryan books-given when the possibility of such retrogression was much greater than now— a good deal of stress is laid on the danger of such reversions. Shrī Kṛiṣhṇa, speaking in much later days, says that नराधमाः "the worst of men only are thrown आसुरीऽवेवयोनिषु "into *āsuric* wombs," are born of evil people, such as He had just been describing as *āsuric*.

The law is that when a man has so degraded himself below the human level that many of his qualities can only express themselves through the form of a lower creature, he cannot, when

24 Bhagavad. Gītā. V. 4.5.

his time for rebirth comes, pass into a human form. He is delayed, therefore, and is attached to the body of one of the lower creatures, as a co-tenant with the animal, vegetable or mineral Jīva, until he has worn out, exhausted, the bonds of these non-human qualities and is fit to again take birth in the world of men. A very strong and excessive attachment to an animal may have similar results, where the man should be far beyond such exaggerated fondness.

The points to be remembered are:

1. The Jīvātmā is Brahman, as a seed is the tree, and remains as a wanderer in Samsāra till he realises his own nature.
2. There is continuity of forms, by a new form separating from an old and leading an independent existence; and continuity of life in each evolving Jīvātmā.
3. The Jīvātmā, embodied in a form, experiences through that form, throws it away when outworn, reaps his reward in the invisible worlds, and returns to the visible.
4. The Jīvātmā may be detained in animal forms by self-degradation.
5. There are three stages of the evolving Manas: (a) subjection to Kāma; (b) conflict with Kāma; (c) triumph over Kāma and development of the higher intellectual powers.
6. Buddhi is evolved, and liberation is reached.
7. There are three paths to liberation, Jnāna, Bhakti, and Kriyā, and these finally blend.

KARMA

KARMA literally means action, but as every action is triple in its nature, belonging partly to the past, partly to the present, partly to the future, it has come to mean the sequence of events, the law of cause and effects, the succession in which each effect follows its own cause. The word Karma, simply meaning action, should however remind us that what is called the consequence of an action is really not a separate thing but is a part of the action, and cannot be divided from it. The consequence is that part of the action which belongs to the future, and is as much a part of it as the part done in the present. Thus suffering is not the consequence of a wrong act, but an actual part of it, although it may be only experienced later. A soldier is sometimes wounded in battle, and in the excitement does not feel any pain; afterwards, when he is quiet he feels the pain; so a man sins and feels no suffering, but later the suffering makes itself felt. The suffering is not separated from the wound, any more than heat from fire, though experienced as a result.

Hence all things are linked together indissolubly, woven and interwoven inseparably; nothing occurs which is not linked to the past and to the future.

अकारणं कथं कार्यं संसारेऽत्र भविष्यति ।[1]

"How shall there be in this Samsāra an uncaused action?"

The Jīvātmā, then, comes into a realm of law and must carry on all his activities within law. So long as he does not know the law in its various branches, called the laws of nature, he is a slave, tossed about by all the currents of natural energies, and drifting whithersoever they carry him; when he knows them, he is able to use them to carry out his own purposes.

So a boat without oars, sails, or rudder is carried about helplessly by the winds and currents, and the sailor finds himself drifting along under the press of forces he can neither change nor direct. But a clever sailor, with oars, sails and rudder, can steer along his boat in any direction he pleases, not because he has changed the winds and the currents, but because he understands their directions, and can use those that are going in the direction he wants, and can play off, the one against the other, the forces that oppose him. So can a man, who knows the laws of nature utilise those whose forces are going his way and neutralise those which oppose.

Therefore is knowledge indispensable; the ignorant are always slaves.

It must be remembered that a law of nature is not a command to act in a particular way, but only a statement of the conditions within which action of any kind can be done. "Water boils at 100°C under normal pressure." This is a law of nature. It does not command a man to boil water, but states the conditions under

1 Devī Bhāgavata. I. v. 74.

which water boils at 100° C. If he wants boiling water at that temperature, these are the conditions which are necessary. If he is on a high mountain where the pressure is much less than the normal, his water will boil at a temperature not sufficiently high for cooking purposes. How then does the law help him? It tells him how to get his boiling water at 100° C by increasing the pressure; let him shut his water up in a pot from which the steam cannot escape, and so add to the pressure the weight of the steam given off, till the temperature of the water rises to 100°. And so also it is with every other law of nature. The laws state conditions under which certain results follow. According to the results desired many conditions be arranged, and, given the conditions, the results will invariably follow. Hence, law does not compel any special action, but only renders all actions possible, and knowledge of law is power.

The Jīvātmā, as we have seen, is three-fold in his nature; he consists of Ichchhā, Jnāna and Kriyā, Will, Wisdom and Activity. These, in the lower world of *upādhis*, of forms, express themselves as Desire, Knowledge and Action, and these three fashion a man's Karma, and each works according to a definite law.

Desire stands behind Thought, stimulating and directing it; Thought, energised and determined by Desire, stands behind Action, expressing itself therein in the world of objects.

काममय एवाय पुरुष इति स यथाकामो भवति तत्क्रतुर्भवति। यत्क्रतुर्भवति तत्कर्मकुरुते यत्कर्मकुरुते तदभिसम्पद्यते।।[2]

"Man verily is desire-formed; as is his desire, so is his thought; as (his) thought is, so he does action; as he does action, so he attains."

2 Brihadāraṇyakop. IV. iv. 5.

On this shloka, Shaṅkara comments that Desire is the root of the world.

We have then to study three laws, which, taken together, make up the Law of Karma. We shall then understand the conditions under which things. happen, and can shape our future destiny according to the results we have chosen.

Desires carry the man to the place where the objects of desire exist, and thus determine the channels of his future activities:

तदेव सक्तः सह कर्मणैति लिङ्गं मनो यत्र निषक्त मस्य ॥[3]

"So indeed, the desirer goes by work to the object in which his mind' is immersed."

Desire attaches a man to the objects of desire, binding him to them with links unbreakable; wherever is the object of desire thither must go the man who desires it. The object of desire is called फल, fruit, and the fruit which the man has sought he must consume, in whatever place it is found.

.... कामकारेण फले सक्तो निबद्ध्यते ॥[4]

The man "impelled by desire, attached to fruit, is bound." Whether the fruit be good or evil, pleasurable or painful, the law is the same. So long as a man desires fruit, he is bound by his attachment to that fruit, and is said to have a "good or bad Karma" according as the fruit is pleasant or painful.

When a man understands this law, he can watch over his desires, and allow them to attach themselves only to objects, the possession of which will yield happiness; then, in another life, he

3 Ibid. 6.

4 Bhagavad-Gītā. v. 12.

will have opportunities of attaining them, for they will come and place themselves in his way. This is the first law, belonging to the desire-nature.

The second law concerns the mind.

Mind is the creative power, and a man becomes that which he thinks.

अथ खलु क्रतुमयः पुरुषो यथा क्रतुरस्मिँल्लोके पुरुषो भवति तथेतः प्रेत्य भवति ।[5]

"Now verily man is thought-formed[6]; as a man thinketh in this world, so, having gone away hence, he becometh."

As Brahmā created by meditation, so does Manas, which is His reflection in man, have creation as its essential activity; Brahmā embodies Kriyā, activity, but we find that his activity consisted in meditation, thought, and this gave birth to the worlds; hence action is only thought thrown outwards, objectivised, and a man's actions are only his past thoughts materialised. As Brahmā created His world, so Manas creates his vehicles, and by the same means, thought.

Character, the nature of the man, is thought-created; this is the first of the three factors of Karma. What the man essentially is in himself, that is the outcome of his thinking. As he is thinking now, so hereafter he will himself be. If he thinks nobly, he will become noble if he thinks basely, he will become base. Thus knowing, a man can deliberately shape his character, by dwelling in his mind on all that is good and pure and elevating, and driving out of it all that is evil, foul, and degrading. This is the second law, belonging to the mind.

---

5 Chhāndogyop. III. xiv. 1.

6 The word is क्रतु

The third law concerns action.

Circumstances are made by actions.

यथा यथा कर्मगुणं फलार्थी
करोत्ययं कर्मफले निविष्टः ।
तथा तथायं गुणसंप्रयुक्तः
शुभाशुभं कर्मफलं भुनक्ति ॥[7]

"Devoted to the fruits of acts, whatever kind of acts a person covetous of fruits accomplishes, the fruits, good or bad, that he actually enjoys, partake of their character. Like fishes going against a current of water, the acts of a past life are flung back on the actor. The embodied creature experiences happiness for his good acts, and misery for his evil ones."

नाबीजाज्जायते किंचिन्नाकृत्वा सुखमेधते ।
सुकृतैर्विन्दते सौख्यं प्राप्य देहक्षयं नरः ॥[8]

"Nothing can sprout forth without a seed. No one can obtain happiness without having accomplished acts capable of leading to happiness."

If a man spreads happiness round him, he will reap happiness hereafter; if he spreads misery, he will reap misery. Thus knowing the law, he can prepare for himself favourable or unfavourable circumstances, as he prepared a good or bad character, and pleasure-giving or pain-giving objects.

This is the third law, belonging to actions.

These three laws cover the making of Karma, for the Jīvātmā consists of Will, Wisdom and Activity, and these show themselves

7 *Mahābhārata*, Shānti Parva, cci. 23.
8 Ibid. ccxcl. 12

in the world by desires, thoughts and actions. When we have divided the factors in a man's destiny into opportunities, character—or capacities—and surrounding circumstances, we have covered them all. Nothing else remains.

We find, then, that we are always making new Karma, and experiencing what we have made in the past. We are obliged to act now in the conditions we have created in our past; we have only the opportunity of obtaining the objects then desired; of using the capacities then created; of living in the circumstances then made. But the living Jīvātmā, that then desired; thought and acted, is still the same powerful agent as he then was, and can put out his powers within the limits he has made, can modify and slowly change them, and create better conditions for the future Therefore Bhīṣhma places exertion above destiny.

A view of Karma that paralyses human efforts is a crude and mistaken one, and men should see in Karma a guide, and not a paralyser, of action.

One very commonly felt difficulty in connection with Karma is this: men ask: "If I am destined by my Karma to be bad or good, to do this or not to do it, it must be so; why then make any effort?" The fallacy of this line of thought should be very clearly understood, if the above has been grasped, for it turns upon a complete misunderstanding of the nature of Karma. The effort is part of the Karma, as much as the goodness or badness; Karma is not a finished thing awaiting us, but a constant becoming, in which the future is not only shaped by the past but is being modified by the present. If a man desires to be good, he is putting forth an energy which presently will make him good, however bad he may be now. A man is not a helpless being, destined by his Karma to be either bad or good, but he becomes that which he daily chooses as desirable—badness or goodness. He always is, and always must be, making efforts, merely because he is alive, and his only choice lies in making an effort to move in one direction rather than in another; his quietude is merely a choice to let past choices have their way, and to go in accordance with them. He does not eliminate the element of choice by doing nothing; he simply chooses doing nothing. A man has only to desire, to think, to act, and he can make his Karma what he chooses. Thus the Gods have risen to their high estate, and thus may others rise.

कर्मणेन्द्रो भवेज्जीवो ब्रह्मपुत्रः स्वकर्मणा ।
स्वर्कमणा हरेर्दसो जन्मादिरहितो भवेत् ॥
स्वर्कमणा सर्वसिद्धिममरत्वं लभेद्ध्रुवम् ।
लभेत्स्वकर्मणा विष्णोः सालोक्यादि चतुष्टयम् ॥
सुरत्वञ्च मनुत्वञ्च राजेन्द्रत्वं लभेन्नरः ।
कर्मणा च शिवत्वञ्च गणेशत्वं तथैव च ॥

"By his Karma may a Jīva become an Indra, by his Karma a son of Brahmā. By his Karma he may become Hari's servant, and free from births.

"By his Karma he may surely obtain perfection, immortality. By his Karma he may obtain the fourfold (Mukti), Sālokya and the rest, connected with Vishṇu.

"Godhood and manhood and sovereignty of a world-empire may a man obtain by Karma, and also the state of Shiva and of Gaṇesha."

The main thing is to see in Karma not a destiny imposed from without, but a self-made destiny, imposed from within, and therefore a destiny that is continually being re-made by its maker.

Another mistake sometimes made as to Karma is that which

leads a person to say respecting a sufferer: "He is suffering his Karma; if I help him I may be interfering with his Karma." Those who thus speak forget that each man is an agent of the Karma of others, as well as an experiencer of his own. If we are able to help a man, it is the proof that the Karma under which he was suffering is exhausted, and that we are the agent of his Karma bringing him relief. If we refuse to carry the *kārmic* relief, we make bad Karma for ourselves, shutting ourselves out from future help, and someone else will have the good Karma of carrying the relief and so ensuring for himself aid in a future difficulty. Further, "if's" and "maybe's" are no ground for action; "If I do not help him I may be interfering with his Karma," is as valid an argument as "If I help him." Action should be based on what we know, and we know it is right and good to help others; it is constantly commanded by the wise. Only a full and clear knowledge of the causes in the past resulting in the suffering of the present could justify refusal to help on *kārmic* grounds.

Karma is said to be the three kinds—प्रारब्धं, Prārabdham, सञ्चितं, Saňchitam, and वर्तमानं, Vartamānam, called also, आगामि, Āgāmī. Prārabdha Karma is that which is ripe for reaping and which cannot be avoided; it is only exhausted by being experienced. Saňchita Karma is the accumulated Karma of the past, and is partly seen in the character of the man, in his powers, weaknesses and capacities. Vartamāna Karma is that which is now being created.

अनेकजन्मसंजातं प्राक्तनं सञ्चितंस्मृतम् ॥
क्रियमाणञ्च यत्कर्मवर्तमानंतदुच्यते ॥
सञ्चितानां पुनर्मध्यात्समाहृत्य कियत्किल ।
देहारम्भे च समये कालः प्रेरयतीव तत् ।

प्रारब्धं कर्म विज्ञेयं ....[9]

"That which was in the olden time प्राक्तन produced in many births, is called Sañchitam..."

"That Karma which is being done, that is called Vartamāna."

"Again, from the midst of the Sañchitas is selected a portion, and, at the time of the beginning of the body, Time energises this: it is known as Prārabdha Karma"

The Sañchita Karma is the Karma which is gathered, collected, heaped together. It is the mass which lies behind a man, and his tendencies come from this. The Vartamāna Karma is the actual, that which is now being made for the future, or the Āgāmī, the coming Karma; while the Prārabdha Karma is that which has begun, is actually bearing fruit.

Now this Prārabdha Karma is, as said in the shloka above quoted, selected out of the mass of the Sañchita Karma. In Vedāntic literature it is sometimes compared to an arrow already shot. That which is sufficiently congruous to be worked out in one physical body is selected by the Devas who rule this department of nature, and a suitable physical body is built for it, and placed with the parents, nation, country, race, and general surroundings, necessary for the exhaustion of that Karma.

Prārabdha Karma, as said above, cannot be changed; it must be exhausted by being experienced. The only thing that can be done is to take it as it comes, bad or good, and work it out contentedly and patiently in it we are paying our past debts, and thus getting rid of many of our liabilities.

प्रारब्धकर्मणां भोगादेव क्षयः ।

---

9 Devī-Bhāgavata. VI. x. 9, 12, 13, 14.

"The exhaustion of Prārabdha Karma is possible only by the suffering of the consequences of it..."

Sañchita Karma may be largely modified by the additions we make to it: vicious tendencies can be weakened, virtuous ones can be strengthened, for with every thought, desire and action we are adding to that which will be the Sañchita Karma in our next birth.

Vartamāna Karma may, to a great extent, be destroyed in the same life, balanced up, by one who deliberately expiates a wrong done by restitution, voluntarily paying a debt not yet due, instead of leaving it to fall due at a future time.

There remains the question: how can a man become free from Karma?

From the general Karma of the universe he cannot be freed so long as he remains in the universe; Devas, men, animals, plants, minerals, all are under the sway of Karma; no manifested life can escape from this everlasting law, without which the universe would be a chaos.

ब्रह्मादीनां च सर्वेषां तद्वशत्वं नराधिप ॥[10]

"All, Brahmā and the rest, are under its sovereign rule, O king!"

If a man has to escape this universal Karma, he must go out of the universe—that is he must merge in the Absolute.

But a man may escape from the wheel of births and deaths, and yet remain manifested so long as Īshvara chooses to manifest, by ceasing to create fresh Karma and by exhausting what already exists. For the tie that binds man to the wheel is desire, and when desire ceases man creates no more bonds:

---

10 Devī Bhāgavata. IV. ii. 8.

यदा सर्वे प्रमुच्यन्ते कामा येऽस्य हृदिश्रिताः ।
अथ मर्त्योऽमृतो भवत्यत्र ब्रह्म समश्नुते ॥[11]

"When all the desires hidden in the heart are loosed, then the mortal becomes immortal, then he here enjoys Brahman."

Such is the re-iterated teaching of the Shruti. Again, we read in the Bhagavad-Gītā:

यस्य सर्वे समारम्भाः कामसंकल्पवर्जिताः ।
ज्ञानाग्निदग्धकर्मणां तमाहुः पण्डितं बुधाः ॥
गतसंगस्य मुक्तस्य ज्ञानावस्थित चेतसः ।
यज्ञायाचरतः कर्म समग्रं प्रविलीयते ॥[12]

"Whose works are all free from the moulding of desire, whose Karma is burned up in the fire of wisdom, him the wise have called a Sage..........."

"From one with attachment dead, free, with his thoughts established in wisdom, working for sacrifice (only), all Karma melts away."

Then freedom is achieved, and the man may either remain, as the Ṛiṣhis have remained, to aid in the evolution going on in the Brahmāṇḍa or may sink to rest.

The points to be remembered are:

1. The nature of action and its consequence.
2. The nature of law.
3. The three laws which make the Karma of the Jīvātmā.
4. The relation between exertion and destiny.
5. The three kinds of Karma.
6. The ceasing of individual Karma.

---

11 Kaṭhop. II. vi. 14.

12 Loc. cit. iv. 19. 23.

SACRIFICE

AS far reaching as the Law of Karma is, the Law of Sacrifice is the Law by which the worlds were builded, the Law by which they are maintained. All lives can only be supported by absorbing other lives: जीवोजीवस्यजीवनम्; all forms can only be preserved by absorbing other forms. Sacrifice permeates all religion as it permeates the universe. Says Shrī Kṛishṇa:

नायंलोकोऽस्त्य यज्ञस्य कुतोऽन्यः कुरुसत्तम ॥[1]

"This world is not for the non-sacrificer: how then the other? O best of the Kurus!"

The Sanatana Dharma has incorporated this Law into its very essence; all the Shrutis declare it; all the Smritis inculcate it; the Purāṇas and the Itihāsa are full of it; the Ṣhaḍāṅgas circle round it; the Six Darsanas lay it down as the pathway to be trodden ere knowledge can be gained.

We shall see in Part II how sacrifices pervade the whole life of the true Aryan; we are here concerned with the general principle, not with the specific applications:

1 Bhagavad Gītā. iv. 31.

Creation began with sacrifice:

ओं उषा वा अश्वस्य मेध्यस्य शिरः ।[2]

"Om! The dawn verily (is) the head of the sacrificial horse."

The dawn is explained as the beginning of the Day of Brahmā, the day of creation. Then is the great horse sacrifice, the horse, whose body is the universe, the sacrifice of The One who carries the Many—Devas, Gandharvas, Asuras, Men—as the next shloka says. And then the Upaniṣhad goes on to describe the beyond, when there was not anything, and the building of the universe.

So also in the *Ṛigveda* the splendid Puruṣha Sūkta describing the sacrificial slaying of Puruṣha[3] tells how all creatures were formed by one-fourth of Him offered up as "victim" in "that great general sacrifice," three-fourths remaining in heaven as the Eternal Life.

The great sacrifice involved in creation is beautifully described in the *Shatapatha Brāhmaṇa*.

ब्रह्म वै स्वयम्भूस्तपोऽतप्यत ।

तदैक्षत न वै तपस्यानन्त्यमस्ति हन्त अहं भूतेष्वात्मानं जुहवानि भूतानि च आत्मनि इति ।

तत्सर्वेषु भूतेष्वात्मानंहुत्वा भूतानि च आत्मनि

सर्वेषां भूतानां श्रेष्ठ्यं स्वाराज्यमाधिपत्यं पर्यैत् ।[4]

"Brahmā, the Self-existent, performed tapas. He considered: 'In *tapas* there is no infinity. Come let me sacrifice myself in living things and all living things in myself.' Then having sacrificed himself in all living things and all living things in himself, he acquired greatness, self-effulgence and lordship."

---

2 Brihadāranyakop. I. i. 1.

3 Loc. cit X. 90.

4 Loc. cit, XIII. vii, 1.

Manu also declares that Brahmā created यज्ञंसनातनम्[5] "the eternal sacrifice" ere He drew forth the Veda.

This profound teaching, that Īshvara sacrificed Himself in order to create His universe, means that He limited Himself in matter—technically died—in order that His life might produce and sustain a multiplicity of separate lives. Every life in His universe is a part of His life ममैवांशः "a portion of Myself."[6] Without this sacrifice, the universe could not come into existence. As a fourth part only of Puruṣha is said to suffice for the bringing forth of all beings, so Shrī Kṛiṣhṇa says:

विष्टभ्याहमिदं कृत्स्नमेकांशेन स्थितो जगत् ॥[7]

"Having pervaded all this universe with a portion of Myself, I remain."

Ishvara is far more than His universe, but it is wholly contained in Him, lives in His life, is composed of His substance.

Shrī Kṛiṣhṇa tells how Prajāpati सहयज्ञाः प्रजाः सृष्ट्वा,[8] "having emanated mankind together with sacrifice," bade man find in sacrifice his Kāmadhuk, the cow whence each could milk the objects he desired. So action is essentially rooted in sacrifice:

भूतभावोद्भवकरो विसर्गः कर्मसंज्ञितः ।[9]

"The pouring out which caused the birth of beings is called Karma."

The pouring out is the pouring out of life, which alone enabled separate beings to live, and this pouring out is that same

---

5 Loc. cit. i. 22.
6 Bhagavad-Gītā. xv. 7.
7 Ibid. x. 42.
8 Ibid. iii. 10.
9 Ibid. viii. 3.

sacrifice described in the Purușha Sukta. So thoroughly has this been recognised that Karma has become the general name for sacrifices, and Karma-kāṇḍa is the name which covers all sacrificial rites.

The essential idea of sacrifice, then, is the pouring out of life for the benefit of others; such pouring out is the law by which life evolves: it is imposed on the lower creation by strife and continual combats; its voluntary acceptance by self-sacrifice is the crowning glory of man. Hence all man's higher evolution is marked out by self-sacrifice, by sacrificing himself and all his actions to the Supreme man obtains liberation.

यत्करोषि यदश्नासि यज्जुहोषि ददासि यत्।
यत्तपस्यासि कौंतेय तत्कुरुष्व मदर्पणम्॥
शुभाशुभफलैरेव मोक्ष्यसे कर्मबन्धनैः।[10]

"Whatsoever thou doest, whatsoever thou eatest, whatsoever thou offerest, whatsoever thou givest, whatsoever thou doest of austerity, O Kaunteya, do thou that as an offering unto Me.

"Thus thou shalt be liberated from the bonds of action, (yielding) good and evil fruits."

Let us see how the Law of Sacrifice is seen in the physical world.

The Life in the mineral kingdom evolves as the mineral forms in which it dwells are broken up to nourish plants of every kind. The mineral forms perish to feed the Life in the vegetable kingdom, and the Life in the mineral forms has grown more complex and developed by this sacrifice.

10 Bhagavad-Gītā. ix. 27-28

The Life in the vegetable kingdom evolves by the sacrifice of the lower plants to nourish the higher, the countless annual plants perishing to enrich the soil in which trees grow. Myriads of others are eaten by animals, and their forms go to build up animal bodies, in which the Life has fuller scope.

The Life in part of the animal kingdom evolves by the sacrifice again of the lower forms to the higher, and also to the maintenance of the human kingdom, within which also the weak are devoured by the strong in the savage state. But here gradually, with increasing development of the animals to keen sensibility, and with the development of conscience and sympathy in man, another form of the law appears, and man begins to refuse to sacrifice to the support of his own life those who share with him the feelings of pleasure and pain. He first revolts against cannibalism—eating his own kind—and then against eating his weaker brothers in the animal kingdom. He realises that the divine nature in him develops by sacrifice of himself to others, and not by the sacrifice of others to himself. He lessens as much as he can his demands on the lives of others, and increases as much as he can his own sacrifices for them. So long as a man identifies himself with his body, he is always trying to take, to absorb, because the body continues only by such taking and absorbing. When he identifies himself as the Self, he is always trying to give, to pour out, because the joy of the Self is in forth-pouring. On the Pravṛitti Mārga he takes; on the Nivṛitti Mārga he gives. Thus evolves the life of man.

The alphabet of the lesson of sacrifice was taught to man by the Ṛiṣhis who watched over the Āryan race in its infancy. They did not attempt to teach men the full lesson of self-surrender, but merely laid down for them a system of sacrifices, in which they should sacrifice some of their possessions with a view to their large increase in the future; the firm grasp with which a man grips the objects on the maintenance of which his life in the body depends was slowly loosened by the sacrifice of some of them, the return for this not being immediate but lying in the future.

आवां राजानावध्वरे ववृत्यां हव्येभिरिन्द्रावरुणा नमोभिः ।
अस्मे इन्द्रावरुणा विश्ववारं रयिं धत्तं वसुयन्तं पुरुक्षुम् ॥
इयमिन्द्रं वरुणमष्ट मे गीः प्रावत्तोके तनये तूतुजाना ।[11]

"O Kings! Indra, Varuṇa, to this our sacrifice be ye turned by offerings and homage.........

"O Indra, Varuna, plenteous wealth and food and blessing give us: ....

"This my song may it reach Indra, Varuṇa and by its force bring sons and offspring."

Such prayers are found on every page of the Samhitās, and thus were men taught to sacrifice what they valued for a future gain.

By these sacrifices they were also taught to see that man is part of a great whole, and related to all around him; and that as his own life was maintained by the sacrifice of other lives, so he must repay that debt by sacrificing to others some of his possessions, sacrificing to the Devas in the fire which was "the mouth of the Gods,"or अन्नादः[12] "the eater of food," and to men by charitable gifts. In this way the sense of obligation was impressed on them, and the interdependence of lives continued.

---

11 Ṛigveda. VII, lxxxiv 1, 4, 5

12 Brihdāraṇyakop. I. iv. 6.

The next step was to train them to sacrifice these same possessions, immediately valuable, for happiness on the other side of death, a far-off invisible reward. स्वर्गकामायजेत; "let him sacrifice who desireth Svarga."

एतेषु यश्चरते भ्राजमानेषु यथाकालं चाहुतयो ह्याददायन्।
तन्नयन्त्येताः सूर्यस्य रश्मयो यत्र देवानां पतिरेकोऽधिवासः॥

एह्येहीति तमाहुतयः सुवर्चसः सूर्यस्य रश्मिभिर्यजमानं वहन्ति। प्रियां वाचमाभिवदन्त्योऽर्च्चयन्त्य एष वः पुण्यः सुकृतो ब्रह्मलोकः॥

"Whoever works (sacrifices), pouring libations into the shining of these [the seven flames previously mentioned), at the proper time, him these sun-rays lead where dwells the one Lord of the Devas."

Saying to him 'Come, come,' these resplendent libations carry the sacrificer by the sun-ray, worshipping him and saying the sweet words; 'This is your pure well-deserved Brahma-world.'

A great step forward was made in this sacrificing of the visible to the invisible, of the present to a far-off future. But the object of this training in sacrifices was no more the enjoyment of Svarga than the enjoyment of wealth on earth. They had learned to curb their greed for possessions by the practice of giving, and to recognise themselves as owing their lives to the larger life around them; they were thus prepared for the third stage, that of sacrifice as duty, for which no reward should be sought.

Men now began to see that the sacrifice of the lower to the higher was "right," a duty that was owed in return for the perpetual sacrifice of the higher to the lower, of the life of Ishvara for the maintenance of His children, and further that the body also owed a debt to the lower creatures who supported it, that ought to be paid by helping and serving them in turn. Then they were ready for the lesson:

कर्मणयेवाधिकारस्ते मा फलेषु कदाचन।
माकमफलहेतुर्भूर्मा ते संगोऽस्त्वकर्मणि॥
योगस्थः कुरुकर्माणि संगंत्यत्का धनंजय।[13]

"Thy business is with the action only, never with its fruits; let not the fruit of action be thy Motive, nor be thou to inaction attached.

"Perform action, O Dhanañjaya, established in Yoga, having renounced attachment."

The wheel of life which is ever turning, this interdependence of lives, being thoroughly understood, men see it as an obvious duty to help in the turning, and readily see the unworthiness of trying to live without doing their share of work:

एवं प्रवर्तितं चक्रं नानुर्वतयतीहयः।
अघायुरिन्द्रियारामो मोघं पार्थ स जीवति॥[14]

"He who on earth does not follow the wheel thus revolving, sinful of life and rejoicing in the senses, he, O Pārtha! liveth in vain."

This, practised for long, led up to the last lesson, the complete self-surrender of the man to Īshvara, recognising himself only as an instrument of the Divine Will carrying out in the physical world the purposes of that Will.

मन्मनाभवमभ्दत्को मद्याजी मां नमस्कुरु।
माभेवैष्यसि सत्यं ते प्रतिजाने प्रियोऽसि मे॥
सर्वधमान्परित्यज्य मामेकं शरणं व्रज।[15]

13 Bhagavad-Gītā. ii. 47-48.
14 2bid. vi, 16.
15 Ibid. xviii. 65. 66.

"Merge Manas in Me, be My devotee, sacrifice to Me, worship Me, thou shalt come to Me; I pledge thee My troth; thou art dear to Me. Abandoning all Dharmas, come unto Me alone for shelter."

Thenceforth the whole life is a sacrifice, and the man lives only to do the Divine Will. Hence, he abandons all separate Dharmas as Dharmas, as having over him no binding force. He has but the one Dharma, of carrying out the Divine Will, and if he fulfils all family and other relationships more perfectly than he ever did before, it is not because they in themselves bind him, but because Īshvara having placed him amid these surroundings as part of Himself, as His representative, he must fully meet all the necessities of the case in this representative character.

During this long training, men were gradually led to see that outer sacrifices of wealth were less valuable than inner sacrifices of virtue, and that the purification of the heart and mind were of more real importance than the external purifications.

While there should not be neglected, the neglect of the other was fatal.

यस्यैते चत्वारिंशत्संस्काराः न चाष्टावात्मगुणाः न स ब्रह्मणः सायुज्यं सालोक्यं च गच्छति यस्य तु खलु चत्वारिंशत्संस्काराणामेकदेशोऽप्यष्टावात्मगुणा अथ स ब्रह्मणः सायुज्यं सालोक्यं च गच्छति ॥[16]

"He who has the forty-two Samskāras, but has not the eight virtues of the Self, will not obtain Brahman, nor will he go to Brahmaloka. But he who has only a part of the forty-two Samskāras, but has the eight virtues of the Self, he will attain to Brahman and go to Brahmaloka."

16 Gautama Dharma Sūtra. viii. 24, 25.

The object of sacrifice is purification, and this has been insisted on over and over again. Says Shrī Kṛiṣhṇa:

यामिमां पुष्पितां वाचं प्रवदन्त्यविपश्चितः।
वेदवादरताः पार्थ नान्यदस्तीति वादिनः॥
कामात्मानः स्वर्गपरा जन्मकर्मफलप्रदाम्।
क्रियाविशेष बहुलां भोगैश्वर्य गतिंप्रति॥
भोगैश्वर्य प्रसक्तानां तयापहृतचेतसाम्।
व्यवसायात्मिकाबुद्धिः समाधौ नविधीयते॥[17]

Flowery speech is uttered by the foolish, rejoicing in the letter of the Vedas, O Pārtha, saying 'There is naught but this.'

"With Kama for Self, with Svarga for goal, they offer rebirth as the fruit of action, and prescribe many and various ceremonies for the attainment of pleasure and lordship.

"To those who cling to pleasure and lord ship, whose minds are captivated by such, cometh not this determinate reason, on Samādhi steadily bent."

And again:

श्रेयान्द्रव्यमयाद्यज्ञाज्ज्ञानयज्ञः परन्तप।
नहि ज्ञानेन सदृशं पवित्रमिह विद्यते॥[18]

"Better than the sacrifice of any objects is the sacrifice of wisdom, O Parantapa.........

Verily there is no purifier in this world like wisdom."

Bhīṣhma, speaking of truth and declaring it to be sacrifice of a high order, says:

अश्वमेधसहस्रं च सत्वं च तुलया धृतं।
अश्वमेधसहस्राद्धि सत्यमेव विशिष्यते॥[19]

---

17 Bhagavad Gītā. ii. 42, 44.

18 Ibid. iv, 33, 38

19 *Mahābhārata*; Shānti Parva. clxii. 26.

"Once upon a time a thousand horse-sacrifices and truth were weighed against each other in the balance. Truth weighed heavier than a thousand horse-sacrifices."

With regard to abstention from cruelty he says:

सर्वयज्ञेषु वा दानं सर्वतीर्थेषु चाप्लुतं ।
सर्वदानफलं चापि नैतत्तुल्यमहिंसया ।
अहिंस्रस्य तपोऽक्षय्यमहिंस्रो यजते सदा ।[20]

"Gifts made in all sacrifices, ablutions performed in all sacred waters, and the merit acquired by making all the possible kinds of gifts—all these do not come up to abstention from cruelty. The penances of a man that abstains from cruelty are inexhaustible. The man who abstains from cruelty is regarded as always performing sacrifices."

To destroy the sense of separateness is to gain the ultimate fruit of all sacrifices—purification and union with the Supreme. This is the road along which the great Ṛishis have led the true followers of the Sanātana Dharma.

The points to be remembered are:

1. The world was created and is maintained by a Divine Sacrifice.
2. Sacrifice is essentially giving, pouring forth.
3. Sacrifice is the law of evolution; compulsory in the lower kingdoms, becoming voluntary in the human.
4. Man rises by definite stages from Vaidika sacrifices to self-sacrifice.
5. Sacrifices of virtue and wisdom are more effective than the sacrifices of external objects.

---

20 Ibid, Anushāsana Parva, cxvi. 40-41.

THE WORLDS—VISIBLE AND INVISIBLE

WE have followed the Jīvātmā in his evolution, and have seen the laws of his growth, the unfolding of his consciousness. We have now to consider the *upādhis* in which he dwells, and the worlds that he inhabits during his long pilgrimage. These upadhis are related to the worlds, and by them the Jīvātmā comes into contact with these worlds, and is able to gain experience from them and to act in them. The *upādhis* are only brought into existence to serve the purposes of the Jīvātmā, moved by desire to taste these worlds. That the Jīvātmā's own desire is at the root of his embodiment is very plainly stated in the *Chhāndogyopaniṣhat*.

First comes the statement:

मघवन्मर्त्यं वा इदं शरीरमात्तं मृत्युना तदस्यामृतस्याशरीरस्यात्मनोऽधिष्ठानम् ।[1]

"O Maghavan, this body truly is mortal, controlled by death. It is the dwelling of the immortal bodiless Ātmā."

Then the wish to experience is said to lead the Ātmā to form organs for receiving and transmitting to himself the experiences. His wish lies at the root of each, and matter obeys his impulse,

1 Chhāndogyop. VIII. xii. 1.

and obediently moulds itself into a form suitable for the exercise of the life-function. (Science in these later days, proves over and over again that an organ is formed under the pressure of the life seeking to function in a particular way.)

यो वेदेदं जिघ्राणीति स आत्मा गन्धाय घ्राणमथ यो
वेदेदमभिव्याहरणीति स आत्माऽभिव्याहाराय वागथ यो
वेदेदं शृण्वानीति स आत्मा श्रवणाय श्रोत्रमथ यो वेदेदं
मन्वानीति स आत्मा मनोऽस्य दैवं चक्षुः ।[2]

"He who has the consciousness, 'may I smell,' he the Ātmā, in order to smell, (makes) the organ of smell; he who has the consciousness, 'may I speak,' he, the Ātmā, in order to speak, (makes) the voice; he who has the consciousness, 'may I hear,' he, the Ātmā, in order to hear, (makes) the organ of hearing; he who has the consciousness, 'may I think,' he, the Ātmā, (makes) the mind, his divine eye."

It is by this subtle organ, the mind, that he sees and enjoys, for the grosser matter cannot affect his fine essence; the Shruti proceeds:

स वा एष एतेन दैवेन चक्षुषा मनसैतान्कामान्पश्यन्रमते ।

"He, verily, this (Ātmā) by this divine eye the mind, sees and enjoys these (objects of) desires."

Here is, at once, the psychology and physiology connected with the Jīvātmā. He is a conscious being, and that consciousness, seeking external experiences, fashions senses and sense-organs for contact with the outer worlds, and a mind of nature more akin to itself as a bridge between the outer and the inner. It is these and

2 Ibid. 4 5

the worlds to which they are related, that we have now to study. Shrī-Kṛiṣhṇa speaks on exactly the same lines, reminding us further of the essential identity between the Jīvātmā and the Supreme Īshvara:

ममैवांशो जीवलोके जीवभूतः सनातनः ।
मनःषष्ठानीन्द्रियाणि प्रकृतिस्थानि कर्षति ॥
श्रोत्रं चक्षुः स्पर्शनं च रसनं घ्राणमेव च ।
अधिष्ठाय मनश्चायं विषयानुपसेवते ।[3]

"A portion of Myself, transformed in the world of life (into an immortal Jīva, draws round itself the senses with Manas as the sixth, placed in Prakriti...........

"Enshrined in the ear, the eye, the organs of touch, taste and smell, and the mind, he enjoyeth the objects of the senses."

There are three worlds in which the Jīvātmā circles round on the wheel of births and deaths.

These are भूलोकः Bhūlokaḥ or Bhūrloka, the physical earth; भुवर्लोकः Bhuvarlokaḥ, the world next to the physical, and closely related to it but of finer matter; स्वर्लोकः Svarlokaḥ, or Svarga, the heavenly world. Beyond these are four other worlds, belonging to the higher evolution of the Jīvātmā महर्लोकः Maharlokaḥ, जनलोकः Janalokah, तपोलोकः Tapolokaḥ, and सत्यलोकः Satyalokaḥ. The first three Lokas, or worlds perish at the end of a Day of Creation, a Day of Brahmā, and are reborn at the dawn of the succeeding Day. The others persist, but as Maharloka is rendered untenable and deserted by all its inhabitants, four Lokas may be regarded as perishing at the Night of Brahmā, while three—Janaloka, Tapoloka, and Satyaloka remain. All these seven Lokas are within

3 Bhagavad Gītā. xv. 7.9.

the Brahmāṇḍa; two others, Vaikuṇṭha and Goloka, lie beyond it, but can be reached from it.[4]

Other Lokas—Such as Indraloka, Sūryaloka, Pitṛiloka, etc.—are special regions situated within these seven great Lokas, as countries make up a continent.

There are seven other worlds, usually called, Talas, literally surfaces, which have to do with regions "within" the earth, that is of grosser matter than the earth. The student may remember that the sons of Sagara, after hunting all over the surface of the earth for the stolen horse, penetrated the lower regions, and came to Rasātala.[5]

The names of these are: पातालं Pātālam; महातलं Mahātalam; रसातलं Rasātalam; तलातलं Talātalam; सुतलं Sutalam; वितलं Vitalam; and अतलं Atalam. They correspond to the Lokas, as an image corresponds to an object, and are on a descending scale, as the Lokas are on an ascending.

These lokas mark the stages of evolution of the consciousness of the Jīvātmā; as his powers unfold, he becomes conscious of these Lokas one after the other, and becomes able to feel, think, and act in *upādhis* made out of the भूतानि Bhūtani, the Bhūtas or elements, which correspond to these stages of consciousness. Each Loka, as a state, represents a form of the consciousness of Īshvara; and, as a place, represents a modification of Prakṛiti, expressing that state of consciousness. As the Jīvātmā is of the nature of Īshvara, he is capable of realising these seven states of consciousness, and of thus living in touch with the seven worlds or modifications of Prakṛiti, which correspond to them.

4 See Viṣhṇu Purāṇa. I. III.

5 See Rāmāyaṇa. I. xl. 22.

These seven, as said above, make up the Brahmāṇḍa, the world Egg, within which the creative work of Brahmā proceeds.

पातालाद्ब्रह्मलोकान्तं ब्रह्माण्डं परिकीर्तितम् ॥
तत ऊर्ध्वं च वैकुण्ठो ब्रह्माण्डाद्बहिरेवसः।
तत ऊर्ध्वं च गोलोकः पञ्चाशत्कोटियोजनः ॥
नित्यसत्यस्वरुपश्च यथा कृष्णस्तथाप्ययम्।
ऊर्ध्वं धराया भूर्लोको भुवर्लोकस्ततःपरः।
ततः परश्च स्वर्लोको जनलोकस्ततःपरः।
ततः परस्तपोलोकः सत्यलोकस्ततःपरः ॥
ततः परोब्रह्मलोकस्तप्तकाञ्चनसन्निभः।
एवं सर्वं कृत्रिमञ्च बाह्याभ्यन्तरमेव च ॥
तद्विनाशे विनाशश्च सर्वेषामेव नारद।
जलबुद्बुद्वत्सर्वं विश्वसंघमनित्यकम् ॥[6]
नित्यौ गोलोक वैकुण्ठौ प्रौक्तौ शश्वद कृत्रिमौ ।।[1]

"From Pātala to Brahmaloka is called the Brahmāṇḍa. Then beyond is Vaikuṇṭha, outside the Brahmāṇda. Yet beyond is Goloka, extending over fifty crores of Yojanas. It is eternal and of the nature of truth. Whatever Kṛiṣhṇa is, such is it.

"Above the earth is Bhūrloka, then Bhuvarloka beyond. Then next is Svarloka, and Janaloka beyond yet beyond is Tapoloka, and again beyond is Satyaloka. Then beyond is Brahmaloka, like burning gold.

"All this is made, one within the other when that perishes, all perish, O Nārada! All this collective universe is like a water-bubble, transient. Goloka and Vaikuṇṭha are called everlasting."

Here "Pātala" is made to cover the seven Talas and Maharloka

6 1Devī Bhāgvata, IX. 8-10, 12-16. A similar statement is made in the Viṣhṇu Bhāgavata. III. x. 7-9, xi. 28-31.

is omitted, Brahmaloka being added at the end to make up the seven.

Let us examine these words more closely.

The first three, Bhūr, Bhuvar and Svar Lokas, are those in which the Jīvātmā lives during his long evolution, in which he dwells while on the wheel of births and deaths. The *Brihadāraṇyakopaniṣhat* says:

अथ त्रयो वाव लोका मनुष्यलोकः पितृलोको देवलोक इति ।[7]

"Now verily there are three worlds, the world of men, the world of the Pitṛis, the world of the Devas."

These three are called the त्रिलोकी Trilokī, the three worlds.

Each of these worlds is a definite region, marked off by the nature of the matter of which it is composed. The Tattva that predominates in Bhūrloka, or Prithvī, the earth, is the Prithvī Tattva; there are seven modifications of it, Prithvī, Āpaḥ, Agni, Vāyu, Ākāsha—solid, liquid, gaseous, radiant matter, etheric, super-etheric and atomic. In all the combinations which make up these modifications of Prakṛiti, the various aggregations of the Aṇu, the Prithvī Tattva is predominant.

In Bhuvarloka, the Āpah Tattva is predominant and in the seven corresponding modifications there, the aggregations of the Aṇu of that world, this Āpah Tattva, is the most prominent characteristic.

In Svarloka, the Agni Tattva is the ruling power, and all the combinations bear the stamp of this fiery Aṇu. All the bodies of the beings belonging to that region are flashing and luminous,

7 Loc cit. I. v. 16.

and from this comes the name of Deva, the Shining.

We then come to Maharloka, in which also the Agni Tattva is predominant, a world composed only of the three finest and subtlest aggregations of the fiery Aṇu.

The three higher Lokas, Jana-Tapa-and Satya-lokas, are not reached by the Jīvātmā till he is very highly evolved. In Janaloka and Tapoloka, the Vayu Tattva predominates, hence all the combinations interpenetrate each other without any difficulty, as gases do down here, and the sense of unity predominates over the sense of separateness.

In Satyaloka the Ākāsha Tattva predominates, and the Jivatma here attains the Shabda Brahma-world, and is on the threshold of mukti. He has reached the limit of the Brahmāṇḍa. Beyond it lies Vaikuṇṭha and Goloka, composed of the two highest Tattvas, the Mahat Tattva sometimes called Anupādaka, because it has as yet no upādaka, receptacle or holder and the Ādi-Tattva, the root of all.

These seven Lokas correspond to seven states of consciousness of the Jīvātmā. The life in man which is consciousness is that of the Self; it is written:

आत्मन एष प्राणो जायते ।।[8]

"Of Ātmā this life is born."

And

तस्मादेताः सप्तार्च्चिषो भवन्ति ।[9]

"From this these seven flames become."

Again, in the *Muṇḍakopaniṣhat*, the seven worlds are

8 Prashnop. iii. 3.

9 Ibid. 5.

connected with the seven flames, and these flames take the departed soul to the heavenly worlds.[10]

And the *Devī Bhāgavata* says:

सप्त प्राणार्चिषो यस्मात समिधः सप्त एव च
होमाः सप्त तथा लोकास्तस्मै सर्वात्मने नम ।।[11]

"From whom the seven Prāṇa flames, and also the seven fuels, the seven sacrifices and worlds to that All-Self we bow."

The seven Prāṇas, or life-breaths, of the body are the representatives of the seven great Prāṇas, the true life-breaths of the Self, consciousness seven-fold divided in man.

This is plainly stated in the *Chhāndogyopaniṣhat*, where it is said that there are five gates out of the heart which lead to a special region, that to which each belongs. Thus Prāṇa itself, the chief life-breath, leads to the Sun, here standing for the chief, or highest Loka, Satyaloka. Vyana, leading southwards, carries to the Moon—here to the dark side of the moon, connected with Bhuvarloka. Apāna leads to the Fire Region, Maharloka, and Samāna, "which is the mind," to Svarloka. Udāna leads to the Air Region, that of Vāyu which includes Janaloka and Tapoloka.

The Prāṇas in man correspond to the cosmic Prāṇas, for man is related to, and reflects in every part, the image of Īshvara and His universe.

In the *Māṇḍūkyopaniṣhat*, the Self is said to have four states, the जाग्रत् Jāgrat, waking, in which he is called Vaishvānara; the स्वप्नः dreaming, in which he is called Taijasa; the third सुषुप्तिः Suṣhuptiḥ, "well sleeping," in which he is called Prājna; and the

10 Loc. cit. I. ii. 3, 6.
11 Loc. cit. VII. xxxiii. 49.

fourth, that which is Brahman. These four states belong to the seven Lokas, as will be clearly seen, if we now consider the देहाः Dehāḥ, bodies, in which the aspects of consciousness are manifested.

We shall return to the aspects of consciousness when we consider them in their several material sheaths.

There are three chief bodies which the Ātmā uses as Upādhis:(1) The स्थूलशरीरम् Sthūla sharīram, sense or gross body; this is the Upādhi of the Vaishvānara consciousness, (2) The सूक्ष्मशरीरम् Sūkṣhma-sharīram, subtle body; this is the Upādhi of the Taijasa consciousness. (3) The कारणशरीरम् Kāraṇa-sharīram, or causal body; this is the Upādhi of the Prājna consciousness.

प्राज्ञस्तु कारणात्मा स्यात्सूक्ष्म देही तु तैजसः ।
स्थूलदेही तु विश्वास्यास्त्रिविधः परिकीर्तितः ॥
एवमीशोऽपि संप्रोक्त ईशसूत्रविराट्पदैः ।
प्रथमो व्यष्टिरूपस्तु समष्टयात्मा परः स्मृतः ॥[12]

"Ātmā in the Kāraṇa is Prājna; He is Taijasa in the Sūkṣhma body; in the Sthūladeha he is named Vishva. Threefold he is thus called."

"The Lord also is thus spoken of as threefold, by the names Isha, Sutra and Virat. The first (Jivas) is the distributive form, while the Collective Self is the Supreme."

As every man has, then, three Upādhis and uses them as the organs of three different forms of consciousness, the Lord has three Dehas, Upādhis, and three different forms of universal consciousness; these are called Īsha, Sūtra and Virāt respectively, corresponding to the three human forms of consciousness—

12 Devī Bhāgavata. VII. xxxii. 47 49.

Prājna, Taijasa, and Vaishvānara.

These Upādhis may be considered as expressions in matter of the three aspects of the Self: Will, Wisdom and Activity. The Sthūla-sharīra is the organ of Activity; the Sukshma-sharira is the organ of Wisdom; the Kāraṇa-sharīra is the organ of Will. And just as these three aspects express themselves in higher and lower states of consciousness—Will and Desire, Wisdom and Knowledge, Creation and Generation—so are the sharīras made up of Sheaths, composed of differing densities of matter, according to the subdivision of the consciousness working in each sheath.

The three sharīras are related to the seven Lokas as follows: The Sthūla-sharīra is the Upādhi in Bhūrloka.

The Sūkṣhma-sharīra:

- Bhūrloka
- Bhuvarloka
- Svarloka
- Maharloka

The Kāraṇa-sharīra:

- Janaloka
- Tapoloka
- Satyaloka

The sharīras, as said above, are made up of sheaths, and here the Vedāntic division of the five कोषाः Koṣhāḥ, sheaths, is very helpful.

The first koṣha is that which is built of the particles of food, and is therefore named अन्नमयकोषः Annamaya-koṣhaḥ, food-sheath. This is identical with the Sthūla-sharīra, the dense body, and is composed of solids, liquids, and gases, in which the Prithvī Tattva predominates. Here the outer expressions of the

Karmendriyas, the organs of action—hands, feet, voice, generation and evacuation—have their place. Here is the nervous system, with its central organ, the brain, through which Vaishvānara, the waking consciousness, acts, and comes into touch with Bhūrloka.

The second, third and fourth koshas—the प्राणमयकोषः prāṇamaya-koṣhaḥ, life-breath sheath; the मनोमयकोषः manomaya-koṣhaḥ, mind sheath; and the विज्ञानमयकोषः vijnānamaya-koṣhaḥ, knowledge sheath-make up the Sūkṣhma sharīra, the subtle body.

ज्ञानेन्द्रियाणि पश्चैव पञ्च कर्मेन्द्रियाणि च ।
प्राणादिपञ्चकञ्चैव धिणा च सहितं मनः ॥
एतत्सूक्ष्मं शरीरं स्यात्ममलिंग बदुच्यते ।[13]

"The five Jnānendriyas, the five Karmendriyas and the five Prāṇas, and Manas with Vijnāna, this is the Sūkṣhma-sharīra, which is called my Type."

The student must here notice the word "Karmendriyas." The absolute organs-hands, feet, etc.—belong obviously to the Sthūlasharīra, but the centres which govern them, the true motor centres, are in the Sūkṣhma-sharīra, as are the sense centres, which have as their organs in the Sthūla-sharīra the eye, ear, nose, tongue and skin. Each Indriya is essentially a subtle centre in the Sūkṣhma-sharīra, and has an organ in the Sthūla-sharīra. If this be grasped, the student will not be puzzled by the verbal contradictions that he may meet with in his reading.

The Sūkṣhma-sharīra is connected with Bhūrloka—by that part of it which is called the Prāṇamaya-koṣha; this koṣha is

13 Devī Bhāgavata. VII. xxxii. 41. 42.

composed of the subtle ethers of the physical world, Bhūrloka, and the Prāṇas move in this etheric sheath, the life-currents which carry on all the functions of the body; of these there are five at work—the remaining two being latent—and these are: प्राणः Prāṇaḥ, the outgoing breath; अपानः Apānaḥ, the incoming breath: व्यानः Vyānaḥ, the held-in breath; उदानः Udānaḥ, the ascending breath; समानः Samānaḥ, the equalising breath, which distributes the digested food throughout the body. In these Prāṇas the magnetic energies of the body exist, and all bodily energies are modifications of these.

अहमेवैतत्पञ्चधात्मानं प्रविभज्यैतद्बाणमवष्ट भ्यविधारयामीति ।[14]

"I, indeed, fivefold dividing myself, by my support maintain this (body)."

यस्मात्कस्माच्चाङ्गात्प्राण उत्क्रामति तदेव तच्छुष्यति ।[15]

"From whatever limb Prāṇa departs, that indeed becomes dried up."

And, as we shall presently see, when Prāna leaves the body, the body dies. For the Puruṣha asks:

कस्मिन्नहमुत्क्रान्त उत्क्रान्तो भविष्यामि कस्मिन्वा प्रतिष्ठिते प्रतिष्ठास्यामीति। सप्राणमसृजत ।।[16]

"Who is it in whose going I shall go, in whose staying I shall stay? He created Prāṇa."

Modern science, it may be remarked, has come to the

14 Prashnop. ii. 3.
15 Brihadāraṇyakop. I. iii. 19
16 Prashnop. vi. 3

conclusion that all these energies are movements in ether, and it is this ether, as said above, which forms that Prāṇamaya-koṣha.

The part of the Sūkṣhma-sharīra connecting it with Bhuvarloka and Svarloka is the Manomaya-koṣha, or mind-sheath. This Manomaya-koṣha is composed of matter from these two worlds, and is the Upādhi of the lower mind, Manas affected by, mingled with, Kāma. This mind, which is never separated from desires, has in this sheath matter of Bhuvarloka, in which desires work, and matter from Svarloka, in which thoughts work.

Lastly, the Sūkshma-sharīra, by its finest particles, is connected with Maharloka, to which pure Manas, free from Kāma, belongs, and these particles, of the matter of Maharloka, form the Vijnānamaya-koṣha.

This body, it will be seen, is a very complicated one, yet it is necessary to understand it, if the path of the man after death is to be followed. It is the Upādhi of the Taijasa consciousness, in which the Self comes into touch with the permanent invisible worlds, the consciousness spoken of sometimes as that of dream. It includes, however, far more than is indicated by the modern use of the word dream, for it includes the high states of trance, attainable by Yoga, in which a man may reach Maharloka.

The third Sharīra, the Kāraṇa-sharīra, is composed of the matter of the three higher and relatively permanent Lokas, Jana-, Tapo-, and Satya-lokas.

The Ānandamaya-koṣha of the Vedāntins is the same as this Kāraṇa-sharīra, and this is composed of the materials of the three Lokas just named.

The name covers the three—as there are really three sheaths under one name; in the bodies of the dwellers in Janaloka, the material of that world predominates and wisdom specially characterises them, that world being the abode of the Kumāras, the Beings whose pure wisdom is untouched by any desire. In the Tapoloka, the great ascetics and devotees live, and in their bodies the materials of Tapoloka predominate, ananda being their chief characteristic. Satya or Brahmaloka is the home of those whose peculiar functions are in activity, closely allied to the nature of Brahma.

In this third Sharīra, the Prājna consciousness, works, not affecting the lower bodies; beyond this is the Brahmāṇḍa, and the Ātmā, rising beyond it, unites with Īshvara.

Consciousness, in the Annamaya-koṣha, works in the brain and is concerned with external activities; it uses at the same time the Prāṇamaya-koṣha, to carry on the life-functions of the body, and affects, by this, all the objects with which it comes into contact; these two koṣhas leave minute particles of themselves on all the objects they touch, and the rules of physical purity are based on this fact.

Consciousness, in the waking state, also uses the Manomaya-koṣha, by which it desires and thinks, and these three sheaths are active during all walking consciousness. A deep thinker, a philosopher or metaphysician, also uses the Vijnānamaya-koṣha in working out his thoughts, but ordinary men do not get beyond the Manomaya-koṣha.

When the time of death comes, the Prāṇamaya-koṣha separates from the Annamaya-koṣha, and leaves the latter inert and helpless, fit only for the burning-ghat. Its elements are scattered, and go back into the general store. The presence of Prāṇa is necessary for its life.

यावद्ध्यस्मिञ्छरिरे प्राणो वसति तावदायुः ।[17]

---

17 *Kaushītaki* Br. Up. iii. 2.

"As long as Prāṇa dwells in the body, so long life." This same Upaniṣhad describes a dying man, and tells how all the powers of the waking consciousness are gathered up in Prāṇa, so that when Prāṇa goes out all these accompany it, and the man, the Self, going out, all these powers go with him.

He is then in the Kāraṇa and Sūkṣhma Sharīras.

The Prāṇamaya koṣha, the part of the subtle body made of ethers, soon drops away, and the man enters the Pretaloka, the world of the departed, a special region in Bhuvarloka; if he has been a bad man, the coarser part of the Manomaya-koṣha is rearranged to form the ध्रुवंशरीरम् Dhruvam Sharīram, the strong body,[18] also called the Yātanā Sharīra, in which he suffers the results of his evil deeds; if he be a good man, these coarser particles gradually drop away, and in the partially purified Manomaya-koṣha he goes to the peaceful Pitṛiloka, the "watery world," still a region in Bhuvarloka. When the Manomaya-koṣha is quite freed from its desire particles, he goes on into the division of Svarga; allotted to the departed, sometimes called the Moon.

ये वैके चास्माल्लोकात्प्रयन्ति चन्द्रमसमेव ते सर्वे
गच्छन्ति.. स्वर्गस्य लोकस्य द्वारं यश्चन्द्रमाः ।[19]

"They who depart from this world, they all go to the Moon...... The Moon is the gate of Svarga."

And again, we read in the *Brihadhrāṇyakopaniṣhat* that the departed go to:

पितृलोकं पितृलोकाच्चन्द्रं ।[20]

"Pitriloka, from Pitriloka to the Moon."

---

18 Manu, xii. 16.
19 Kaushītaki Br. Up. i. 2.
20 Loc. cit. VI. ii. 16.

The Manomaya-koṣha is called the lunar body, and, as we shall see in a moment, is also called Soma, the Moon.

This path, from the earth to Pitṛiloka, from Pitṛiloka to the Moon, or the part of Svarga allotted to ordinary men between death and birth—other than Indraloka, Sūryaloka, etc., divisions of Svarga gained by special merits—is called Pitṛiyāna, the path of the Pitṛis.[21] From this Moon they return to the earth, the first stage being that in which a new Manomaya-koṣha is obtained; this is the Soma-rājā, brought out of the Fire-Region—Svarga—by the Devas. Then the Devas put the Soma-rājā into the fire of Parjanya, the "Watery World," once more, and the watery particles are built into the Manomaya-koṣha, those belonging to Kāma, to desire. This is brought down to Bhūrloka, where the Prāṇamaya and Annamaya-koṣhas are formed, and so rebirth is gained.[22]

The Devayāna, the path of the Devas, is trodden only by those who do not compulsorily return to the earth during this Kalpa. They depart as do the others, but they pass on from the Moon, casting off the Manomaya-koṣha, to the Deva-world, and from that to the Sun and the Lightning, to Brahmaloka:

तेषु ब्रह्मलोकेषु पराः परावतो वसन्ति ।[23]

"In those Brahma-worlds they dwell immemorial years."

Shankara remarks that these are not absolutely free from transmigration, but that they will not be reborn within this Kalpa. These are they of whom the *Vishṣu Purāṇa* says that they dwell in

---

21 See Ibid. 2; Prashnop. I. 9. and Chhāndogyop. V. x. 4.

22 Chhāndogyop. V. iv-viii.

23 Brihadāraṇyakop. VI. ii. 15, and see Chhāndogyop. V. x. 2.

the higher Lokas while Brahma sleeps.[24]

One other matter of importance remains in connection with man's bodies and the seven Lokas. By Yoga, a man may, during his life-time, separate himself from his lower sheaths and rise into the higher worlds; and, far more, he may reach the Vidyā which liberates.

अथ यदिदमस्मिन्ब्रह्मपुरे दहरं पुण्डरीकं वेश्म दहरोस्मिन्नन्तराकाशः ।[25]

"Now within this Brahmapura (the body) there is a minute lotus-like chamber, and within it a minute inner space."

Therein dwells the Ātmā, unobserved by ordinary men;

यथापि हिरण्यनिधिं निहितमक्षेत्रज्ञा उपर्युपरि सञ्चरन्तो न विन्देयुरेवमेवेमाः सर्वाः प्रजा अहरहर्गच्छन्त्य एतं ब्रह्मलोकं न विन्दन्ति ।[26]

"As those ignorant of the nature of the field pass over a hidden gold-mine and do not find it, so all men daily go to this Brahmaloka and do not find it."

Leaving the body in sleep, they as it were, walk over it, but do not know it. But he who knows it, daily retires to this region in the heart:

अस्माच्छरीरात्समुत्थाय परं ज्योतिरुपसम्पद्य स्वेन रूपेणाभिनष्पद्यत एष आत्मेति ।[27]

"Having risen from this body, he attains a splendid body of light, and dwells in his own form. This is the Ātmā."

By Yoga this separation is effected, and it is written:

24 Loc, cit I. iii.
25 Chhāndogyop. VIII. i. 1.
26 Ibid. iii 2.
27 lbid.4.

तं स्वाच्छरीरात्प्रबृहेन्मुञ्जदिवेषीकां धैर्येण ।[28]

"That (Puruṣha) let him draw out from his own body with self-possession, like a grass-stalk from its sheaths."

This is not the place to enter into details with respect to Yoga. It is enough to know that such high possibilities are within the reach of man, and may be realised by purity, by knowledge and by love.

The following points should be remembered:

1. The Jīvātmā, seeking experience, forms bodies.
2. He dwells in three worlds, during the cycle of births and deaths.
3. There are seven Lokas within the Brahmāṇḍa, and seven Talas.
4. There are three great Sharīras, corresponding to three main states of consciousness, and these are subdivided into seven, corresponding to the seven Lokas.
5. At and after death, the Jīvātmā throws off the lower koṣhas, dwelling finally in Svarga in the purified Manomaya-koṣha, after leaving Pitṛiloka.
6. The Jīvātmā may, by Yoga, free himself from the lower koṣhas during physical life.

28 Kaṭhop. II. vi. 17.

Name of Jīvātmā	States of Consciousness	Sub States of Consciousness	Sharīras or Bodies	Koṣhas or Sheaths	Lokas
Vaishvānara	Jagrat	Physical or walking	Sthūla-sharīra	Annamaya	Bhūrloka
Taijasa	Svapna	Physical Dream Highest Trance	Sūkṣhma-sharīra	Prāṇamaya Manomaya Vijnānamaya	Bhurloka. Bhuvarloka Svargaloka Maharloka
Prājna	Sushupti	Kumāra Nārada Manu (prājāpatya)	Kāraṇa-sharīra	Ānandamaya, triple 1.c. Jana-Ān, Tapa-Ān, Satya-Ān.	Janaloka Tapoloka Satyaloka

PART II

GENERAL HINDU RELIGIOUS CUSTOMS AND RITES

THE SAMSKĀRAS

CERTAIN general principles pervade all religious ceremonies, and these principles must be clearly grasped; otherwise, these ceremonies will be unintelligible, and the mind will, sooner or later, revolt against them.

These principles are:

1. Man is a composite Being, a Jīvātmā, enclosed in various sheaths; each sheath is related to one of the visible or invisible worlds, and therefore also to its inhabitants. He is thus in touch with these worlds, and in continual relations with them.
2. The Jīvātmā and Prakṛiti are in a state of unceasing vibration; these vibrations vary in rapidity, regularity and complexity.
3. The vibrations of the Jīvātmā are rapid and regular, becoming more and more complicated as he unfolds his powers.
4. The vibrations of the matter of the sheaths are continuously affected by those of the Jīvātmā, and non-continuously by the various vibrations which reach from the world to which its materials belong. In addition, each vibrates continuously according to the fundamental vibration of its world.
5. The Jīvātmā endeavours to impose his own vibrations on his sheaths, so that they may respond to him, and work harmoniously with him.

6. He is constantly frustrated in these attempts by the vibrations that reach his sheaths from outside, and set up vibrations in them that are independent of him.
7. He may be very much assisted in his labour by the setting up of vibrations which are in harmony with his own efforts.

These principles must be studied carefully and thoroughly understood.

Then we come to certain special facts, a knowledge of which is also necessary:

A mantra is a sequence of sounds, and these sounds are vibrations, so that the chanting, loud or low, or the silent repetition, of a mantra sets up a certain series of vibrations. Now a sound gives rise to a definite form, and a series of pictures is made by successive musical notes; these may be rendered visible, if suitable scientific means are taken to preserve a record of the vibrations set up by the sounds. Thus the forms created by a mantra depend on the notes on which the mantra is chanted; the mantra, as it is chanted, gives rise to a series of forms in subtle matter. The nature of the vibrations—that is their general character, whether constructive or destructive, whether stimulating love, energy, or other emotions—depends on the words of the mantra. The force with which the mantra can affect outside objects in the visible or invisible worlds depends on the purity, devotion, knowledge and will-power of the utterer. Such vibrations are included among the "various vibrations" mentioned under Principle 4 as affecting the sheaths, and are also referred to under Principle 7.

The repeated recitation of a mantra, that is, the repeated setting up of certain vibrations, gradually dominates the vibrations going on in the sheaths, and reduces them all to a regular rhythm, corresponding to its own. Hence the feeling of peace and calm which follows on the recitation of a mantra.

The name of a Deva, or other Being, mentioned in a mantra, sets up vibrations similar to those present in the Deva and his sheaths, and, as the mantra is repeated many times with cumulative effects, the sheaths of the utterer—or of any hearer—gradually repeat these vibrations with ever increasing force.

यस्य यस्य च मन्त्रस्य प्रोद्दिष्टा या च देवता ।
तदाकारं भवेत्तस्य दैवतं देवतोच्यते ॥[1]

"Whatever the Devatā concerned with a mantra, his is the form of it the mantra of the Deva is said to be the Deva."

Piṅgala, the writer on Vaidika mantras, divides the metres according to the seven fundamental vibrations, and gives the name of the Devatā corresponding to each vibration.

As the matter of the sheaths thus vibrates, it becomes easily penetrable by the influence of the Deva, and very impervious to other influences. Hence the Deva's influence reaches the Jīvātmā, and other influences are shut out.

If the sheaths contain much coarse matter which cannot vibrate in answer to the subtle and rapid vibrations set up by the mantra, the repetition of the mantra may cause pain, disease, death. It is therefore dangerous for an impure person to recite a mantra, or to listen to the recitation of a mantra, or even for a mantra to be inaudibly recited in his presence.

If the sheaths contain some coarse matter, and some pure,

1 Yogi Yājnavalkya, quoted in the Āhnika-Sūtrāvalī, p. 13.

the coarse matter will be shaken out, as the sheaths vibrate in answer to the mantra, and pure matter will be drawn in to replace that which is shaken out.

But one important fact must be remembered, since, in a mantra, the *sound* and rhythm are all important:

मन्त्रोहीनः स्वरतो वर्णतो वा मिथ्याप्रयुक्तो न तमर्थमाह
स वाग्व्रजो यजमानं हिनस्ति यथेन्द्रशत्रुः स्वरतोपराधात् ॥

"When the mantra is defective in Svara or Varṇa, it is incorrectly directed and does not declare the true meaning. That lightning-word (then reacts upon and) slays the performer (of the sacrifice) himself as (the word) 'Indra-Shatru' for fault of Svara (slew Vṛittra, the performer of the sacrifice, and the enemy of Indra, instead of slaying Indra the enemy of Vṛittra, as intended)."

A good knowledge of Samskrit is therefore necessary.

The magnetic properties of objects are also important in this matter of vibrations. *All* objects are always vibrating, and thus affect the sheaths of other objects near them. To affect the sheaths in any particular way, it is necessary to choose objects which have the desired vibrations.

All rites and ceremonies ordained by Seers and Sages are based on these principles and facts, which govern the mantras and the objects used with them. They are all intended to aid the Jīvātmā in reducing his sheaths to obedience, in purifying them, and in making them strong against evil; or else to shape external conditions to man's benefit, protection and support.

If these principles and facts are understood, the student will see clearly the reason of many injunctions and prohibitions which he finds in the Sanātana Dharma as to by whom and in whose presence, mantras may be recited, what substances should be used in different ceremonies, what offerings should be made, and so on. Instead of a meaningless labyrinth of ceremonies, sounds, objects and gestures, he will see an ordered system, intended to help the Jīvātmā to unfold his powers more rapidly, and to overcome the obstacles in his way.

The संस्काराः Samskārah, are variously given, some lists enumerating only ten, others rising to a higher and higher number up to fifty-two. Among those which are specially called the ten Samskāras, some mark the important stages of a man's life up to and including his marriage; the remainder are ceremonies which may be performed daily or on special occasions, or are subsidiary to some of the Ten.[2]

The Ten principal and generally recognised Samskāras are:

1. गर्भाधानं Garbhādhānam
2. पुंसवनं Pumsavanam
3. सीमन्तोन्नयन Sīmantonnayanam
4. जातकर्म Jātakarma
5. नामकरण Nāmakaraṇam
6. अन्नप्राशनं Annaprāshanam
7. चूड़ाकरणं Chūdākaraṇam
8, उपनयन Upanayanam
9. समार्वतन Samāvartanam
10. विवाह Vivāhaḥ

वैदिकैःकर्मभिःपुण्यैनिर्षेकादिर्द्विजन्मनाम्।
कार्यःशरीरसंस्कारःपावनःप्रेत्यचेहच ॥[3]

2 In the Introduction to Māṇdlik's edition of the Yājnavalkya Smriti several lists are given, pp. xxx-xxxii

3 Manusmriti, ii. 26.

"With sacred Vaidika rites should be performed the Samskāras of the body, namely, Niṣheka and the rest, of the twice-born, which purily here and here-after."

The whole life of the Āryan is thus guarded from conception to cremation.

The Garbhādhānam sanctifies the creative act, not to be undertaken carelessly, lightly, nor during the presence of any evil emotion in the mind of husband or wife, nor for the sake of mere enjoyment, but with the purpose of exercising the divine power of creation, the creating of a human body. The husband prays that a child may be conceived. Thus the first dawning of the new life is amid the vibration of a mantra (*Rigveda* X. lxxxv. 21, 22).

The Annamaya-koṣha and Prāṇamaya-koṣha are being formed within the mother's womb, and in the third month the Pumsavanam is performed with mantras—*Rigveda*. I. i. 3; III. iv. 9; V. xxxvii. 2; II. iii. 9—for the forming of a male child.

At the seventh month takes place the Sīmantonnayanam, or parting of the hair of the mother, at which the *Rigveda* mantras, X. cxxi, 10; clxxxiv 1; II. xxxii 4-8, are recited, guarding her from evil influences, and bringing to bear on the growing sheaths the most harmonious and health-giving vibrations.

These three Saṃskāras protect both mother and child, and to the latter bring all helpful vibrations to shape the developing body. The occult knowledge, which was thus utilised for the health and beauty of the evolving form, having disappeared for the most part, these useful and beautiful ceremonies have fallen into desuetude, to the great loss in health and vigour of the race.

The next Saṃskāra, the ceremony performed at birth, is the Jātakarma, the father welcoming his new-born child, praying for its long life, intelligence, wisdom, and well-being, and feeding it with gold, honey and butter.[4]

Shāṅkhāyana *Grihya Sūtras* (i. 24), Āshvalāyana Grihya *Sūtras* (i. I5), and Āpastamba *Grihya Sūtras* (i. 15) refer to this ceremony. Āshvalāyana gives *Rigveda* II. xxi. 6. and III. xxxvi. I0 to be recited at the conclusion of the Jātakarma ceremony.

When the child is eleven days old, or on the tenth or twelfth day, the Nāmakaraṇam, the naming ceremony, is performed, with the *Rigveda* mantra, I. xci. 7. The name given should be according to caste:

मङ्गल्यं ब्राह्मणस्य स्यात्क्षत्रियस्य बलान्वितम् ।
वैश्यस्य धनसंयुक्तं शूद्रस्य तु जुगुप्सितम् ॥
शर्मवद्ब्राह्मणस्य स्याद्राज्ञो रक्षासमन्वितम् ।
वैश्यस्य पुष्टि संयुक्तं शूद्रस्य प्रैष्यसंयुतम् ॥
स्त्रीणां सुखोद्यमक्रूरं विस्पष्टार्थंमनोहरम् ।
मङ्गल्यं दीर्घवर्णान्तमाशीर्वादाभिधानवत् ॥[5]

"Let a Brāhmaṇa's be auspicious, a Kshattriya's full of power, a Vaiṣhya's connected with wealth, and a Shūdra's with lowliness.

"A Brāhmaṇa's implying happiness; a Kshattriya's protection; a Vaiṣhya's, prosperity; a Shūdra's, service.

"Women's easily pronounceable, not harsh, with a clear meaning, pleasing, auspicious, ending in a long vowel, (soft) like the utterance of a benediction."

In the sixth month comes the Annaprāshanam, the first feeding with solid food, with the *Rigveda* mantras, IV. xii. 4, 5; IX. lxvi. 19; and I. xxii. 15.

4 Manusmriti, ii, 29.
5 Ibid, 31-33.

In the first or third year—or, according to the *Grihya Sūtras*, in the fifth for a Kshatriya and the seventh for a Vaiṣhya—the Chūdākaraṇam, the tonsure, or shaving of the head, is performed.

The Karṇavedha, or ear-boring ceremony, is performed at the fifth or seventh year, or even later. In Southern India, it is sometimes performed on the twelfth day after birth or at the close of the first year, or with the Chūdakaraṇam. It is not mentioned in the authoritative lists of Saṃskāras, but in modern Indian life it is regularly performed.[6]

By these ceremonies the young body is constantly harmonised and guarded, and says Yājnavalkya:

एवमेनः शमं याति बीजगर्भसमुद्भयम् ।[7]

"Thus is the sin (hereditary defect) arising from defect of seed and embryo allayed."

These Saṃskāras belong to the child-stage of life. With the next, the Upanayanam, the stage of youth may be said to begin. The lad is now to put away the toys of childhood, and is to begin the life of study which is to equip him to take his place in the world.

The Upanayanam is the ceremony of the investiture with the sacred thread, the initiation which is the second birth, given by the Āchārya, and which constitutes the boy a द्विजः Dvijaḥ, twice-born.

कामान्माता पिता चैनं यदुत्पादयतो मिथः ।
संभूतिं तस्य तां विद्याद्यद्योनावभिजायते ॥
आचार्यस्त्वस्य यां जातिं विधिवद्वेदपारगः ।
उत्पादयति साविल्या सा सत्या साऽजराऽमरा ॥

6 See Pāraskara Grihya Sūtra, II. i. and Gadādhara-Bhāṣhaya thereon.

7 Loc. cit. i, 13.

"That the father and mother give birth to him from mutual desire, so that he is born from the womb, let this be known as his physical birth."

"But that birth which is given, according to the ordinance, through the Sāvitrī, by the preceptor who has mastered the Vedas, that is the true birth, the unageing and immortal."

The word Upanayana means bringing near—bringing near to the preceptor, who initiates the boy, by giving him the sacred mantra called गायत्री Gāyatrī.[8]

Shāṅkhāyana, Ashvalāyana and Āpastamba agree with Yājnavalkya in their age limits. Manu gives the age at the fifth year for a Brāhmaṇa, the sixth for a Kshattriya and the eighth for a Vaiṣhya, making the limit, up to which initiation may be given, the sixteenth, twenty-second and twenty-fourth years respectively.[9]

Yājnavalkya puts the lower limits at the eighth, eleventh and twelfth years, and the higher at the same ages as Manu.[10]

The boy is dressed in a kaupīna, and then in a new garment, and wears a girdle of Munja grass, if a Brāhmaṇa; of a bowstring, if a Kshattriya; of woollen thread, if a Vaiṣhya; The Āchārya puts on him according to his caste an antelope skin, a spotted deer skin, or a cow skin, and knots the girdle round him.[11] He then invests him with the यज्ञोपवीतं, Yajnopavitam, the sacrificial thread, and after certain questions and answers he sprinkles him with water, recites certain formulas and mantras, and, placing his hand on the pupil's heart, he says: "Under my will I take thy heart;

8 So named because it protects him who chants it: गायन्तंत्रायतेइत ।

9 Loc, cit, ii. 37. 38.

10 3Loc, cit, i, 14. 37.

11 These significant symbols have been dropped in modern India, and all castes wear the same.

my mind shall thy mind follow; in my word thou shalt rejoice with all thy heart; may Bṛihaspati join thee to me." He then teaches him the Gāyatrī, and gives him a staff, the length and the wood of which vary according to the caste of the boy.[12]

The whole ceremony represents the spiritual birth of the Ārya, and all its parts are significant. As spirits are sexless, the *kaupīna* symbolically makes him sexless, and being such the Brahmachārī is bound to lead a life of chastity or celibacy. The new garment represents the new body. The girdle is wound round thrice to show that the boy has to study the Samhitās, the Brāhmaṇas and the Upanishads. The skin represents the ascetic life he should lead.

The sacrificial thread consists of three threads, knotted together, and signifies the various triads which exist in the universe: the triple nature of Spirit, Sat-Chit-Ānanda; the triple nature of matter, Sattva, Rajas, Tamas; the Trimurti; the triple Jīvātmā, Jnāna Ichchhā-Kriyā; the three words, Bhūḥ, Bhuvaḥ, Svaḥ, mind, speech and body, each again divided into three as regards action; and so on, and he who wears the thread should exercise a triple control, over his mind, speech and body[13]

The staff represents, as a rod, like the triple wand of the Sannyāsī the control that a student should exercise over thoughts, words and actions.

वाग्दण्डोऽथ मनोदण्डः कर्मदण्डस्तथैव च ।
यस्यैते निहिता बुद्धौ त्रिदण्डीति स उच्यते ॥
त्रिदण्डमेतन्निक्षिप्य सर्वभूतेषु मानवः ।
कामक्रोधौ तु संयम्य ततः सिद्धिं निगच्छति ॥[14]

12 See, for full details, the Shāṅkhāyana Grihya Sūtra, II. i-vi.
13 See Manusmriti, xii, 4-11.
14 Manusmriti, xii, 10, 11.

"The rod that rules the voice, the rod that rules the mind, the rod that rules the acts—he in whose Buddhi these are maintained is called a Tridaṇḍī."

"The man who exercises this triple rod in respect to all creatures, controlling desire and anger, he attains perfection."

Then came the end of the student stage, the Samāvartanam; the pupil presented his teacher with a gift, and received permission to take the formal bath, which marked the close of his pupil age.

गुरवे तु वरं दत्त्वा स्नायीत तदनुज्ञया।
वेदं व्रतानि वा पारं नीत्वा ह्युभयमेव वा।।[15]

"To the teacher having given what is wished for, let him bathe with his permission, having completed the Vedas, the Vratas, or both."

Then he returned home and performed the Samāvartanam, the returning ceremony. He was then called a Snātaka, and was ready to marry and enter the household state.

गुरुणानुमतः स्नात्वा समावृत्तो यथाविधि।
उद्वहेत द्विजो भार्यां सवर्णां लक्षणान्विताम्।।[16]

"Having bathed, with the permission of his teacher, and having become Samāvritta (returned) according to rule, let a twice-born man marry a wife of his caste, endowed with auspicious marks."

Thus closed the student stage, and with the Vivāha, the marriage, the life of the householder began. Now he was to take up his duties as man and begin the payment of his debts by sacrifice, by study and by begetting children.

---

15 Yājnavalkya, i. 51.
16 Manusmriti, iii. 4.

The ceremonies accompanying marriage vary much with local custom, and the simple and dignified original ceremony has become much overlaid by show and pomp. The Vaidika mantras show the spirit in which marriage should be undertaken, and it is these which the true Aryan should lay stress on, not the modern glitter and show.

The Sūkta of Sūrya's bridal gives a picture of the marriage ceremony.

गृहान्गच्छ गृहपत्नी यथासो वशिनी त्वं विदथमा वदासि ॥
इह प्रियं प्रजयाते समृध्यतामस्मिन्गृहे गार्हपत्याय जागृहि ।
एना पत्या तन्वं संसृजस्वाधाजिव्री विदथमावदाथः ॥[17]

"Go to the house as the house's mistress; as ruler, speak thou to the household folk.

"Here be thou beloved with thy children; in this house be vigilant to rule thy household. With this man, thy husband, be productive; speak ye to your household-folk full of years."

The bridegroom speaks to the bride:

गृभ्णामि ते सौभगत्वाय हस्तं मया पत्या जरदष्टिर्यथासः ।[18]

"I take thy hand for good fortune; mayst thou grow old with me, thy husband."

They walk round water and the sacred fire hand-in-hand, and the bride sacrifices grains in the fire, praying:

आयुष्मानस्तु मे पतिरेधन्तां ज्ञातयो मम ।[19]

"May my husband live long; may my kinsfolk increase."

17 Rigveda, X. lxxxv. 26, 27.
18 Ibid, 36.
19 Shāṅkhāyana's Grihya Sūtras, I. xiv, I.

Agni is said to give the bride to the bridegroom, he who is ever the Lord of the Hearth.

The Sūkta prays, when the bride goes to her new home:

इहैव स्तं मा वियौष्टं विश्वमायुर्व्यश्नुतम्।
क्रीडन्तौ पुत्रैर्नप्तृभिर्मोदिमानौ स्वे गृहे ॥[20]

"Here dwell ye, be not parted; enjoy full age, Play and rejoice with sons and grandsons in your own house."

And it prays that the bride, lovely and gentle hearted, may bring bliss to the home, to men and animals, ruling the home, pious, mother of heroes.

The law of marriage is given by Manu:

अन्योन्यस्याव्यभीचारो भवेदामरणान्तिकः।
एष धर्मः समासेन ज्ञेयः स्त्रीपुंसयोः परः ॥
तथा नित्यं यतेयातां स्त्रीपुंसौ तु कृतक्रियौ।
यथा नातिचरेतां तौ वियुक्तावितरेतरम् ॥[21]

"Let there be faithfulness to each other until death; this, in short, should be known as the highest duty of husband and wife.

"So let husband and wife ever strive, doing all their duties, that they may not, separating from each other, wander apart."

Such was the Āryan ideal of marriage, perfect faith of each to each till death, and Āryan literature shows how nobly that ideal was fulfilled. Let the student look on marriage in the old light, and we may see men and women again of the old type.

Thus, in the ancient days, was the young man launched into

---

20 Rigveda, X, lxxxv. 42.
21 Manusmriti ix. 101, 102.

manhood, with mantras and with prayers; but Gautama's saying already quoted[22] must ever be laid to heart:

"He who has the forty-two Saṃskāras, but has not the eight virtues of the self, will not obtain Brahman, nor will he go to Brahmaloka. But he who has only a part of the forty-two Saṃskāras but has the eight virtues of the self, he will attain to Brahman and go to Brahmaloka."

22 P. 135.

SHRADDHĀ

THE longer lists of Saṃskāras include the various ceremonies performed on behalf of those who have departed from the physical world, the ceremonies that fall under the general name of श्राद्धम् Shrāddham. The Āryan has never felt the presence of a thick barrier between the visible and invisible worlds, between the "living" and the "dead". All his religion brings the invisible worlds into continual contact with the visible, the Devas are as real as the men. And he recognises the continued existence of the Jīvātmā so vividly that the death of the body is not to him a matter of terror and anxiety, but a habitual thought, and "the dead" are never regarded as dead, but merely as living elsewhere. The habitual thought of transmigration, linking life with life, reduces any particular death to a mere incident in an indefinite series, and the Jīvātmā, not the body, assumes predominant importance. Still more vividly is this idea that the Jīvātmā is the man impressed on the minds of Āryans by the recurring Shrāddhas, in which the continued existence of those who have left the physical world is brought before the eyes of the present dwellers upon earth.

The duties an Āryan owes to the dead commence from the moment the life departs, and are divided into two classes—Preta-kriyā and Pitṛi-kriyā or Shrāddha—funeral and ancestral ceremonies. The dead is called the प्रेतः Pretaḥ, the departed, till the Sapiṇḍīkaraṇa is performed, when he becomes a Pitṛi.

At death, the man, clothed in the Prāṇamayakoṣha, leaves the Annamaya-koṣha, and as all the Vaidika Saṃskāras have been framed to help the processes of nature, the Preta-kriyā is intended to neutralise the tendency of the Prāṇamaya-koṣha to hang about the Annamaya-koṣha as long as the latter is whole, and thus to retain the real man in Bhūrloka after the normal course of nature requires him to leave it.

The first important thing to be done is to destroy the Annamaya-koṣha, and this is done by cremation. In the words of the Chhāndogyopaniṣhat:

तं प्रेतं दिष्टमितोऽग्नय एव हरन्ति यत ऐवेतो यतः सम्भूतो भवति ।[1]

"They carry him who has departed, as ordained, to the fire whence he came, whence he was born."

Before the fire is applied to the corpse, the celebrant walks three times round the spot where it is laid, and sprinkles water on it with the verse *Rigveda* X, xiv. 9:

अपेत वीत विच सर्पतातः... ।

"Go away, withdraw, and depart from here. While the body is burning," *Rigveda* X, xiv. 7:

प्रेहि प्रेहि पथिभिः... ।

"Go on, go on, on the ancient paths" is to be recited.

On the third day after the cremation the remnants of the bones are gathered and buried, or thrown into running water, thus completing the disintegration of the Annamaya-koṣha. The Prāṇamaya-koṣha then rapidly disintegrates.

---

1 V. ix. 2.

The next work to be done is to help to disintegrate the lowest part of the Manomaya-koṣha and thus change the Preta, the departed, into the Pitṛi, the ancestor.

For this purpose have been framed the Ekoddishta-shrāddha and the Sapiṇḍana-shrāddha. The Ekoddishta-shrāddha is one directed to a single dead person, whereas a shrāddha proper is directed to three generations of Pitṛis or to all Pitṛis. The offerings connected with it are intended to be offered during a whole year. No āvāhana, inviting, takes place in this ceremony, nor the putting of food into the fire, nor do the Vishvedevas take part in it.[2]

The Ekoddishta- shrāddha are completed by the performance of the Sapiṇḍīkaraṇa, the reception of the Preta, into the community of the Pitṛis. According to Shāṅkhāyana, the celebrant fills four water-pots with sesamum, scents, and water—three for the fathers, one for the newly dead person—and pours the pot that belongs to the newly dead person into the pots of the Pitṛis with the two verses, *Vājasaneya Samhitā* xix. 45, 46.[3]

If these ceremonies should be properly performed, the subtle parts of the offerings made during their performance feed the deceased till he goes to Pitṛiloka. The mantras facilitate his passage thereto and he takes his place among the Pitṛis.

Then "the fourth is dropped", i. e., in the ceremonies the great-grandfather of the deceased person is not invoked, the deceased, his father and grandfather forming the three Pitṛis.

The numerous periodical ceremonies that are performed to the Pitṛis are technically Shrāddhas. At a Shrāddha, the Pitṛis are the deities to whom the sacrifice is offered; the Brāhmaṇas who are fed represent the Āhavanīya fire.[4]

---

2 Shānkhāyana's Grihya Sūtras iv. 2. 5.

3 Ibid. iv. 3.

4 Āpastamba's Dharma Sūtras, II. vii. 16 (3).

The Ābhyudayika-shrāddhas or Nāndī-shrāddhas are performed on the occasions of rejoicings, such as the birth of a son, the marriage of a son or daughter, nāmakaraṇa, jātakarma, chūdākaraṇa etc. In this ceremony, the Nāndī–mukha Pitṛis, glad-faced ancestors, those that have gone to the Svarga Loka, are invoked, and an even number of Brāhmaṇas are fed in the forenoon.

Of all the ancient ceremonies, Shrāddhas alone are still performed with any appreciable degree of religious fervour and it is hoped that an intelligent understanding of the rational basis of them will increase the Shrāddha, faith, without which a Shrāddha cannot properly deserve the name.

We shall see, in studying the Five Daily sacrifices—Chapter IV—that the Pitṛi-Yajna has its place among them. On the new-moon day this is followed by the monthly Shrāddha ceremony, called the, पिण्डान्वाहार्यकं,Piṇḍānvāhāryakam, and, पार्वणश्राद्धम्, Pārvaṇa-shrāddham, one of the seven, पाकयज्ञः, Pākayajnaḥ, or sacrifices with baked offerings.

Sacrifices to the Pitṛis are offered in the afternoon, facing south,[5] and the ground should slope southwards.[6] On the new moon day, Kusha or Darbha grass is arranged for seats, and an odd number of Brāhmaṇas are invited. Great stress is laid on the character and learning of these Brāhmaṇas.

यथेरिणे बीजमुप्ता न वप्ता लभते फलम्।
तथानृचे हविर्दत्त्वा न दाता लभते फलम् ॥[7]

"As the sower having sown feed in barren soil, obtains no

5 Āpastamba's Yajna Paribhāṣha, Sūtra LX.
6 Manusmriti, iii, 206.
7 Ibid. 142.

harvest, so the giver, having given sacrificial food to one ignorant of the Ṛichas, obtains no harvest."

नश्यन्ति हव्यकव्यानि नराणामविजानताम् ।
भस्मभूतेषु विप्रेषु मोहाद्दत्तानि दातृभिः ।।[8]

"The offerings of ignorant men to Devas and Pitṛis perish, being gifts from deluded givers to Brāhmaṇas who are ashes."

ब्राह्मणो ह्यनधीयानस्तृणाग्निरिव शाम्यति ।
तस्मै हव्यं न दातव्यं न हि भस्मनि हूयते ॥[9]

"A Brāhmaṇa who is ignorant goeth out like a grass fire; to him sacrificial food ought not to be given; offerings are not poured into ashes."

So, also, Hiraṇyakeshin says that the Brāhmaṇas invited to the Shrāddha must be pure and versed in the mantras.[10]

Having gathered these and prepared the materials for the sacrifice, and offered Haviḥ in the Dakshiṇāgni, the sacrificer calls to the Pitṛis, and sprinkles water. According to Manu, he should make three cakes, offering them to his father, grandfather and great grandfather, pour cut water near the cakes, and give to the Brāhmaṇas very small portions of them; after this the Brāhmaṇas should be fed in the afternoon.[11]

In the *Grihya Sūtras* it is directed that the Brāhmaṇas are first fed, and that then the offerings are to be made to the Pitṛis. The domestic Bali offerings should follow the Shrāddha.[12]

Similar ceremonies may be performed in the dark fortnight,

8 Manusmriti iii. 97.
9 Ibid, 168
10 Grihyasūtras ll. iv. 10.
11 Manusmriti, iii. 208-237.
12 2Ibid. 265.

and the Aṣhtakā ceremony is sometimes offered to the Pitṛis.

It must be remembered that Pitṛiloka and Pretaloka, or Yamaloka, are both regions in Bhuvarloka (see Part I. ch. vi.) and influence from the earth, Bhūrloka, reaches both of these. The influence of Piṇḍa offerings reaches throughout Preta-loka; the three higher generations (fourth, fifth and sixth) are affected by offerings of remnants of food. Including the offerer, only seven generations can mutually influence each other by the giving and receiving of food. Three generations beyond these can receive only libations of water.

Influence from below can go no further, for by that time an average man is supposed to have passed into Svarga, and the whole object of Shrāddha is to facilitate his passage thither.

The general principles of the Shrāddha of a person recently departed are adaptations of the principles underlying all Saṃskāras.

Shrāddhas may, generally speaking, be regarded as serving the same purpose with reference to the subtler bodies, as is served by the pre-natal and natal Saṃskāras with reference to the gross physical body. Having helped the Jīvātmā going from here to a fair birth in the other world, the human helper has completed his duty, and cannot go any further or give other help. The agencies of the other world thereafter take up the Jīvātmā into their own exclusive charge.

SHAUCHAM

THE rules for purifying the body are based on scientific facts as to the Annamaya and Prāṇamaya-koṣhas.

The Annamaya-koṣha is composed of solids, liquids and gases, and infinitesimal particles of these are constantly passing off from the body. Apart altogether from the obvious daily losses sustained by the body in the excrements and sweat, there is this ceaseless emission of minute particles, alike in night and day, whether the body is waking or sleeping. The body is like a fountain, throwing off a constant spray. Every physical object is in this condition, stones, trees, animals, men; all are ceaselessly throwing off these tiny particles, invisible because of their extreme minuteness, and are, as ceaselessly, receiving the rain of particles from others which fills the air in which they live, and which they breathe in with every breath. A continual interchange is thus going on between all physical bodies; no one can approach another without being sprinkled by the other, and sprinkling him in turn, with particles from their respective bodies. Everything a man goes near receives some particles from his body, every object he touches retains a minute portion of his body on its surface; his clothes, his house, his furniture, all receive from him this rain of particles, and rain particles from themselves on him in turn.

The Prāṇamaya-koṣha, composed of the physical ethers and animated by the life-energies, affects all around it, and is affected by all around it, not by emitting or receiving particles, but by sending out, and being played upon by, vibrations, which cause waves, currents, in the etheric matter. The life-waves, magnetism-waves, go out from each man as ceaselessly as the fine rain of particles from his Annamaya-koṣha. And similar waves from others play upon him, as ceaselessly as the fine rain of particles from others falls on him.

Thus every man is being affected by others, and is affecting them, in the physical world, in these two ways: by a rain of particles given off from the Annamaya-koṣha, and by waves given off from the Prāṇamaya-koṣha.

The object of the rules of Shaucham is to make this inevitable influence of one person on another, a source of health instead of a source of disease, and also to preserve and strengthen the bodily and mental health of the performer. The Annamaya koṣha is to be kept scrupulously clean, so that it may send off a rain of health on everyone and everything that is near it and the Prāṇamaya-koṣha is to be reached by the mantra-produced vibrations in the etheric matter which permeates the things used in the ceremonies—as etheric matter permeates everything—so that these vibrations may act beneficially on it, and may cleanse and purify it.

The rules affecting bodily cleanlines are definite and strict. On rising, the calls of nature are first to be attended to,[1] plenty of water being used for cleansing purposes, and then the mouth and teeth are to be washed, and a bath taken, A man is to be careful that no unclean matters remain near his dwelling;

---

1 Manusmriti, iv. 45—12. 56—152

दूरादावसथान्मूत्रं दूरात्पादावसेचनम |
उच्छिष्टान्नं निषेकं च दूरादेव समाचरेत् ॥[2]

"Far from his dwelling let him cast excrement, far the water used for washing his feet, far the leavings of food, and bath-water."

Much disease is caused by the neglect of this rule, the filthy surroundings of dwellings causing ill-health and general loss of vigour. In modern city life, the community takes on this duty by an organised system or drainage, but this should be on the same principle of conveying noxious matters far away from all habitations; and it is part of the duty of a good citizen to see that rivers in the neighbourhood of cities are not poisoned, nor filth allowed to accumulate to the injury of the public health.

A man must wash, in some cases bathe the whole body, before taking part in any religious ceremony, and sip water with appropriate mantras.

आचम्य प्रयतो नित्यमुभे संध्ये समाहितः ।
शुचौ देशे जपञ्जप्यमुपासीत यथाविधि ॥[3]

"Being purified by sipping water, he shall always daily worship in the two twilights with a collected mind, in a pure place, performing Japa according to rule."

He must wash before and after meals;

उपस्पृश्य द्विजो नित्यमन्नमद्यात्समाहितः ।
भुत्त्का चोपस्पृशेत्सम्यगद्भिः खानि च संस्पृशेत् ॥[4]

2 Ibid. iv. 151.
3 Manusmriti ii. 222.
4 Manusmriti ii. 53.

"Having washed, the twice-born should eat food always with a collected mind; having eaten, let him wash well with water, sprinkling the sense-organs."

If a man has touched anything impure, a person or an object:

स्नानेन शुध्यति ।[5]

"By bathing he is purified."

मृत्तोयैः शुध्यते शोध्यं ।[6]

"By Earth and water that which should be made pure is purified."

These are the two great purifiers, though alkalis and acids may be used for cleaning copper, iron, brass, pewter, tin and lead; earthen vessels can be purified by burning, houses by sweeping, cowdung and whitewash; other methods are given for special substances. So long as any smell or stain remains on an object it is not to be considered pure.[7]

ज्ञानं तपोऽग्निराहारो भृन्मनो वार्युपाञ्जनम् ।
वायुः कर्मार्ककालौ च शुद्धेः कर्तृणि देहिनाम् ॥[8]

"Wisdom, austerity, fire, food, earth, mind, water, plastering, wind, rites, the sun and time, are the purifiers of human beings."

But nobody can be truly pure unless the mind and heart be pure:

अद्भिर्गात्राणि शुध्यन्ति मनः सत्येन शुध्यति ।
विद्यातपोभ्यां भूतात्मा बुद्धिर्ज्ञानेन शुध्यति ॥[9]

5 Ibid. V. 85.
6 Ibid. 108.
7 Ibid. 105—27.
8 Ibid 105.
9 Manusmriti v. 109

"The body is purified by water, the mind by truth, the soul by knowledge and austerity, the reason by wisdom."

Besides the impurities due to obvious causes, the birth or death of Sapiṇḍas, or of relatives not Sapiṇḍas, causes impure magnetic currents in the Prāṇamaya-koṣha and therefore sullies the Annamaya-koṣha. In the case of Sapiṇḍas, the impurity lasts from ten days to one month according to the caste of the parties concerned. In the case of the death of little children, the impurity lasts for a very short time.

The relationship of Sapiṇḍa ceases with the seventh remove of relationship through males. In the case of relations, not Sapiṇḍas, the impurity lasts three days, or less, decreasing according to the remoteness of the relationship. During the period of impurity, sacrificial oblations, recitation of mantras, and some other religious duties have to be given up.

No one must eat the food of, or touch, one impure. But the customs vary much in these respects in the different parts of the country and even the word Sapiṇḍa is differently interpreted.

Further details may be studied in the Smritis, and may be applied by the student to his own life, in conformity with caste and family customs and having regard to the changed conditions of life. Infectious diseases of all kinds run riot where the rules of individual purity are disregarded, and where houses, clothes and articles in daily use are not scrupulously cleaned. Modern science is re-establishing, with infinite labour and pains, the facts on which these ancient rules were based, and a dear understanding of the reason for their imposition will render obedience to them willing and cheerful.

THE FIVE DAILY SACRIFICES

THE application of the great Law of Sacrifice to the daily life of the Āryan was made by the laying down of rules for making sacrifices, by which he gradually learned to regard himself as part of a connected whole, a whole of which the parts were mutually interdependent, owing to each other's mutual aid and support. When this lesson had been thoroughly assimilated, then, and then only, might the man lay aside these duties, entering on the life of the Sannyāsī, who having sacrificed all his possessions and himself, had nothing left to offer.

The various bodies or vehicles of man are nourished and helped to grow severally, by the initial energy received from parents, by food, by sympathy and help from his fellow-beings, by magnetic influences, and by knowledge and illumination. He therefore owes a fivefold debt to nature: and it is but meet and proper that, if he would flourish, he should fully recognise his indebtedness and do his best to pay back his debt. As stated before, he is not an isolated creature, and his whole well-being depends upon his co-operation with nature, which works not so much for the exaltation of individuals as for the steady evolution of all creation. The sacrifices prescribed by Hindu law-givers are nothing more than an enumeration of the duties which thus devolve on every man. They embrace all the planes of his existence, and are therefore conducive to his highest growth.

There are thus five: महायज्ञः, Māhayajnaḥ, great sacrifices, to be offered every day, and seven: पाक्यज्ञः, Pākayajnaḥ, literally cooked sacrifices, occurring at stated intervals. In addition to these, there are the fourteen Shrauta sacrifices, divided into हविर्यज्ञः, Haviryajnaḥ, offerings of grains, etc., and सोमयज्ञः Soma-yajnah, offerings of Soma. Some of these are of daily, others of occasional, obligation.

The five-great sacrifices are as follows:

1 ब्रह्मयज्ञः Brahmayajnaḥ, called also, वेदयज्ञः, Vedayajnaḥ, Sacrifice to Brahman or the Vedas.

2 देवयज्ञः Devayajnaḥ, Sacrifice to Devas.

3 पितृयज्ञः Pitṛiyajnaḥ, Sacrifice to Pitṛis.

4 भूतयज्ञः Bhutayajnaḥ, Sacrifice to Bhūtas.

5 मनुष्ययज्ञः Manuṣhyayajnaḥ, Sacrifice to men.

These are laid down by Manu among the duties of the householder.

अध्यापनं ब्रह्मयज्ञः पितृयज्ञस्तु तर्पणम्।
होमो दैवो बलिर्भौतो नृयज्ञोऽतिथिपूजनम्॥
अहुतं च हुतं चैव तथा प्रहुतमेव च।
ब्राहम्यं हुतं प्राशितं च पञ्चयज्ञान्प्रचक्षते॥
जपोऽहुतं हुतोहोमः प्रहुतो भौतिको बलिः।
ब्राह्मयं हुतं द्विजाग्र्यर्चा प्राशितं पितृतर्पणम्॥
स्वाध्याये नित्ययुक्तः स्याद्दैवे चैवेहं कर्मणि।
दैवे कर्मणि युक्तोहि बिभर्तीदं चराचरम्॥

"Teaching is the Brahma sacrifice, Tarpaṇa (the offering of

water) is the Pitṛi sacrifice, Homa (the pouring into the fire) the Deva sacrifice, Bali (food) is the Bhūta sacrifice, hospitality to guests the Mānuṣhya sacrifice.

"They call the five sacrifices Ahuta, Huta, Prahuta, Brāhmyahuta, and Prāshita.

"Japa is Ahuta, Homa is Huta, the bali given to Bhūtas is Prahuta, respectful reception of the twice-born is Brāhmyahuta, and the Pitṛi-tarpaṇa is Prāshita.

"Let a man ever engage in Veda study, and in the rites of the Devas; engaged in the rites of the Devas, he supports the movable and immovable kingdoms."

And again—

ऋषयः पितरो देवा भूतान्यतिथयस्तथा ।
आशासते कुटुम्बिभ्यस्तेभ्यः कार्यं विजानता ॥
स्वाध्यायेनार्चयेतर्षीन्होमैर्देवान्यथाविधि ।
पितृञ्छ्राद्धेन नृनन्नैर्भूतानि बलिकर्मणा ॥[1]

"The Ṛiṣhis, the Pitṛis, the Devas, the Bhūtas and guests expect (help) from the householders: hence he who knows should give to them.

"Let him worship, according to the rule, the Ṛiṣhis with Veda study, the Devas with Homa, the Pitris with Shrāddha, men with food, and the Bhūtas with Bali."

We have here very plainly indicated the nature of the sacrifices to be offered; the sacrifice to Brahman, called also that of the Vedas and the Ṛiṣhis, is study and teaching: this is a duty every man owes to the Supreme—to cultivate his intelligence and to share his knowledge with others. Every day the Āryan should devote a portion of time to study; the man who lives without daily

1 Manusmriti, iii. 80.

study becomes frivolous and useless. This duty is enjoined by the first of the great sacrifices.

Then comes the sacrifice to the Devas—the recognition of the debt due to those who guide nature, and the "feeding" them by pouring ghee into the fire, the Homa sacrifice. The Devas are nourished by exhalations as men by food, their subtle bodies needing no coarser sustenance.

The sacrifice to the Pitṛis follows, consisting of the offerings of cakes and water. The Pitṛis are the sons of Marīchi and the Ṛiṣhis produced by Manu, and are of many classes, the progenitors of the various divine and human races. From the Somasad Pitṛis the Sādhyas and pure Brāhmaṇas are descended, and from the Agniṣhvātta Pitṛis the Devas and also some Brāhmaṇas. The Daityas, Dānavas, Yakshas, Gandharvas, Uragas, Rākshasas, Suparṇas and Kinnaras descend from the Barhiṣhad Pitṛis, as do also some Brāhmaṇas. The Pitṛis of Kshattriyas are the Havirbhuks, of Vaiṣhyas the Ājyapas, of Shūdras the Sukālins. Countless descendants become associated with them, so that the sacrifice may be said to be to ancestors. In this a man is taught to remember the immense debt he owes to the past, and to regard with loving gratitude those, whose labours have bequeathed to him the accumulated stores of wealth, learning and civilisation. He is reminded also of the time when he will pass into the great ancestral host, and of his duty to hand down to posterity the legacy he has received, enriched, not diminished, by his life. The full meaning of descent from Pitṛis is ascertainable only by study of occult science.

The sacrifice to Bhūtas consists of Bali, or offerings of food placed on the ground in all directions, intended for various beings of the invisible worlds, and also for stray animals of all kinds and wandering outcasts and diseased persons. The injunction as to this should be remembered:

शुनां च पतितानां च श्वपचां पापरोगिणाम् ।
वायसानां कृमीणां च शनकैर्निर्वपेद्भुवि ।।[2]

"Let him gently place on the ground (food) for dogs, outcasts, Shva-pachas, those diseased from sins, crows and insects."

It is not to be thrown down carelessly and contemptuously, but put there gently, so that it may not be soiled or injured. It is a sacrifice, to be reverently performed, the recognition of duty to inferiors, however degraded.

Lastly comes the sacrifice to men, the feeding of guests—or generally of the poor—the giving of food to the homeless and the student:

कृत्वैतद्बलिकर्मैवमतिथिं पूर्वमाशयेत् ।
भिक्षां च भिक्षवे दद्याद्विधिवद्ब्रह्मचारिणे ॥[3]

"The Bali offering made, let him feed first the guest, and let him give food, according to rule, to a beggar and a student."

In this, man is taught his duty to his brother-men, his duty of brotherly help and kindness. He feeds humanity in feeding some of its poorer members, and learns tenderness and compassion. The giving of food is illustrative of all supply of human needs. Manushyayajna includes *all* philanthropic actions. As in the old days, want of food was the chief want of man, that is mentioned prominently. The complexities of life have given rise to other wants now. But they are all included in the Manushyayajna, provided they are legitimate wants, and it becomes the duty of

2 Manusmriti, iii. 92.
3 Ibid iii, 94

each man to remove them, so far as lies in his power.

Thus these five great sacrifices embrace man's duty to all the beings round him; and the man who truly performs them in spirit as well as in letter, day by day, is doing his share in turning the wheel of life and is preparing for himself a happy future. We may glance briefly at the other sacrifices.

The Pāka-yajnas are seven in number:

1 पितृश्राद्धं	Pitṛi-shrāddham
2 पार्वणश्राद्धं	Pārvaṇa-shrāddham
3 अष्टका	Aṣhtakā
4 श्रावणी	Ṣhravaṇī
5 अश्वयुजिः	Ashvayujiḥ
6 आग्रहायणी	Āgrahāyaṇī
7 चैत्री	Chaitrī

The first two of these are ceremonies in honour of the Pitṛis, and have been dealt with in Chapter II, under Shrāddha. The remainder, except the fourth, are now rarely met with.

The seven Haviryajnas:

1.	अग्न्याधेयं	Agnyādheyam
2.	अग्निहोत्रं	Agnihotram
3.	दर्शपूरणमासं	Darsha-pūrṇamāsam
4.	आग्रयणां	Āgrayaṇām
5.	चातुर्मास्यं	Chāturmāsyam
6.	निरूढपशुबन्धः	Nirūḍha-pashu-bandhaḥ
7.	सौत्रमणिः	Sautramaniḥ

In these, milk, ghee, grains of various kinds, and cakes were offered, and Manu says that a Brāhmaṇa should daily offer the Agnihotra in the morning and evening, the Darsha and

Pūrṇamāsa at the end of each fortnight, the Āgrayaṇa with new grain—before which the new grain should not be used—the Chāturmāsya at the end of the three seasons, the Nirūḍha-pashubandha at the solstices.[4]

The seven Somayajnas are:

1. अग्निष्टोमः Agniṣhṭomaḥ
2. अत्यग्निष्टोमः Atyagniṣhṭomaḥ
3. उक्थ्यः Ukthyaḥ
4. षोडषी Ṣhodaṣhī
5. वाजपेयः Vājapeyah
6. अतिरात्रः Atirātraḥ
7. आप्तोर्यामः Āptoryāmaḥ

In these sacrifices Brāhmaṇa priests must be employed, the number varying with the sacrifice, the man on whose behalf they are offered being called the: यजमानः,Yajamānah; the husband and wife light the three sacred fires—the Āhavanīya fire on the east, for offerings to the Devas; the Dakshiṇa fire on the south, for performing the duties to the Pitṛis; the Gārhapatya fire on the west; sometimes a fourth is mentioned, the Anvāhārya—and these are not allowed to go out; this is the Agnyādhāna ceremony. All the Shrauta sacrifices are offered in these.

According to some authors, the domestic or household—the Āvasathya or Vaivāhika—fire is lighted by the student on his return home when his pupilage is completed, but on this point there are many varieties of custom. The Pāka-yajnas are offered in the household fire.

4 Manusmriti, iv, 25, 26.

A description of the daily life of a Brāhmaṇa is given in the *Āhnika Sūtrāvalī*,[5] and may be summarised as follows:

He should wake up in the Brāhma-muhūrta[6] and think of Dharma and Artha, of the evils of the body, and of the Vedas. At the dawn he should rise, follow the Shaucha rules, and take his bath, then perform Sandhyā. Then, he should perform the Agnihotra, and worship the Devas and the Gurus (teacher and parents). After this, he should study the Vedas and Vedāngas. Then, he should work for those dependent on him—parents, guru, wife, children, relatives, friends, the aged, infirm, friendless, poor, and those who have no means.

Then, he should bathe, perform the mid-day Sandhyā, feed the Pitṛis, Devas, men and animals, and take his own meal. After this, he should read Purāṇas, Itihāsa, and Dharmashāstras, avoiding idle talk and discussion. Then, he should go out, visit temples and friends, returning to his evening Sandhyā and Agnihotra. After this, he should eat, attend to any family duties, and finally, after a brief reading of the Vedas, retire to bed. Any special duty should be attended to when it presents itself; as to these no rule can be laid down.

The general principle of this is that a man's life should be orderly, regulated, and balanced, due time being given to each part of his duty so that none should be slighted or omitted, and none allowed to monopolise his time. Above all he should realise the idea that man has no separate individual existence, but is indissolubly linked with the universe, and his whole life must be

---

5 Edited by Pandit VaidyanārāyaṇaVitthala.

6 There are thirty Muhūrtas in 24 hours, a Muhūrta being 48 minutes. The Brāhamamuhūrta is the third Muhūrta of the last quarter of the night.

a life of sacrifice and duties, if he is to fulfil the very law of his being. Such deliberate regulation of life is wise—necessary, even, if the most is to be made of life—and conduces to peacefulness and absence of hurry. In modern life, the details cannot be carried out but the general principle of regularity, balance and a sustained spirit of self-sacrifice and duty should be maintained, so that all-round and harmonious progress may be made.

WORSHIP

WE have already seen that the work of the Devas was recognised and duly honoured among the Āryans, and that the duty of sacrificing for their support was regularly performed. But the truly religious man's relations with the invisible Powers are not confined to these regular and formal sacrifices. Īshvara Himself, the Supreme Lord, will attract the heart of the thoughtful and pious man, who sees, beyond these many ministers, the King Himself, the ruling Power of His universe, the life and support of Devas and men alike. It is towards Him that love and devotion naturally rise—the human spirit, who is His offspring, a fragment of Himself, seeking to rise and unite himself to his Parent. These feelings cannot find satisfaction in sacrifices offered to Devas, connected as they are with the outer worlds, with the Not-Self; they seek after the inner, the deepest, the very Self, and remain craving and unsatisfied until they rest in Him.

Worship is the expression of this craving of the part for the whole, of the separate for the One, and is not only due from man to the source of his life, but is a necessary stage in the evolution of all those higher qualities in the Jīvātmā which make possible his liberation and his union with the Supreme. An Object of worship is therefore necessary to man.

That Object will always be, to the worshipper, the Supreme Being. He will know intellectually that the Object of his worship is a form of manifestation of the Supreme, but emotionally that Form is the supreme-as in truth it is, although the Supreme includes and transcends all forms.

Now a Form is necessary for worship. The Nirguṇa Brahman, the Absolute, the All, cannot be an Object of worship. It is not an Object, but is beyond all Subject and Object, including all, in separate. But from that

वाचो निवर्तन्त अप्राप्य मनसा सह ॥[1]

"Words return with the mind, not having reached."

Words fall into silence, mind disappears, It is all in all.

The Saguṇa Brahman may be the object of worship for those whose minds are of metaphysical nature, and who find rest and peace in the contemplation of Brahman in His own nature as Sat-Chit-Ānanda, the Universal Self, the One, the Supreme.

Such contemplation is worship of a lofty kind, and is peculiarly congenial to philosophical minds, who find in it the sense of peace, rest, unity, which they cannot feel in any more limited conception. But to most it is easier to rise to Him through His manifestation as the Lord and Life of His worlds, or through one of the manifestations, as Mahādeva, Nārāyaṇa, or more concrete yet, Shrī Rāma or Shrī Kṛiṣhṇa, or other embodiment. These arouse in them the Bhakti, the love and devotion, which the other conception fails to stir, and all the tendrils of the human heart wind themselves round such an image, and lift the heart

1 Taittirīyop, II. iv. I.

into Ānanda, into bliss unspeakable.

Whether one of these two ways is the better is an oft-disputed question, and the answerers on either side are apt to be impatient with those on the other, intolerant of the uncongenial way. But the answer has been given with perfect wisdom and all-embracing comprehension by Shrī Kṛiṣhṇa Himself.

Arjuna was troubled by the question, five thousand years ago, and put it to his divine Teacher:

एवं सततयुक्ता ये भक्तास्त्वां पर्युपासते ।
ये चाप्यक्षरमव्यक्तं तेषां के योगवित्तमाः । ।
श्रीभगवानुवाच ।
मय्यावेश्य मनो ये मां नित्ययुक्ता उपासते ।
श्रद्धया परयोपेतास्ते मे युक्ततमा मताः । ।
ये त्वक्षरमनिर्देश्यमव्यक्तं पर्युपासते ।
सर्वत्रगमचिंत्यं च कूटस्थमचलंध्रुवम् ॥
सनियम्येन्द्रियग्रामं सर्वत्र समबुद्धयः ।
ते प्राप्नुवन्ति मामेंव सर्वभूताहिते रताः । ।
क्लेशोऽधिकतरस्तेषामव्यक्तासक्तचेतसाम् ।
अव्यक्ता हि गतिर्दुःखं देहवद्भिरवाप्यते । ।
ये तु सर्वाणि कर्माणि मयिसंन्यस्य मत्पराः ।
अनन्येनैव योगेन मां ध्यायंत उपासते ॥
तेषामहं समुद्धर्ता मृत्युसंसारसागरात् ।
भवामि न चिरात्पार्थ मय्यावेशितचेतसाम् ॥[2]

"Those Bhaktas, who, ever controlled, worship Thee, and those also (who worship) the Indestructible, the Unmanifested, of these which are the more skilled in Yoga?

"The Blessed Lord said:

---

2 Bhagavad Gītā, xii. 1—7

"They who with Manas fixed on Me, ever controlled, worship Me, with faith supreme endowed, these I hold as best in Yoga.

"They who worship the Indestructible, the Ineffable, the Unmanifested, the Omnipresent, the Unthinkable, the Unchangeable, the Immutable, the Eternal.

"Renouncing and subduing the senses, every-where equal-minded, in the welfare of all creatures rejoicing, these also come unto Me.

"Greater is the difficulty of those whose minds are set on the Unmanifested, for the path of the Unmanifested is hard for the embodied to reach.

"Those verily who, renouncing all actions in Me and intent on Me, worship, meditating on Me with whole-hearted Yoga.

"These I speedily lift up from the ocean of death and existence, O Pārtha, their minds being fixed on Me."

This is the final answer; both achieve, both gain Mukti, but the worship of Īshvara in a Form is easier than the worship of Him without a Form, and escape from the cycle of rebirth is easier for those who thus worship.

The simplest form of worship is that generally spoken of as Pūjā, in which an image representing some divine Form is used as the Object, and the Being thus represented is adored; flowers are used, as beautiful symbols of the heart—flowers of love and reverence; water is sanctified with a mantra, poured on the image, and sprinkled over the worshipper; a mantra, in which the name of the Object of worship occurs, is repeated inaudibly a certain number of times, and the invisible bodies are thus rendered receptive of His influence, as before explained. Then the worshipper passes on according to his nature into spontaneous praise or prayer, aspiration and meditation, and becoming oblivious of the external object, rising to the One imaged in that object, and often feeling His presence, becomes suffused with peace and bliss. Such worship steadies the mind, purifies and ennobles the emotions, and stimulates the unfolding of the germinal spiritual faculties.

The use of an image in such worship is often found most helpful, and is well-nigh universal. It gives an object to which the mind can at first be directed and thus steadiness is obtained. If it be well chosen, it will attract the emotions, and the symbols, always present in such an image, will direct the mind to the characteristic properties of the Object of worship.

Thus the Liṅgam is the symbol of the great Pillar of Fire, which is the most characteristic manifestation of Mahādeva, the destroying element which consumes all dross but only purifies the gold. The four-armed Viṣhṇu represents the protecting support of the deity, whose arms uphold and protect the four quarters, and the objects held in the hands are symbols of His creative, ruling, destroying forces, and of the universe He governs.

The Shālagrāma is used in the household as the symbol of Viṣhṇu. But all these are already familiar.

When the worshipper passes from the external worship to the internal, the image is reproduced mentally and carries him on into the invisible world, where it may change into a living Form, animated by the One it represents. Further, a properly prepared image-sanctified by mantras and by the daily renewed forces of the worshipper's devotion—becomes a strong magnetic centre which issues powerful vibrations, which regularise and steady the invisible bodies of the worshipper, and thus assist him in gaining the quiet and peaceful conditions necessary for effective prayer and meditation.

Apart from these definite uses, the Bhakta feels a pleasure in contemplating such an image, similar in kind to, but greater in degree than, any one finds in having with him the picture of a beloved but absent friend.

For all these reasons, no one should object to the use of images in religious worship by those who find them helpful; nor should any one try to force their use on those who are not helped by them. Tolerance in these matters is the mark of the truly religious man.

The special Form to which pūjā is addressed is sometimes the Kula-deva, or Kula-devī, the family Deva or Devī, and sometimes is the one chosen for the worshipper by his Guru, or chosen by himself as the one which most appeals to him. This Form is the Ishta-deva, the Deva sacrificed to, or desired.

Other forms of worship are generally classed under the name Upāsanā. Flowers are not employed, nor is an image necessary, though it is often used, for the reasons already given. The daily Sandhyā is a form of such worship in which all students should be properly instructed. It is of two types, Vaidika and Tāntrika, and varies according to caste and family customs. The complicated Sandhyā ceremony as performed nowadays in various parts of India does not exactly represent the oldest form of it, as taught in the *Taittīriya* Brāhmaṇa, and the early Smritis. But the Arghya-pradāna to the Sun and the meditation on and recitation of the Gāyatrī, which form the heart of the ceremony, are the oldest parts of it too. Unless it is performed at the proper Sandhyās it cannot be of much profit to the performer. A Sandhyā is the meeting point of two periods of time, great or small, or of two different states of one and the same subject. It is the teaching of the ancient Ṛiṣhis of India that at Sandhyās, there is always a special manifestation of force which vanishes when the Sandhyā is past.

The broad features are:

1. Āchamana and Mārjana, purifying the body with water sanctified by a Mantra.
2. Prāṇāyama, control of the breath.
3. Agha-marṣhaṇa, expiatory of all sins to which the Ego, not the Personality, is attached; the worshipper goes back in mind to the time when there was no manifestation and no sins.
4. Gāyatrī, either Vaidika or Tāntrika, followed by
5. Worship of the Sun-God—Arghya and Upasthāna.
6. Japa, recitation, a certain number of times, of the Mantra of the Ishṭa-deva, including adoration and salutation.

The Vaidika sacrifices and Saṃskāras are mostly out of use, but this Sandhyā Vandana is a living thing, the last remnant, and the student must jealously keep to it and must perform it every day.

Another kind of Upāsanā is meditation, and the treatise of Patanjali, the Patanjala-sūtrāṇi, should here be carefully studied, when the time for systematic meditation arrives. In student days, the due performance of Sandhyā and of some form of Pūjā may suffice, but the theoretical outline of the practice of meditation may be given. Paṭanjali says:

यमनियमासनप्राणायामप्रत्याहारधारणाध्यानसमाधयोऽष्टावङ्गानि ।[3]

"Yama, Niyama, Āsana, Prāṇāyama, Pratyāhāra, Dhāraṇa, Dhyāna, Samādhi, the eight limbs."

The first two of these, Yama and Niyama, have to do with conduct, for without good conduct and purity there can be no meditation.

3 Op.cit. ii. 29.

तत्राहिंसासत्यास्तेयब्रह्मचर्याऽपरिग्रहायमाः ।[4]

"Harmlessness, truth, honesty, chastity, absence of greed—these are Yamas."

शौचसंतोषतपः स्वाध्यायेश्वरप्रणिधानानि नियमाः ।[5]

"Purity, contentment, austerity, Veda-study, yearning after Īshvara—(these are) Niyamas."

These qualities acquired; a man may sit for meditation. There are two preliminaries. Any posture which is steady and pleasant is suitable:

स्थिरसुखमासनम् ।[6]

"Firm, pleasant—(that is) Āsana."

Prāṇāyama is the regulation of the breath, and this has to be learned from a teacher.

Then comes the immediate preparation, the closing of the senses against external objects, and the drawing of them and placing them in the mind: this is Pratyāhāra.

Now follows meditation, consisting of three stages, Dhāraṇā, Dhyāna and Samādhi.

देशबन्धश्चित्तस्य धारणा ।[7]

"The binding of the mind to (one) object is Dhāraṇā."

This is concentration, the steadying of the mind on one point, in one place, so that it is fixed, one-pointed. Only such a mind can pass on to Dhyāna.

4 Ibid. 30.
5 Ibid. 32.
6 Ibid. 46.
7 Ibid. iii.1.

तंत्र प्रत्ययैकतानता ध्यानम् ।[8]

"The steady (and uninterrupted) flow of cognition towards that (object) is Dhyāna."

When this is reached, the mind, fixing itself thus, loses the consciousness of itself and remains identified with the object of thought, and this state is Samādhi.

तदेवार्थमात्रनिर्भासं स्वरूपशून्यमिव समाधिः ।[9]

"That same (Dhyāna) showing the object only, and devoid, as it were, of self-consciousness, (is) Samādhi."

These are the preparations for and the stages of meditation. By this, a man rises to knowledge; by this, he loses himself in the divine Being he worships; by this, he disengages himself from the bonds of action. Without meditation no truly spiritual life is possible.

Manu has declared, after describing the life of the Sannyāsī:

ध्यानिकं सर्वमंवैतद्यदेतदभिशब्दितम् ।
न ह्यनध्यात्मवित्कश्चिक्रियाफलमुपाश्नुते ।।

"All this that has here been declared depends on meditation; for no one who does not know the Supreme Self can fully enjoy the fruit of rites."

It is therefore a thing to be looked forward to and prepared for, and every student who desires the higher life should begin his preparation by practising Yama and Niyama.

8 Ibid 2.
9 Ibid. 3.

THE FOUR ĀSHRAMAS

THE student will have noticed the extremely systematic and orderly arrangement of life which characterises the Sanātana Dharma. It is in full keeping with this, that the whole life should be arranged on a definite system, designed to give opportunity for the development of the different sides of human activity and assigning to each period of life its due occupations and training. Life was regarded as a school in which the powers of the Jīvātmā were to be evolved, and it was well or ill spent according as this object was well or ill achieved.

The life was divided into four stages, or Āshramas: that of the ब्रह्मचारी, Brahmachārī, the student, bound to celibacy; that of the गृहस्थः, Grihasthaḥ, the householder; that of the वानप्रस्थः, Vānaprasthaḥ, the forest-dweller; that of the सन्यसि, Sannyāsī, the ascetic, called also the यतिः,Yatiḥ, the controlled, or the endeavourer.

ब्रह्मचारी गृहस्थश्च वानप्रस्थो यतिस्तथा।
एते गृहस्थप्रभवाश्चत्वारः पृथगाश्रमाः ॥[1]

1 Manusmriti, vi. 87.

"The Student, the Householder, the Forest-dweller, the Ascetic-these, the four separate orders, spring from the Householder."

A man should pass through these regularly, and not enter any prematurely. Only when each had been completed might he enter the next.

वेदानधीत्य वेदौ वा वेदं वापि यथाक्रमम् ।
अविप्लुतब्रह्मचर्यो गृहस्थाश्रममावसेत् ॥[2]

"Having studied the Vedas, or two Vedas, or even one Veda, in due order, without breaking celibacy, let him dwell in the householder order."

गृहस्थस्तु यदा पश्येद्वलीपलितमात्मनः ।
अपत्यस्य तथापत्यं तदारण्यं समाश्रयेत् ॥[3]

"When the householder sees wrinkles (in his skin) and whiteness (in his hair) and the son of his son, then let him retire to the forest."

वनेषु तु विहृत्यैवं तृतीयं भागमायुषः ।
चतुर्थमायुषो भागंत्यक्त्वासङ्गान्परिव्रजेत् ॥[4]

"Having passed the third portion of life in the forests, let him, having abandoned attachments, wander (as an ascetic) the fourth portion of life."

This succession is regarded as so important for the due development of the Jīvātmā, and the proper ordering of society, that Manu says:

---

2 Ibid.iii.2.
3 Ibid. vi.2.
4 Ibid. 33.

अनधीत्य द्विजोवेदाननुत्पाद्य तथा प्रजाम् ।
अनिष्ट्वा चैव यज्ञैश्च मोक्षमिच्छन्व्रजत्यधः ॥[5]

"A twice-born man who seeketh Mokṣha without having studied the Vedas, without having produced offspring, and without having offered sacrifices, goeth downwards."

The offering of sacrifices, we shall see, is the chief duty of the forest-dweller, and therefore indicates the Vānaprastha state.

In rare and exceptional cases, a student was allowed to become a Sannyāsī, his debts to the world having been fully paid in a previous birth; but these rare cases left the regular order unshaken. Strictly speaking, indeed, even he was not called a Sannyāsī, and did not receive the initiations of Sannyāsa proper; but was called a Bāla or Naiṣhṭhika Brahmachāri, like Shuka and the Kumāra Ṛiṣhis. The great multiplication of young Sannyasis found in modern days is directly contrary to the ancient rules, and causes much vice and trouble and impoverishment of the country.

We will now consider the Āshramas in order.

The student life began, as we have seen, with the Upanayana ceremony, the boy being then committed to the care of his teacher, with whom he lived while his pupilage continued. His life thereafter was simple and hardy, intended to make him strong and healthy, independent of all soft and luxurious living, abstemious and devoid of ostentation. He was to rise before Sunrise and bathe and then perform Sandhyā during the morning twilight till the sun rose; if it rose while he was still sleeping, he had to fast during the day, performing Japa. Then he went out to beg for food which was placed at his teacher's disposal, and was to take the portion assigned to him cheerfully:

5 Manusmriti, vi. 37.

पूजयेदशनं नित्यमद्याच्चैतदकुत्सयन् ।
दृष्ट्वा हृष्येत्प्रसीदेच्च प्रतिनन्देच्च सर्वशः ॥
पूजितं ह्यशनं नित्यं बलमूर्जं च यच्छति ।
अपूजितं तु तद्भुक्तमुभयं नाशयेदिदम् ॥[6]

"Let him ever honour (his) food, and eat it without contempt; having seen it, let him be glad and pleased, and in every way welcome it.

"Food which is honoured ever gives strength and nerve-vigour; eaten unhonoured, it destroys both these."

The day was to be spent in study and in the service of his teacher:

नोदितो गुरुणा नित्यमप्रणोदित एव वा ।
कुर्यादध्ययने योगमाचार्यस्य हितेषु च ॥[7]

"Directed or not directed by his teacher, let him ever engage in study, and in doing benefits to his preceptor."

At sunset he was again to worship till the stars appeared. Then the second meal was taken. Between these two meals he was generally not to eat, and he was enjoined to be temperate as to his food.

अनारोग्यमनायुष्यमस्वर्ग्यं चातिभोजनम् ।
अपुण्यं लोकविद्विष्टं तस्मात्तत्परिवर्जयेत् ।[8]

"Over-eating is against health, long life, (the attainment of) heaven and merit, and is disapproved by the world; therefore, let him avoid it."

---

6 Manusmriti, ii. 54, 55.

7 Manusmriti. ii. 191.

8 Ibid.57.

The rules laid down as to his general conduct show how frugality, simplicity and hardiness were enforced, so that the youth might grow into a strong and vigorous man; it was the training of a nation of energetic, powerful, nobly-mannered and dignified men.

वर्जयेन्मधु मांसं च गन्धमाल्यं रसांस्त्रियः।
शुक्तानि चैव सर्वाणि प्राणिनां चैव हिंसनम्।
अभ्यङ्गमञ्जनं चाक्ष्णोरुपानच्छत्त्रधारणम्।
कामं क्रोधं च लोभं च नर्तनं गीतवादनम्।
द्यूतं च जनवादं च पारवादं तथानृतम्।
स्त्रीणां च प्रेक्षणालम्भमुपघातं परस्य च॥
एकः शयीत सर्वत्र न रेतः स्कन्दयेत्क्वचित्।
कामाद्धि स्कन्दयन रेतो हिनस्ति व्रतमात्मनः॥
स्वप्ने सिक्त्वा ब्रह्मचारी द्विजः शुक्रमकामतः।
स्नात्वार्कमर्चयित्वा त्रिः पुनर्मामित्यृचं जपेत्॥[9]

"Let him refrain from wine, meat, perfumes, garlands, tasty and savoury dishes, women, all acids, and from injury to sentient creatures.

"From unguents, collyrium to the eyes, the wearing of shoes and umbrellas, from lust, anger and greed, dancing, singing and playing on musical instruments.

"Dice-playing, gossip, slander and untruth, from staring at and touching women, and from striking others.

"Let him always sleep alone, and let him not waste his seed; he who from lust wastes his seed, destroys his vow (and its valuable fruits.)

"A twice-born Brahmachārī who loses seed in sleep without lust, having bathed and worshipped the sun, should repeat the

9 Manusmriti, ii, 177-181

rik, पुनर्माम्, etc., three times."

The student will see that all the injunctions of Manu above quoted apply perfectly to the present day, except the prohibition as to shoes and umbrellas. Changed social conditions make modifications necessary on this point, as well as on certain other matters not included in the quotation.

The great stress laid upon chastity and purity during youth is due to the fact that the vigour and strength of manhood, freedom from disease, healthy children, and long life, depend more on this one virtue of complete continence than on any other one thing, self-abuse being the most fertile breeder of disease and premature decay. The old legislators and teachers therefore made a vow of celibacy part of the obligation of the student, and the very: name of the student, the Brahmachārī, has become synonymous with one who is under a vow of celibacy. The injunction quoted above, to avoid dancing, singing, playing on musical instruments, dicing, gossip, staring at and touching women, has as aim to keep the lad out of the company and the amusements that might lead him into forgetfulness of his vow, and into temptations for its breach. The simple food, the hard work, the frugal living, all build up a robust body, and inure it to hardships.

Over and over again Manu speaks on this:

इन्द्रियाणां विचरतां विषयेष्वपहारिषु ।
संयमे यत्नमातिष्ठेद्विद्वान्यन्तेव वाजिनाम् ॥[10]

"Let the wise man exercise assiduity in the restraint of the senses, wandering among alluring objects, as the driver (restrains) the horses,"

10 Manusmriti. ii. 88.

वशेकृत्वेन्द्रियग्रामंसंयम्यचमनस्तथा।
सान्संसाधयेदर्थानक्षिण्वन्योगतस्तनुम्।।[11]

"Having brought into subjection all his senses, and also regulated his mind, he may accomplish all his objects by Yoga, without emaciating his body."

The *Chhāndogyopaniṣhat* declares that Yajna, Iṣhta, the feeding of the poor, the dwelling in forests, are all summed up in Brahmacharya, and that the third heaven of Brahmā is only thus obtained.[12]

The practice of self-control and complete continence was rendered much easy than it would otherwise have been, by the care bestowed on the physical development and training of youth by physical exercises and manly games of all kinds.

In the *Rāmāyaṇa* and the *Mahābhārata*, we read of the way in which the youths were practised in the use of weapons, in riding and driving, in sports and feats of skill. These physical exercises formed a definite part of their education, and contributed to the building up of a vigorous and healthy frame.

Having thus fulfilled, in study and strict chastity, the student period, the youth was to present His teacher with a gift, according to his ability, and return home to enter the household life.

Then, and then only, he was to take a wife, and the responsibilities of man's estate. After marriage, great temperance in sexual relations was enjoined, marital connexion being only permissible on any one of ten nights in a month (see Manu, iii. 45-49). Women were to be honoured and loved, else no welfare could attend the home:

11 Manusmriti ii. 100.

12 Loc. cit. VIII. iv. 3 and v.1—4.

पितृभिर्भ्रातृभिश्चैताः पतिभिर्देवरैस्तथा।
पूज्या भूषयितव्याश्च बहुकल्याणमीप्सुभिः॥
यत्र नार्यस्तु पूज्यन्ते रमन्ते तत्र देवताः।
यत्र तास्तु न पूज्यन्ते सर्वास्तत्राफलाः क्रियाः॥
शोचन्ति जामयो यत्र विनश्यत्याशु तत्कुलम्।
न शोचन्ति तु यत्रैता वर्धते तद्धि सर्वदा।[13]

"They must be honoured and adorned by fathers, brothers, husbands and brothers-in-law, desiring, welfare.

"Where women are honoured, there verily the Devas rejoice; where they are not honoured, there indeed all rites are fruitless.

"Where the female relatives grieve, there the family quickly perishes; where they do not grieve, that family always prospers."

संतुष्टो भार्यया भर्ता भर्त्रा भार्या तथैव च।
यस्मिन्नेव कुलेनित्यं कल्याणं तत्र वै ध्रुवम्॥[14]

"In the family in which the husband is contented with his wife, and the wife, with the husband, there happiness is ever sure."

The Grihastha is the very heart of Aryan life; everything depends on him.

यथा वायुं समाश्रित्य सर्वे जीवन्ति जन्तवः।
तथा गृहस्थमाश्रित्य वर्तन्त इतराश्रमाः॥[15]

"As all creatures live supported by air, so the other orders exist supported by the householder."

सर्वेषामपि चैतेषाम्वेदश्रुतिविधानतः।
गृहस्थ उच्यते श्रेष्ठः स त्रीनेतान्बिभर्तिहि॥
यथा नदीनदाः सर्वे सागरे यान्ति संस्थितिम्।

13 Manusmriti iii. 55-57.
14 Manusmriti, iii, 60.
15 Ibid.77.

तथैवाश्रमिणः सर्वे गृहस्थे यान्ति संस्थितिम् ॥[16]

"Of all these, by the precepts of the Veda-Shruti, the householder is called the best; he verily supports the other three.

"As all streams and rivers flow to rest in the ocean, so all the Āshramas flow to rest in the householder."

Hence the householder is the best of the orders, ज्यष्ठाश्रमोगृही. He has the duty of accumulating wealth—in this the Vaiṣhya is the typical householder—and of distributing it rightly. Hospitality is one of his chief duties, and in this he must never fail.

तृणानि भूमिरुदकं वाक्चतुर्थी च सूनृता ।
एतान्यपि सतां गेहे नोच्छिद्यन्ते कदाचन ॥[17]

"Grasses, earth, water, the kind word, these four are never lacking in the houses of the good."

He must ever feed first his guests, Brāhmaṇas, his relatives and his servants, and then he and his wife should eat, but even before these he should serve brides, infants, the sick, and pregnant women.[18]

The householder must duly offer the five great sacrifices, and by Brāhmaṇa householders the duty of the monthly Shrāddhas should be observed.

The Brāhmaṇa should maintain his studies, and not follow occupations which prevent study, but earn his living in some business that does not injure others.[19] Careful rules are laid down for conduct, which will be dealt with in Part III, as they belong to the general conduct of life, the householder being the typical

16 Ibid.89-90.
17 Manusmriti, iii. 101.
18 Ibid. 114—116
19 Ibid. 2.

human being. His special virtues are hospitality, industry, truth, honesty, liberality, charity, purity of food and life. He may enjoy wealth and luxury, provided he gives alms.

The householder may quit the household life, and become a Vānaprastha, going to the forest when, as before said, he is growing old and has grandchildren. His wife may go with him, or remain with her sons, and he goes forth, taking with him the sacred fire and sacrificial instruments. His duty to the world is now to help it by prayer and sacrifice, and he is accordingly to continue to offer the five daily sacrifices, together with the Agnihotra, the new and full moon sacrifices and others. The rule of his life is to sacrifice, study, austerity, and kindness to all:

स्वाध्याये नित्ययुक्तः स्याद्दान्तो मैत्रः समाहितः ।
दाता नित्यमनादाता सर्वभूतानुकम्पकः ॥[20]

"Let him ever be engaged in Veda study, controlled, friendly, collected; ever a giver, not a receiver, compassionate to all beings."

This simple ascetic life leads him on to the last stage, that of the Sannyāsī, the man who has renounced all. He no longer offers sacrifices, having given all his property away; he lives alone, with tree for shelter, his life given to meditation.

अनग्निरनिकेतः स्याद् ग्राममन्नार्थमाश्रयेत् ।
उपेक्षकोऽसंकुसुको मुनिर्भावसमाहितः ॥[21]

"Let him be without fire, without dwelling, let him go to a village for food, indifferent, firm of purpose, a muni of collected mind."

20 Manusmriti. vi. 8.
21 Mid. 43.

Then follows a beautiful description of the true Sannyāsī:

नाभिनन्देत मरणं नाभिनन्देत जीवितम् ।
कालमेव प्रतीक्षेत निर्देशं भृतको यथा ॥
दृष्टिपूतं न्यसेत्पादं वस्त्रपूतं जलं पिबेत् ।
सत्यपूतं वदेद्वाचं मनःपूतं समाचरेत् ॥
अतिवादांस्तितिक्षेत नावमन्येत कंचन ।
न चेमं देहमाश्रित्य वैरं कुर्वीत केनचित् ॥
क्रुध्यन्तं न प्रतिक्रुध्येदाक्रुष्टः कुशलं वदेत् ।
सप्तद्वारावकीर्णां च न वाचमनृतां वदेत् ॥
अध्यात्मरतिरासीनो निरपेक्षो निरामिषः ।
आत्मनैव सहायेन सुखार्थी विचरेदिह । ।[22]

"Let him not wish for death, let him not wish for life, let him wait for the time, as a servant for his wages.

"Let him set feet purified (guided) by sight, let him drink water purified by (strained through a) cloth, let him speak words purified by truth, let him do acts purified (governed) by reason.

"Let him endure harsh language, and let him not insult any one; nor, relying on this (perishable) body, let him make an enemy of anyone.

"Let him not return anger to the angry, let him bless when cursed; let him not utter lying speech, scattered at the seven gates (i. e. speech showing desire for the fleeting and false objects of the five outer senses and Manas and Buddhi.)

"Rejoicing in the Supreme Self, sitting indifferent, refraining from sensual delights, with himself for his only friend, let him wander here (on the earth), aiming at liberation."

22 Manusmriti. vi. 45—49.

He is to meditate constantly on transmigration and suffering, on the Supreme Self and Its presence in high and low alike, to trace the Jīvātmā through its many births, and to rest in Brahman alone.

Thus doing, he reaches Brahman.

Such were the four Āshramas of Sanātana Dharma, designed for the training of man to the highest ends. In modern days they cannot be completely revived in their letter, but they might be revived in their spirit, to the great improvement of modern life. The student period must now be passed in school and college, for the most part, instead of in the Āshrama of the Guru; but the same principles of frugal, hardy, simple living might be carried out, and Brahmacharya might be universally enforced.

The Grihastha ideal, commenced at marriage, might be very largely followed in its sense of duty and responsibility, in its discharge of religious obligations, in its balanced ordering of life, in its recognition of all claims, of all debts. The third Āshrama could not be lived in the forest by many, and the fourth Āshrama is beyond the reach of most in these days; but the idea of the gradual withdrawal from worldly life, of the surrender of the conduct of business into the hands of the younger generation, of the making of meditation, study and worship the main duties of life—all this could be carried out. And the presence of such aged and saintly men would sanctify the whole community, and would serve as a constant reminder of the dignity and reality of the religious life, setting up a noble ideal, and raising, by their example, the level of the whole society.

A life which is well-ordered from beginning to—that is what is implied in the phrase "The four Āshramas." Two of them—namely that of the student and that of the householder—may be said to represent in the life of an individual that outward-going energy which carries the Jīva into the Pravṛitti Mārga. The two later stages—the life of the Vānaprastha and that of the Sannyāsī—these are the stages of withdrawal from the world, and may be said to represent the Nivṛitti Mārga in the life of the individual. So wisely did the ancient ones mark out the road along which a man should tread, that any man who takes this plan of life, divided into four stages, will find his outgoing and in drawing energies rightly balanced. First, the student stage properly lived and worthily carried out; then the householder stage, with all its busy activity in every direction of worldly business; then the gradual withdrawal from activity, the turning inward, the life of comparative seclusion, of prayer and of meditation of the giving of wise counsel to the younger generation engaged in worldly activities, and then, for some at least, the life of complete renunciation.

It must not be forgotten that the passing through these Āshramas and the reaching of liberation has for its object—as we may see from the stories of Muktas in the Purāṇas and Itihāsas—the helping of the worlds, and the co-operating with Ishvara in His benevolent administration, and His guidance of evolution. In the outward life of Sannyāsa the Jīvātmā learns detachment and indifference, but the highest Sannyāsa is that of the inner, not that of the outer life, in which a man, who is completely detached and indifferent, mingles in the life of men for their helping and uplifting.

अनाश्रितः कर्मफलं कार्यं कर्म करोति यः।
स सन्यासी च योगी च न निरग्निर्न चाक्रियः।।[23]

23 Bhagavad Gītā iv. i.

"He who performeth such action as is duty, independently of the fruit of action, he is a Sannyāsī and Yogī also, not be that is without fire and rites."

Such a man lives in the midst of objects of attachment and is yet without attachment, regarding nothing as his own though possessed of wealth.

He then becomes the ideal householder, whom the Gṛihastha reflects, and verifies in its fullest sense the dictum of Manu, that the householder order is the highest of all because it is the support of all.

And the household life is truly lived only where a man sets before himself that high ideal of administrator rather than owner, servant rather than master of all.

THE FOUR CASTES

JUST as the Four Āshramas serve as a school for the unfolding of the Jīvātmā during a single life, so do the Four Castes serve as a similar school for its unfolding during a part of the whole period of its transmigrations. Looked at in the broadest sense, they represent the complete period, but, as an external system, the Jīvātmā is in them only for a portion of his pilgrimage. The present confusion of castes has largely neutralised the use they once served. In the ancient days the Jīvātmā was prepared for entrance into each caste through a long preliminary stage outside India; then he was born into India and passed into each caste to receive its definite lessons; then was born away from India to practice these lessons; usually returning to India, to the highest of them, in the final stages of his evolution.

It is necessary to see the great principles underlying the Caste System in order to estimate its advantages at their proper value; and also in order to distinguish rightly between these fundamental principles and the numerous non-essential, and in many cases mischievous, accretions which have grown up around it, and have become interwoven with it, in the course of ages.

The first thing to understand is that the evolution of the Jīvātmā is divided into four great stages, and that this is true of every Jīvātmā, and is in no sense peculiar to those who, in their outer coverings, are Āryans and Hindus. Jīvātmās pass into and out of the Hindu Religion, but every Jīvātmā is in one or other of the four great stages. These belong to no age and to no civilisation, to no race and no nation. They are universal, of all times and of all races.

The first stage is that which embraces the infancy, childhood and youth of the Jīvātmā, during which he is in a state of pupilage, fit only for service and study, and has scarcely any responsibilities.

The second stage is the first half of his manhood, during which he carries on the ordinary business of the world, bears the burden of household responsibilities, so to say, the accumulation, enjoyment and proper disposal of wealth, together with the heavy duties of organising, training and educating his youngers in all the duties of life.

The third stage occupies the second half of his manhood, during which he bears the burden of national responsibilities, the duty of protecting, guiding, ruling, others, and utterly subordinating his individual interests to the common good, even to the willing sacrifice of his own life for the lives around him.

The fourth stage is the old age of the Jīvātmā, when his accumulated experiences have taught him to see clearly the valuelessness of all Earth's treasures, and have made him rich in wisdom and compassion, the selfless friend of all, the teacher and counsellor of all his youngers.

These stages are, as said above, universal. The peculiarity of the Santana Dharma is that these four universal stages have been made the foundation of a social polity, and have been represented by four definite external castes, or classes, the characteristics laid down as belonging to each caste being those which characterise the stage of the universal evolution to which the caste corresponds.

The first stage is represented by the Shūdra caste, in which, as we shall see, the rules are few and the responsibilities light. Its one great duty is that of service; its virtues are those which should be evolved in the period of youth and pupillage—obedience, fidelity, reverence, industry and the like.

The second stage is represented by the Vaiṣhya, the typical householder, on whom the social life of the nation depends. He comes under strict rules, designed to foster unselfishness and the sense of responsibility, to nourish detachment in the midst of possession, and to make him feel the nation as his household. His virtues are diligence, caution, prudence, discretion, charity, and the like.

The third stage is represented by the Kshattriya, the ruler and warrior, on whom depends the national order and safety. He also lives under strict rules, intended to draw out all the energy and strength of his character and to turn them to unselfish ends, and to make him feel that everything he possesses, even life itself, must be thrown away at the call of duty. His virtues are generosity, vigour, courage, strength, power to rule, self-control, and the like.

The fourth stage is represented by the Brāhmaṇa, the teacher and priest, who lives under the strictest of all rules directed to make him a centre of purifying influence, physically as well as morally and spiritually. He is to have outgrown the love of wealth and power, to be devoted to study, learned and wise. He is to be the refuge of all creatures, their sure help in time of need. His virtues are gentleness, patience, purity, self-sacrifice, and the like.

The Jīvātmā who, in any nation, at any time, shows out these types of virtues, belongs to the stage of which his type is characteristic, and, if born in India as a Hindu, should be born into the corresponding caste. In this age one can only say "should be," as the castes are now confused and the types are but rarely found. These characteristic virtues form the "Dharma" of each caste, but these Dharmas are now, unhappily, disregarded.

It is easy to see that the broad dividing lines of classes everywhere follow these lines of caste. The manual labour class, the proletariat—to use the Western term—should consist of Jīvātmās in the Shūdra stage. The organisers of industry, the merchants, bankers, financiers, large agriculturists, traders, should be Jīvātmās in the Vaiṣhya stage. The legislators, warriors, the judicial and administrative services, the statesmen and rulers, should be Jīvātmās who are in the Kshattriya stage. And the teachers, savants, clergy, the spiritual leaders, should be Jīvātmās in the Brāhmaṇa stage.

There are Jīvātmās of the four types everywhere, and there are social offices of the four kinds everywhere; but now, in the Kali Yuga, the four types of Jīvātmās and the four departments of national life are mixed up in inextricable confusion, so that every nation presents a whirl of contending individuals, instead of an organised community moving in harmony in all its parts.

Another fundamental principle of caste was that as the Jīvātmā advanced, his external liberty, as seen above, became more and more circumscribed and his responsibilities heavier and heavier. The life of the Shūdra was easy and irresponsible, with few restrictions as to food, amusement, place of residence or form of livelihood. He could go anywhere and do anything. The Vaiṣhya had to bear the heavy responsibilities of mercantile life, to support needful public institutions with unstinted charity, to devote himself to business with the utmost diligence; and he was required to study, to make sacrifices, to be pure in his diet, and disciplined in his life. The Kshattriya, while wielding power, worked to the fullest extent, and his laborious life, when he was a monarch, would alarm even a diligent king of the present day; the property, the lives of all, were guarded by the warrior caste, and any man's grievance unredressed was held to dishonour the realm. The heaviest burden of all was laid on the Brāhmaṇa, whose physical life was austere and rigidly simple, who was bound by the most minute rules to preserve his physical and magnetic purity, and whose time was spent in study and worship. Thus the responsibility increased with the superiority of the caste, and the individual was expected to subordinate himself more and more to the community. The rigid purity of the Brāhmaṇa was far less for his own sake than for that of the nation. He was the source of physical health by his scrupulous cleanliness, continually purifying all the particles of matter that entered his body, and sending forth a pure stream to build the bodies of others, for health and gladness are contagious and infectious, for the same reasons as disease and sorrow. The rules which bound him were not intended to subserve pride and exclusiveness, but to preserve him as a purifying force, physical as well as moral and mental. The whole purpose of the caste system is misconceived, when it is regarded as setting up barriers which intensify personal pride, instead of imposing rules on the higher classes, designed to forward the good of the whole community. As Manu said:

सम्मानाद्ब्राह्मणो नित्यमुद्विजेत विषादिव।
अमृतस्येव चाकाङ्क्षेदवमानस्य सर्वदा॥[1]

---

1 *Manusmriti*, ii. 162.

"Let the Brāhmaṇa flee from homage as from venom: let him ever desire indignity as nectar."

Let us now study some of the statements made on this subject in the Shruti and Smṛiti.

The general principle laid down above as to the universality of the four great stages and as to their being founded on natural divisions is enunciated by Shrī Kṛishṇa:

चातुर्वर्ण्यं मया सृष्टं गुणकर्मविभागशः ।
तस्य कर्तारमपि मां विद्धि .... ।[2]

"The four castes, were emanated by me, by the different distribution of the energies (attributes) and actions; know me to be the author of them."

This distribution it is which marks out the castes, and it is not, of course, confined to India. But in the land in which settled the first family of the Āryan stock, the Manu established a model polity or social order, showing in miniature the course of evolution, and into this were born Jīvātmās belonging to the different stages, who showed out the characteristics of the several castes, and thus formed a truly model state. This was "The Golden Age" of India, and the traditions of this still linger, the splendid background of her history.

When humanity is figured as a vast man or when the Īshvara is spoken of as emanating men, then we have the following graphic picture of the four castes:

ब्राह्मणोऽस्य मुखमासीद्बाहूराजन्यः कृतः ।
ऊरू तदस्य यद्वैश्यः पद्भ्यां शूद्रो अजायत ।।[3]

2 *Bhagavad Gītā*, iv, 13.

3 *Ṛigveda, X. xc. 12.*

"The Brāhmaṇa was His mouth; the Rājanya was made His two arms; His two thighs the Vaiṣhya; the Shūdra was born from His two feet."

The teacher is the mouth, and the ruling power the arms; the merchants are the pillars of the nation, as the thighs of the body, while all rest on the manual worker. As we see the facts and necessities of social organisation, we cannot but recognise the inevitableness of the division, whether it be represented or not by a system of four castes.

The virtues that constitute the four castes are thus described by Shrī Kṛiṣhṇa:

ब्राह्मणक्षत्रियविशां शूद्राणां च परंतप।
कर्माणि प्रविभक्तानि स्वभाव प्रभवैर्गुणैः ॥
शमो दमस्तपः शौचं क्षांतिरार्जवमेव च।
ज्ञानं विज्ञानमास्तिक्यं ब्रह्मकर्म स्वभावजम् ॥
शौर्यं तेजो धृतिर्दाक्ष्यं युद्धे चाप्यपलायनम्।
दानमीश्वरभावश्च क्षात्रं कर्म स्वभावजम् ॥
कृषिगोरक्ष्यवाणिज्यं वैश्यकर्म स्वभावजम्।
परिचर्यात्मकं कर्म शुद्रस्यापि स्वभावजम् ॥[4]

"Of Brāhmaṇas, Kshattriyas, Vaiṣhyas and Shūdras, O Parantapa! the Karmas have been distributed according to the Guṇas born of their own natures.

"Serenity, self-restraint, austerity, purity, forgiveness, and also uprightness, wisdom, knowledge, belief in God, are the Brahmana-karma, born of his own nature."

"Prowess, splendour, firmness, dexterity, and also not fleeing

4 *Bhagavad Gītā*, xviii. 41-44

in battle, generosity, rulership are the Kshattriya-karma, born of his own nature."

"Agriculture, protection of kine, and commerce are the Vaiṣhya-karma, born of his own nature.

Action of the nature of service is the Shūdra-karma, born of his own nature."

Thus clearly are outlined the Dharmas of the four castes, the qualities which should be developed in each of the four great stages of the pilgrimage of the Jīvātmā through Samsāra.

Manu explains the occupations of each caste very clearly:

सर्वस्यास्य तु सर्गस्य गुप्त्यर्थं स महाद्युतिः ।
मुखबाहूरुपज्जानां पृथक्कर्माण्यकल्पयत् ॥
अध्यापनमध्ययनं यजनं याजनं तथा ।
दानं प्रतिग्रहं चैव ब्राह्मणानामकल्पयत् ॥
प्रजानां रक्षणं दानमिज्याध्ययनमेव च ।
विषयेष्वप्रसक्तिं च क्षत्रियस्य समादिशत् ॥
पशूनां रक्षणं दानमिज्याध्ययनमेवच ।
वणिक्पथं कुसीदं च वैश्यस्य कृषिमेव च ॥
एकमेव तु शूद्रस्य प्रभुः कर्म समादिशत् ।
एतेषामेव वर्णानां शुश्रूषामनसूयया ॥[5]

"He, the Resplendent, for the sake of protecting all this creation, assigned separate Karmas to those born of His mouth, arms, thighs and feet."

"Teaching and studying the Veda, sacrificing and also guiding others in offering sacrifices, gifts and receiving of gifts, these He assigned to the Brāhmaṇas."

5 *Manusmriti*, i. 87—91.

"The protection of the people, gifts, sacrificing, and study of the Vedas, non-attachment amid the objects of the senses, these He prescribed to the Kshattriyas."

"The protection of cattle, gifts, sacrificing, and study of the Vedas, commerce, banking, and agriculture, to the Vaiṣhyas."

"The Lord commanded one Karma only to the Shūdras, to serve ungrudgingly these castes."

Thus the Brāhmaṇas alone might teach the Vedas, but the duty of studying them belonged equally to the three twice-born castes.

A man who did not show forth the Dharma of his caste was not regarded as belonging to it, according to the teachers of the ancient days. We have already seen that ignorant Brāhmaṇas were mere ashes, unfit for the discharge of their duties, and even more strongly Manu says,

यथा काष्ठमयो हस्ती यथा चर्ममयो मृगः ।
यश्च विप्रोऽनधीयानस्त्रयस्ते नामधारकाः ॥
योऽनधीत्य द्विजो वेदमन्यत्र कुरुते श्रमम् ।
स जीवन्नेव शूद्रत्वमाशु गच्छति सान्वयः ॥[6]

"As a wooden elephant, as a leathern deer, such is an unlearned Brāhmaṇa; the three bear only names.

"The Brāhmaṇa who, not having studied the Vedas, labours elsewhere, becomes a Shūdra in that very life together with his descendants."

And again:

शूद्रो ब्राह्मणतामेति ब्राह्मणश्चैव शूद्रताम् ।
क्षत्रियाज्जातमेवन्तु विद्याद्वैश्यात्तथैव च ॥[7]

---

6 *Manusmriti*, ii. 157, 168.

7 Ibid. x. 65.

"The Shūdra becomes a Brāhmaṇa and a Brāhmaṇa a Shūdra (by conduct). Know this same (rule to apply) to him who is born of the Kshattriya or of the Vaiṣhya."

So also Yudhishthira, taught the fundamental distinctions, without the existence of which caste becomes a mere name:

सत्यं दानं क्षमा शीलमानृशंस्यं तपो घृणा।
दृश्यन्ते यत्र नागेन्द्र स ब्राह्मण इति स्मृतः ॥
शूद्रे तु यद्भवेल्लक्ष्यं द्विजे तच्च न विद्यते।
नैव शूद्रो भवेच्छूद्रो ब्राह्मणो न च ब्राह्मणः ॥
यत्रैतल्लक्ष्यते सर्प वृत्तं स ब्राह्मणः स्मृतः।
यत्र नैतत्भवेत्सर्प तं शूद्रमिति निर्द्दिशेत्।[8]

"Truth, gift, forgiveness, good conduct, gentleness, austerity, and mercy, where these are seen, O king of serpents, he is called a Brāhmaṇa.

"If these marks exist in a Shūdra and are not in a twice-born, the Shūdra is not a Shūdra, nor the Brāhmaṇa a Brāhmaṇa.

"Where this conduct is shown, O serpent, he is called a Brāhmaṇa; where this is not, O serpent, he should be regarded as a Shūdra."

In the *Viṣhṇu-Bhāgavata* we read:

यस्य यल्लक्षणाप्रोक्तं पुंसो वर्णाभिव्यञ्जकम्
यदन्यत्रापि दृश्येत तत्ते नैव विनिर्दिशेत् ॥[9]

"What is said as to the marks of conduct indicative of a man's caste, if those marks are found in another, designate him by the caste of his marks (and not of his birth)."

8 *Mahābhārata*, Vanaparva, clxxx. 21, 25, 26.
9 Loc. cit. VII. xi. 35

Commenting on this Shrīdhara Swāmī says:

"Brāhmaṇa and others are to be chiefly recognised by Shama and other qualities, and not by their birth alone."

जन्मना जायते शूद्रःसंस्काराद्द्विज उच्यते।

"By birth every one is a Shūdra. By Samskāra he becomes twice-born."

So also we find that the preceptor Haridrumata of the Gotama gotra, approached by Satyākama, desirous of becoming his pupil, asked him his gotra; the boy answered that his mother did not know his gotra, for he was born when she was engaged in waiting on guests, and he could only go by her name; he was therefore merely Satyākama, the son of Jabālā. Haridrumata declared that an answer so truthful was the answer of a Brāhmaṇa, and he would therefore initiate him.[10]

Further it must be remembered:

आचारहीनं न पुनन्ति वेदाः।[11]

"The Vedas do not purify him who is devoid of good conduct."

Much question has arisen as to the possibility of a man passing from one caste to another during a single life. It is, of course, universally granted that a man raises himself from one caste to another by good conduct, but it is generally considered that the conduct bears fruit by birth into a higher caste in the succeeding life. The texts quoted in support of passage from one caste to another will mostly bear this interpretation, just as by degradation from one caste to another rebirth in a lower caste was generally meant. But there are cases on record of such passage during a single life.

---

10 *Chhāndogyop.*, IV. iv.

11 *Vasiṣhṭha-Smriti*, vi. 3.

The history of Vishvāmitra, a Kshattriya, becoming a Brāhmaṇa is familiar to everyone,[12] but equally familiar are the tremendous efforts he made ere he attained his object—a proof of the extreme difficulty of the change, Gārgya, the son of Shini, and Trayyāruṇi, Kavi and Pushkarāruṇi, the sons of Duritakṣhaya, all Kshattriyas, became Brāhmaṇa, as did Mudgala, son of Bharmyāshva, also a Kshattriya.[13] Vītahavya, a Kṣhattriya, was made a Brāhmaṇa by Bhṛigu, in whose Āshrama he had taken refuge.[14]

The truth probably is that changes of caste were made in the ancient days, but that they were rare, and that good conduct for the most part took effect in rebirth into a higher caste. Even the famous shloka:

न योनिर्नापिसंस्कारो न श्रुतं न च सन्ततिः ।
कारणानि द्विजत्वस्य वृत्तमेव तुरणं ॥[15]

"Not birth, nor Saṃskāras, nor study of the Vedas, nor ancestry, are causes of Brahmanahood. Conduct alone is verily the cause thereof," may apply as well to rebirth into a higher caste as to transference into it. In ancient days the immediate present was not as important as it is now, the continuing life of the Jīvātmā being far more vividly kept in mind, and the workings of kārmic law more readily acquiesced in. Nor were the divisions of castes then felt to be an injustice, as they now are when the Dharmas of the castes are neglected, and high caste is accompanied by a feeling of pride instead of by one of responsibility and service.

---

12 *Rāmāyaṇa*, Bālakāṇḍa, lvii-lxv.

13 *Viṣhṇu Bhāgavata*, IX. xxi, 19, 20, 33.

14 *Mahābhārata*, Anushāsanaparva, xxx.

15 *Mahābhārata*, Vanaparva cccxiii. 108.

Innumerable subdivisions have arisen within the great castes, which have no foundation in nature and therefore no stability nor justification. By these much social friction is caused, and petty walls of division are set up, jealousies and rivalries taking the place of the ancient co-operation for the general good. The circles of inter-marriage become too restricted, and local and unimportant customs become fossilised into religious obligations, making social life run in narrow grooves and cramping limitations, tending to provoke rebellion and exasperate feelings of irritation. Moreover, many of the customs regarded as most binding are purely local, customs being vital in the South which are unknown in the North, and vice versa. Hence Hindus are split up into innumerable little bodies, each hedged in by a wall of its own, regarded as all important. It is difficult, if not impossible, to create a national spirit from such inharmonious materials, and to induce those who are accustomed to such narrow horizons to take a broader view of life. While a man of one of the four castes, in the old days, felt himself to be an integral part of a nation, a man of a small sub-caste has no sense of organic life, and tends to be a sectarian rather than a patriot.

At the present time a man of any caste takes up any occupation, and makes no effort to cultivate the characteristic virtues of his caste. Hence the inner and the outer no longer accord, and there is jangle instead of harmony. No caste offers to incoming Jīvātmās physical bodies and physical environments fitted for one caste more than for another, and the castes consequently no longer serve as stages for the evolving Jīvātmās. Hence the great value of the Hindu system as a graduated school, into which Jīvātmās could pass for definite training in each stage, has well-nigh ceased, and the evolution of the human race is thereby delayed.

The caste system is one on which the student, when he goes out into the world; will find great difference of opinion among pious and highly educated men, and he will have to make up his own mind upon it, after careful study and deliberation. It is the system which Manu considered best for the fifth, or, Āryan, race, the Pañchajanas, and in its early days ensured order, progress and general happiness, as no other system has done. It has fallen into decay under those most disintegrating forces in human society—pride, exclusiveness, selfishness, the evil brood of Ahamkāra wedded to the personal self instead of to the Supreme Self.

Unless the abuses which are interwoven with it can be eliminated, its doom is certain; but equally certain is it, that if those abuses could be destroyed and the system itself maintained, Hinduism would solve some of the social problems which threaten to undermine Western civilisation, and would set an example to the world of an ideal social state.

PART III

ETHICAL TEACHINGS

ETHICAL SCIENCE, WHAT IT IS

MORALITY, or Ethic, is the Science of Conduct, the systematised principles on which a man should act. The conduct of man has reference to his surroundings as well as to himself. We have to ascertain what is good in relation to those who form our surroundings, as well as in relation to the time and place of the actor, and we may take a wider and wider view of our surroundings, according to the knowledge we possess. We have to also ascertain what is good for ourselves and in relation to ourselves. What is good for one man may not be good for another man. What is good at one time, and at one place may not be good at another time, and at another place.

Ethical Science is therefore a relative science—it is relative to the man himself and to his surroundings.

The object of morality is to bring about happiness by establishing harmonious relations between all the Jīvātmās that belong to any special area; harmonious relations between the members of a family; harmonious relations between the families that make up a community; harmonious relations between the communities that make up a nation; harmonious relations between the nations that make up humanity; harmonious relations between humanity and the other inhabitants of the earth, harmonious relations between the inhabitants of the earth and those of other worlds of the system.

The great circle goes on spreading outwards indefinitely, and including larger and larger areas within its circumference. But still, whether the area be large or small, Ethic is "the principles of harmonious relations." Thus we have family morality, social morality, national morality, international morality, human morality, inter-world morality; and all these concern us. With the yet wider sweeps of the Science of Conduct we are not yet concerned, but the basic principle is the same throughout.

It is obvious that the establishment of harmonious relations between a man and his surroundings, near and remote, means happiness. We are always suffering from the want of harmony, from jarring wishes, from friction between ourselves and others, from the lack of mutual support, mutual assistance, mutual sympathy. Where there is harmony, there is happiness; where there is disharmony, there is unhappiness. Morality, then, in establishing harmony establishes happiness, makes families and communities and nations and humanity and all dwellers in this and other worlds happy. The ultimate object of Morality, of Ethic, of the Science of Conduct, is to bring about universal Happiness, Universal Welfare, by uniting the separated selves with each other and with the Supreme Self. All the six Darshanas are agreed as to this summum bonum of man.

The student must grasp this thought, and realise it very clearly. Morality brings about Universal Happiness at last. Let us pause for a moment on this word, "Happiness." Happiness does not mean the transitory pleasures of the senses nor even the more durable pleasures of the mind. It does not mean the satisfaction of the cravings of the Upādhis, nor the joys which are tasted in the possession of outer objects. Happiness means the deep, inner, enduring bliss which is the satisfaction in the Self. It means perfect harmony, lasting peace. Happiness is

यत्रोपरमते चित्तं निरुद्धं योगसेवया।
यत्र चैवात्मनाऽऽत्मानं पश्यन्नात्मनि तुष्यति॥
सुखमात्यंतिकं यत्तद् बुद्धिग्राह्यमतींद्रियम्।
वेत्ति यत्र न चैवायं स्थितश्चलति तत्त्वतः॥
यं लब्ध्वा चापरं लाभं मन्यते नाधिकं ततः।
यस्मिन्स्थितो न दुःखेन गुरुणापि विचाल्यते॥[1]

"That in which the mind finds rest, quieted by the practice of Yoga; that in which he, seeing the Self by the Self, in the Self is satisfied;

"That in which he findeth the supreme delight which the Buddhi can grasp, beyond the senses, wherein established, he moveth not from the Reality;

"That which, having obtained, he thinketh there is no greater gain beyond it; wherein established, he is not shaken even by heavy sorrow."

Nothing less than this is Happiness, and this is the Happiness which Morality brings about. The student must not allow his clear vision of this truth to be clouded by superficial appearances, which seem to be at variance with it. However difficult and painful it may sometimes be to do right; however tiresome and burdensome obedience to moral precepts may sometimes be; none the less, in the long run, doing right means to be happy, and

1 *Bhagavad-Gītā*, vi. 20-22

doing wrong means to be miserable. "As the wheels of the cart follow the ox," said the great Indian teacher, the Buddha, "so misery follows sin." Thus also speak all the Shāstras.

All this is inevitable, as we shall see later on. We have spoken of harmony, of happiness, of right, of wrong, and of the inhabitants of the earth and those of other worlds of the system.

But if we are to go to the root of things, to first principles, we cannot but seek the help of Religion. For Religion gives us the ultimate data upon which Ethical Science may be built. Morality has only one basis, on which it is built up, as a house is built on its foundation. And just as a house will become crooked and fall, if it be built on a shaky foundation, so will any Morality fall which is not built on that sound basis.

THE FOUNDATION OF ETHICS, AS GIVEN BY RELIGION

(1) THE first thing we learn from religion is the Unity of all selves, and this is the foundation of Ethics. Ethics is built upon:

THE RECOGNITION OF THE UNITY OF THE SELF
AMID THE DIVERSITY OF THE NOT-SELF

There is but One Self, and all the separate selves are अशाःamshāḥ, parts or reflections of the One, are the One.

यथा प्रकाशयत्येकः कृत्स्नं लोकमिमं रविः ।
क्षेत्रं क्षेत्री तथा कृत्स्नं प्रकाशयति भारत ॥[1]

"As one sun illuminates this whole world, so the Lord of the Field illuminates the whole Field, O Bharata!"

एको देवः सर्वभूतेषु गूढः सर्वव्यापी सर्वभूतांतरात्मा ॥[2]

"One God is hidden in all beings, all-pervading, the inmost Self of all."

One sun is shining, and it shines into every separate place,

1 *Bhagavad-Gītā*. xiii. 33.
2 *Shvetāshratarop*, vi. 11.

every separate enclosure. There may be a thousand gardens, separated from each other by high walls, but the one sun shines into all, and the light and heat in each are from the one sun, are parts of himself. So the JīvāJīvātmās in all creatures, separated from each other by the walls of Prakṛiti, the walls of their bodies, are rays from the one Sun, sparks from the one Fire, portions of the one Ātmā, the one Self. We cannot fully realise this, be conscious of it and live in it always, until we have become perfectly pure; but we can recognise it as a Fact, as the one all-important Fact, and in proportion as we try to make our conduct accord with this Fact, we shall become moral. We shall see, as we study morality, that all its precepts are founded on this recognition of the unity of the Self. If there is only one Self, any act by which I injure my neighbour must injure me. A man will not deliberately cut his hand, or his foot, or his face, because all these are parts of his own body, and though a cut on his hand does not directly make his foot ache, he feels the pain from any part of his body. The foot, being ignorant and limited, is not conscious at once of the wound made in the hand, but the man is conscious of it, and will not let the foot carry his body into a place where the hand will be injured.

Of course, the foot ultimately suffers from the general fever of the whole body caused by a severe injury to any part of it, as ignorance of the unity of the body does not alter the fact of unity. And so the man who believes that the Self is one, in him and in all others, also necessarily believes that in injuring any part he is injuring himself, though, being limited and ignorant, he may not then feel it; and he learns to look on all as parts of one body, and on his innermost Self as the one who uses that one body, and lives and moves in all.

If we could realise this, feel it always, there would be no need of any Science of Conduct, for we should always act for the highest good of all; but as we do not realise it, and feel it very seldom, we need rules of conduct, which are all based on this principle, to prevent us from injuring others and ourselves, and to help us to do good to others and ourselves.

The great Ṛiṣhis, knowing the supreme fact that the Self of all beings is one, based on this all their precepts, and on this rock they built the morality they taught. The authoritative declarations of the Shruti on general morality are final because based on this fact, and they can be defended by reason, and shown to be of binding and universal obligation.

All the laws of nature are expressions of the Divine Nature, and, as one of the aspects of that Nature is Chit, the Reason can grasp and verify them. They are supremely rational, nay Reason itself, and Reason in man is fitly concerned with their study. Now "the Reason" must not be confused with the process of reasoning, the passing from one link of an argument to another by logical sequence. This process is only one of the functions of the Reason, and is called the ratiocinative faculty, and belongs to the concrete Reason, the lower mind.

"The Reason" is Chit, and includes all mental processes, concrete and abstract, the perception in the higher as well as in the lower worlds, direct clear vision of truths as of objects. As knowledge is the rightful source of authority, and as the knowledge of the Ṛiṣhis was the product of their Reason, working in assonance with the Divine Reason, the Shruti, given to the Hindus through the Ṛiṣhis, are authoritative. Their authority is thus based on Reason, on the Divine Wisdom primarily, and on the illuminated human Reason secondarily. The Ṛiṣhis, as we saw in the Introduction, have modified the Shruti to meet the needs of special ages, for precepts useful at one time are not useful at another. It is further possible by the use of the Reason to distinguish between precepts of universal and those of local and temporary obligation.

The system of morality inculcated in the Sanātana Dharma may therefore be said to be authoritative: for being founded on the recognition of the Unity of the Self, and drawing its precepts and its sanctions from that supreme fact, it is capable of appealing to and being verified by the Reason, and a perfect harmony can be established between the commands of the Shruti and the dictates of the Reason.

This harmony has prevented the arising in India of independent ethical schools, such as have arisen in the West, the doctrines of which become familiar to students in their studies in Western Moral Philosophy.

The Scriptures of other nations, which have not stated clearly the Unity of the Self, have necessarily been unable to state clearly the highest sanction for morality, and have directed reliance mainly to a Divine authority, the source of which is not universally seen as identical in nature with the Spirit (Jīvātmā) in man. Hence a certain divorce between Authority and Reason, injurious to both, and this divorce has led to the growth of two ethical schools, that stand in opposition to authoritative, i. e., scriptural morality, and also in opposition to each other.

One of these schools, the intuitional, finds its basis for morality in intuition, in the dictates of the conscience, but fails to escape from the difficulties involved in the variations of conscience with racial and national traditions, social customs, and individual development.

The second, the utilitarian, has its ethical basis in "the greatest good of the greatest number," but fails to justify the exclusion of the minority from its canon, and to supply a sanction of sufficiently binding force. Besides, what constitutes "the greatest good of the greatest number" is always a debatable point; hence the "canon" is useless as a practical guide.

The student can study these systems in the works of their exponents, and he will do well to understand that the reconciliation of these schools lies in the recognition of the Unity of the Self, and the consequent completion of the partial truths on which these are based. He will then see that this principle accords to the teachings of the scriptural school their proper support in Reason; that this supplies the intuitionalist with the explanation of the variations of conscience,[3] which is the voice of the Jīvātmā, and depends on the stage of evolution reached and the experiences assimilated; that this shows to the utilitarian that there is no ultimate good for any which is not also good for all, that there is no question of majority and minority, but of unity, and that the sanction of morality lies in this very unity of interests, this identity of nature.

We have, then, as the basis of morality in the Sanātana Dharma, the recognition of the Unity of the Self, and therefore the establishment of mutually helpful relations between all separated selves. Every moral precept finds its sanction in this Unity, and we shall presently see that the Universal Love, which is the expression of the Unity, is the root of all virtues, as its opposite is the root of all vices.

---

3 There is no exact Samskrit equivalent for the word "conscience."

Universal Brotherhood has its basis in the Unity; men are divided by their Upādhis, both dense and subtle, but they are all rooted in the one Self. Only this teaching, when generally realised, can put an end to wars, and serve as a foundation for peace. This alone can eradicate racial and national hatreds, put an end to mutual contempt and suspicion, and draw all men into one human family, in which there are elders and youngers, indeed, but no aliens.

Nor, indeed, can the Brotherhood based on the Unity of the Self be limited to the human family. It must include all things within its circle, for all, without exception, are rooted in the Self. In the 10th Adhyāya of the *Bhagavad-Gītā*, Shrī Kṛiṣhṇa declares:

अहमात्मा गुडाकेश सर्वभूताशयस्थितः ।
अहमादिश्च मध्यं च भूतानामंत एव च ॥[4]

"I am the Self, O, Guḍākesha, seated in the heart of all beings: I am the beginning, the middle, and also the end of beings."

He then names himself as many objects, as sun and moon, as mountain and tree, as horse and cow, as bird and serpent and many others, and sums up in one all-embracing declaration:

यच्चापि सर्वभूतानां बीजं तदहमर्जुन ।
न तदस्ति विना यत्स्यान्मया भूतं चराचरम् ॥[5]

"Whatsoever is the seed of all beings that I am, O Arjuna! Nor is there aught, moving or unmoving that may exist bereft of Me."

Over and over again He insists on the all-importance of this recognition of the Unity of the Self and of the presence of the Self in each and all.

---

4 *Bhagavad Gītā* x. 20,

5 Ibid. 39.

समं सर्वेषु भूतेषु तिष्ठंतं परमेश्वरम् ।
विनश्यत्स्वविनश्यंतं यः पश्यति स पश्यति ॥
समं पश्यन्हि सर्वत्र समवस्थितमीश्वरम् ।
न हिनस्त्यात्मनाऽऽत्मानं ततो याति परां गतिम् ॥
यदा भूतपृथग्भावमेकस्थमनुपश्यति ।
तत एव च विस्तारं ब्रह्म संपद्यते तदा ।।[6]

"Seated equally in all beings, the Supreme Īshvara, indestructible within the destructible—he who thus seeth, he seeth.

"Seeing; indeed, everywhere the same, Īshvara equally dwelling, he doth not destroy the Self by the self, and thus reacheth the supreme goal.

"When he seeth the diversified existence of beings as rooted in One, and proceeding from It, then he reacheth Brahman."

All human relations exist because of this Unity, as Yājnavalkya explained to his wife Maitreyī when she prayed to him to know the secret of immortality:

न वा अरे पत्युः कामाय पतिः प्रियो भवत्यात्मनस्तु कामाय पतिः प्रियो भवति ।[7]

"Behold! Not indeed for the love of the husband is the husband dear: for the love of the Self is the husband dear."

And so with wife, sons, property, friends, worlds and even the Devas themselves, all are dear because the One-Self is in all.

न वा अरे सर्वस्य कामाय सर्वं प्रियं भवति आत्मनस्तु कामाय सर्वं प्रियं भवति ।

"Behold! Not for the love of the all, the all is dear, but for the love of the Self verily the all is dear."

6 *Bhagavad-Gītā* xiii 27, 28, 30.

7 *Brihadāraṇyakop*, IV. iv. 5.

घृतात्परं मण्डमिवातिसूक्ष्मं ज्ञात्वा शिवं सर्वभूतेषु गूढं।
विश्वस्यैकं परिवेष्टितारं ज्ञात्वा देवं मुच्यते सर्वपाशैः॥

"Having known the Auspicious, the exceedingly subtle, hidden in all beings, like cream in butter, having known the Supreme God, the one Pervader of the universe, he is freed from bonds."

But it is useless to multiply texts, when the Shruti at every step proclaim the truth. In this and in this alone is the sure Basis of Morality, for this Unity of the Self is the real cause and explanation of Love; One Self, embodied in Many forms, is ever seeking to draw the forms together in order to again realise its own unity. This is why the recognition of the Unity of the Self by the Reason, which is Wisdom, shows itself in a world of separate forms as Love. So also the many-ness of the Not-Self is the cause and explanation of Hate, each separate form setting itself up against others. The full significance of this will be seen by the student on maturer study; but he should grasp the Fact—which will become clearer as we proceed—that all virtue, all that is good, is the immediate result of the pure Love which springs from recognising the Unity of the Self, and that all vice, all that is evil, similarly arises from disregard of this truth, and from the feeling that the Self is not one, but many, as the bodies are many.

RIGHT AND WRONG

THE student will remember the description of the Trilokī in Part I. At the beginning of a new Trilokī, life evolution begins. This evolution takes place in all the three worlds, but we may confine ourselves to our Earth. First the life forms appear. The Purāṇas speak in veiled words as to how sheath after sheath the life is enclosed under the influence of the five forms of Avidyā (Avidyā, Asmitā, Rāga, Dvesha and Abhinivesha), we have the process of manifestation, till we find all the forms of creation manifested on our Earth. During this process, the idea of multiplying governs all beings. This idea breaks through the innate inertia, the remnant of *pralayic* tendency with which all beings start. This idea becomes refined and is then called Pravṛitti, or Inclination, the desire for objects; the world is then on the Pravṛitti Mārga, the Path of going forth.

Beings become materialised, and as they become consciously separate, their self-seeking tendencies become very strong. Every such being forms a world in himself, and tries to exclude others. Men live for enjoyment, and they care for the present only. The idea of separateness develops the intellect, which works from the standpoint of individuality. This element is necessary in man in order to bring out his individual faculties, and to cultivate them in such a way as will make the intellectual development fairly complete.

But the idea of separateness becomes after a while a drawback to further progress. Man has to gradually transcend it. He has to recognise the Unity of all selves, and, in practice, to do everything that helps to strengthen the recognition of that Unity, and at last make that recognition a part of his life. This may be called the process of spiritual evolution, and man is then on the Nivṛitti Mārga, the Path of Return.

Lastly, Pralaya comes and the Brahmāṇḍa ends.

During all but the latest stages of the Pravṛitti Mārga that which favours separateness is RIGHT, and that which goes against it is WRONG.

Then follows a transition stage, preparing man to enter on the Nivṛitti Mārga; during that, and on the Nivṛitti Mārga, that which favours the tendency towards Unity is RIGHT and that which goes against it is WRONG.

When the time of Pralaya comes, all that helps it will be RIGHT, all that opposes it is WRONG.

Speaking generally, that which is suitable to the stage of evolution which the world has reached, that which helps it onwards, is RIGHT; that which obstructs and hinders evolution is WRONG. For the will of Īshvara points steadfastly to the highest good, and guides His universe towards good. To work with this will is to be in harmony with the great movement of the world-system, and thus to be carried on with the stream of evolution; while to go against it is like beating against an overwhelming current, which dashes us against the rocks, bruises and wounds us. To do right is to be at peace with ourselves and with God, and is therefore happiness; to do wrong is to be at war with ourselves and with God, and is therefore misery. Hence bad people tend to become, after a time, discontented, irritable, unsatisfied, however outwardly favourable may be their circumstances; while the good are inwardly at peace and contented, even when their outer circumstances are very unfavourable. Here again, the essential fact is the same, for the will of Īshvara, being guided by the highest wisdom and love, ever necessarily and constantly points to the highest good—the more and more perfect realisation of the Unity of the Self amid the endless diversity of forms.

Let us look further into this matter, as the question is all important.

For this purpose we have to refer back again to the nature of evolution described before. This evolution of the Jīvā gives rise to that variety of relations and situations between Jīvā and Jīvā, out of which the actions arise to which the epithets "right" and "wrong" become applicable; and therefore the nature of "right" and "wrong" depends upon the nature of the scheme of evolution to which the Jīvās concerned belong, and cannot be described independently of that scheme.

We have gathered from the first part of this work what evolution means. Generally speaking, a world-system has a life in the same way as a single human being; and as a single human being grows in physical life for the first half of his lifetime and decreases in respect thereof during the second half, so too a world-system, a Brahmāṇḍa, grows more and more material during the first half of its life, the Pūrvārdha or Prathama Parārdha of the Kalpa, and more and more spiritual during the second half or Dvitīya Parārdha thereof. This process from birth to death, from death to a higher birth, from that to a deeper death and thence again to a still higher birth—repeated endlessly—the general plan of life and evolution.

In our own world-system, the process takes the shape of a gradual descent of Spirit into the dense matter of the mineral kingdom and a reascent therefrom through the Arvāksrotas or the vegetable kingdom, the Tiryaksrotas or the animal kingdom, the Urdhvasrotas or men, and higher forms, into the realised union of Mukti. Coming into still minuter detail, we find that amongst men the process reappears as the descent of the primeval and simple-minded childlike human races, governed and guided by divine beings, through growth of materialism and the sense of separateness, and consequent selfishness and exclusiveness in the appropriation of the stores of nature and the gifts of Providence, into the condition of ever-warring tribes.

Then a slow reascent therefrom, through despotic and military government, to constitutional monarchy and organised society, to reach at last those distant and happy times of universal brotherhood when unselfishness and altruism shall reign supreme, and men will see their common unity far more than their separateness from each other.

Finally, in the individual Jīvā, we see that evolution, or the life process, appears as the gathering of experience and information in the first years after birth, then the utilisation of that experience for the founding of a family, then the instruction of the new generation and the helping of them to take up the life of the householder themselves, and ultimately retirement from life into Sannyāsa and the peace of renunciation and of a happy death.

Such being the general order of evolution, that course of conduct which helps it on is Right; all else is Wrong. If we have to go to a certain place, then all appliances that make the journey easier and help us to move forward in that direction are good; all obstacles that make it more difficult and retard our progress are evil. If we had a different goal, if we were desirous of going to a place in the exactly opposite direction, then the first-mentioned appliances, which would be taking us away from our new goal, would become evil. So long then as we are on the line of our present evolution, the actions that help us forward on it are good and right, and the opposite ones evil and wrong. And in order to find out what is right conduct and what is wrong in any particular situation, we must judge it according to its conduciveness or otherwise to the particular end in view, and judge the particular end again with reference to its congruity with the general goal of human evolution Without such reference, it is impossible to say what is right and what is wrong. With such reference, on the other hand, we may map out easily the details of our path in life and through evolution and then we shall have at every step, a standard of right and wrong by which to guide our actions.

These details have been supplied to us, out of their knowledge and compassion, by the ancient Sages and Seers. They have left to us a complete outline of the scheme of evolution of our world system, and have also left to us general rules for so dealing with our own life and the lives of others, not only of the human but also of the lower kingdoms, that the advance of all Jīvās through the various stages of evolution, mineral, vegetable, animal, human, celestial, shall be made as easy as possible. These general facts and rules are outlined in the various parts of this work.

For instance, the rules of the four Āshramas are dictated by the facts and laws of individual evolution; and the rules of the four castes by the facts and laws of human evolution at large.

The conditions of the four castes and the four Āshramas exhaust all possible situations in the whole life of the present-day humanity, and the Sanātana Dharma therefore provides general rules for all such situations, grouping them into general classes.

The casual observer might think that because there are no expressly recognised castes and Āshramas amongst many nations of modern humanity, therefore general conditions are radically different for different nations; but this is not so. Though not expressly recognised, the divisions themselves are to be found everywhere, under other names and forms it may be, but still in all the races of the present day and that they are not expressly recognised is in some respects product of inconvenience and waste of time and trouble, economically speaking to those nations, even as over recognition and exaggeration are product of inconvenience and mischief here in India.

The natural conditions of the present evolution unavoidably force upon humanity the relations of teacher and student, ruler and ruled, producer and consumer, master and servant, parent and son, husband and wife, brother and sister, worker and pensioner, employer and employed, soldier and civilian, agriculturist and tradesman, layman and priest, householder and recluse. The Sanātana Dharma, instead of leaving these relations to vague and groping experiments, rationally orders and systematises them, and teaches generally the duties and virtues proper to each relation and situation, with the injunction that the duties and virtues of two different relations and situations should never be mixed up together indiscriminately, for thus great danger and confusion result:

स्वधर्मे निधनं श्रेयः परधर्मो भयावहः ।[1]

"Better to die in (the performance of) one's own duty; the duty of another is full of danger."

If a king, in the exercise of his office, come to behave as a merchant, and instead of exercising the king's virtues exhibit those of the tradesman; if a judge, in the decision of a case, instead of being guided by the virtue of justice, show active physical fighting as a soldier, or compassion as a priest; if a priest, in his ministrations, behave as an executioner; if one who should be a Brahmachārī or a Grihastha in the ordinary course, should without good special reason, become a Vanāprasthī or a Sannyāsī, or vice-versa; if one who is fitted by nature to be a soldier should become a merchant, or one fitted for study only should take up the work of agriculture—then the whole economy of the state and the nation would be more or less disturbed.

What is right then in one situation is not right in another; and the most general definition that can be given of right and wrong is, that right conduct is that which helps on a known scheme of evolution, to its recognised goal, and wrong conduct is the opposite.

For an instance of how the epithets right and wrong may be applied to the very same action looked at from different points of view, take this case. Two men come together: one confines the other in a closed house by force, takes away all liberty of movement from him, and also all moveable property he may have about him, and places it in the possession of others who help and obey him. This act taken by itself, without any reference to previous facts, is wrong; it hinders the life and evolution of the man

1 *Bhagavad-Gītā*, iii. 35.

confined and that of his family and dependants; in fact it amounts to robbery with wrongful confinement of an aggravated character. But suppose that the man confined had forcibly deprived a third person of some property, and the man who ordered his confinement was a judge, and the closed house a public jail, then the same act becomes the rightful imprisonment of a thief, and the removal of property from this person a necessary act of prison-discipline, all of which is perfectly right and even necessary, for thereby the evolution of society and of the thief himself is generally helped. But yet again, if the imprisoned man had forcibly deprived the other of property not belonging to that other but to himself, property which that other had stolen, then the action of the judge becomes wrong again, and his order reversible on appeal to a higher judge.

It is the same on a larger scale in the larger life of the world. The Purāṇas say that in the beginning of the world, when the immediate object was to multiply the human population and engage it in the life of the household, Dakṣha Prajāpati created certain classes of children, like the Haryashvas.

The Ṛiṣhi Nārada, whose duty it is to bring about certain adjustments of good and evil forces and generally to promote the life of renunciation in our world, commenced his work too soon, and persuaded the Haryashvas to avoid the life of the household and take up the life of the recluse. His action, because of its inopportuneness, was found to be wrong, and he was punished by a curse under which he himself had to be born in the animal and human kingdoms and lead the life of the household with other Jīvās. So, again, in the earliest days of the race, the worship of Brahmā, the embodiment of Rajas and action, the cause of Sarga, creation, was enjoined. Later on, the worship of Viṣhṇu, the embodiment of Sattva, Knowledge and Love, the cause of Sthiti, maintenance, becomes appropriate. In the last days of a cycle, the worship of Shiva, the embodiment of Tamas, Vairāgya or Self Sacrifice and Renunciation, the cause of the Pralaya, the dissolution of the material world, finds place.

Thus we see that right and wrong are always relative to the surrounding circumstances. If it were necessary to define them generally, without such reference, then the nearest approach to accuracy is to be found in the Samskrit verse which is on the lips of all Samskrit-knowing Indians:

अष्टादशपुराणेषु व्यासस्य वचनद्वयम् ।
परोपकारः पुण्याय पापाय परपीडनम् ॥

"Vyāsa has said but two things in the whole of the eighteen Purāṇas: Doing good to another is Puṇya, (right); causing injury to another is Pāpa (wrong)."

As a general rule, when one Jīvā helps another, makes him happy, then, whether he wish it consciously or not, that happiness comes back to him by the law of action and reaction; this is expressed by the rule that Puṇya brings happiness. Exactly similar is the case regarding misery and Pāpa.

The three processes of creation, preservation and dissolution which have just been described are based upon the three fundamental attributes of the matter side of Nature, or Prakṛiti—Sattva, Rajas and Tamas. To begin with, we have *pralayic* inertia due to Tamas influencing the matter, or *prākṛitic*, side of Jīvās. Then we have *kāmic* and *mānasic* activity, developing the Emotions and the Intellect. This is due to the prevalence of Rajas, acting on the *prākṛitic* basis of Jīvās. Lastly, we have a tendency to free ourselves from distraction, from desires for objects, from selfish pursuits, and to attain calm, peace and bliss, whatever be the outer surroundings at any time. This spiritual evolution is brought about by the prevalence of Sattva in us. Then, on the eve of Pralaya, Tamas overtakes us once again.

Every man has in him a predominance of Sattva, Rajas, or Tamas, and his development depends upon the relative proportions of each of these attributes. When a man is predominantly *tāmasic*, he is indolent, inactive, dull and ignorant.

He requires at first a *rājasic* development. Anything that draws him out, attracts curiosity, and makes him active, is good and right for him. The constant rebuffs and touches of joy that he gets in his active life, the accumulation of painful and pleasurable experiences, develop his intellect.

Under *rājasic* predominance, a man is eager in material pursuits, his intellect soars high and spreads wide, he goes backwards and forwards, his cravings ever increasing, and his efforts to satisfy them take him through different intellectual channels. Action becomes the rule of his nature, self—the personal self, becomes the centre of all his actions, like (Rāga) and dislike (Dveṣha) are the motive powers which drive him in his actions.

When Sattva asserts itself, man begins to realise the littleness of efforts directed towards the personal self, the transitoriness of worldly aspirations, the unrest and disquietude attending all actions. He takes a calm and broad view of all things. He discriminates between the real and the unreal, the lasting and the fleeting, the bliss eternal and the pleasures of the moment. He loves peace, calm, and quietude.

Every man has thus his own evolutionary stage, which is generally indicated by the circumstances attending his birth, but more precisely by the attributes which characterise him. Though particular rules may be laid down for the particular stages of development of a man, such as the Varṇa and Āshrama rules of old, yet for the average civilised man in general, some rules of conduct may also be laid down, and these forms the general rules of Ethics.

We have now to see how on the basis above sketched a Science of Conduct is built up, a Science which cannot be overrated as to its importance.

For this Science of Conduct is, in truth, considering its relations to human happiness, the most important study in many ways that can engage human attention; and it is one which, to the youth, is all-important in its bearing on his own future. For character is that which tells most in human life, and on it chiefly depend both inner happiness and outer success. We have already seen that virtue and happiness are bound up together, and, in the life of the world, character is that on which lasting success depends. A man of a brilliant intellect may carry all before him, for a time, but if he be found to be a man of bad character, his fellows cease to trust him and he falls into discredit. In every walk of life, character is the thing most sought after and most trusted, and a man of good character is respected and admired everywhere.

The time of youth is the time for improving character, the time when the germs of vices can most easily be eradicated, and the germs of virtues can most easily be cultivated.

Each comes into the world with a character made by his past, and he must work upon this character, his self-created friend or foe. He can work on it at the greatest advantage if he understands clearly what he should aim at, and by what means his aim can be reached. He needs to understand the roots of virtues and vices, to learn how to distinguish one from the other, to learn how to cultivate virtues and how to eradicate vices, as a gardener cultivates flowers and eradicates weeds. For each man has a garden in him-self, and should learn to be a skilful gardener.

THE STANDARD OF ETHICS

WE have already seen that the measure used in Ethics at the present stage of evolution, by which the rightness or wrongness of an action is decided, is the tendency of the action to promote or to hinder Union.

The whole tendency of evolution at the present stage is towards the assertion of the Unity of all selves, is to seek the one Life amidst the diverse forms of life, and thus to follow the path that leads to Union, i. e., the path of Truth.

The standard of Ethics is in other words to *unite* and not to *divide*. We can unite by the establishment of harmonious relations between all the Jīvātmās.

It may now be seen why it is said in the first chapter that the object of morality is to bring about happiness by establishing harmonious relations.

The "establishment of harmonious relations," which is said above to be the work of Ethic, is now seen to be the leading of the different parts of the great human body to work in harmony with each other. It is no mere figure of speech that all races of men, all nations, make up one great Man; it is a fact, "Puruṣha," the Inner Man, the Self, is indeed Puruṣhottama, the Lord, Īshvara Himself.

But there is also the Purușha which is His body, and this is Humanity as a whole, and each separate being is a cell in that vast body. All the troubles which make us unhappy, the wars between nations and the quarrels between individuals, the poverty and starvation, the competition and the crushing of the weak, and the countless evils around us, are all diseases of this great body, due to the parts of it getting out of order, and working separately and competitively without a common object, instead of working together as a unity for the good of the whole.

The moral tendencies of man were classified by Shrī Krișhṇa under two broad divisions—Divine qualities (Daivī Sampat) and infernal qualities (Āsurī Sampat).

Under Daivī Sampat, Shrī Krișhṇa placed the virtues that go towards bringing about harmonious feelings amongst all beings, towards accentuating a feeling of unity and friendliness, towards securing peace and calm, in fact towards carrying out the law of evolution in its entirety.

अभयं सत्त्वसंशुद्धिर्ज्ञानयोगव्यवस्थितिः ।
दानं दमश्च यज्ञश्च स्वाध्यायस्तप आर्जवम् ॥
अहिंसा सत्यमक्रोधस्त्यागः शांतिरपैशुनम् ।
दया भूतेष्वलोलुप्त्वं मार्दवं ह्रीरचापलम् ॥
तेजः क्षमा धृतिः शौचमद्रोहो नातिमानिता ।
भवंति संपदं दैवीमभिजातस्य भारत ॥[1]

"Fearlessness, *sāttvic* purity, steadfast pursuit of wisdom, charity, control of the senses, sacrifice, study, austerity, uprightness,

1 *Bhagavad Gītā* xv. 1-3.

"Harmlessness, truthfulness, absence of anger, resignation, peace of mind, avoidance of calumny, pity for all beings, absence of greed, gentleness, modesty, absence of restlessness,

"Energy, forgiveness, endurance, purity, freedom from hatred and from pride—these are his who is born to the divine qualities, O Bhārata."

Under Āsurī Sampat, He placed all the opposite vices-all that tends to divide the Jīvātmās, and to accentuate the feeling of Egotism, of the separated self. He described as *āsuriç* those qualities which have their root in and grow out of the delusion of separateness.

दंभो दर्पोऽभिमानश्च क्रोधः पारुष्यमेव च ।
अज्ञानं चाभिजातस्य पार्थ संपदमासुरीम् ॥[2]

"Hypocrisy, arrogance and conceit, wrath and also harshness and unwisdom, are his, O Pārtha, who is born to the Āsuric qualities."

आत्मसंभाविताः स्तब्धा धनमानमदान्विताः ।
यजन्ते नाम यज्ञैस्ते दंभेनाविधिपूर्वकम् ॥
अहंकारं बलं दर्पं कामं क्रोधं च संश्रिताः ।
मामात्मपरदेहेषु प्रद्विषंतोऽभ्यसूयकाः ॥
त्रिविधं नरकस्येदं द्वारं नाशनमात्मनः ।
कामः क्रोधस्तथा लोभस्तस्मादेतत्त्रयंत्यजेत् ॥[3]

"Self-important, obstinate, filled with the pride and intoxication of wealth, they perform lip-sacrifices for ostentation, contrary to scriptural ordinance.

2 *Ibid.*xvi.4.
3 Ibid. 17, 18, 21

"Given over to egotism, violence, insolence, lust and wrath, these malicious ones ever hate Me in the bodies of others and in their own.

"Triple is the gate of this hell, destructive of the Self-lust, wrath and greed; therefore let a man renounce these three."

The whole of Chapter XVI of the *Bhagavad-Gītā* should be carefully pondered by the student in this connection.

VIRTUES AND THEIR FOUNDATION

THE establishment of harmonious relations means mutual sacrifice of the personal selves. It means that all beings should realise that they form component parts of one Being, and that they must all subordinate themselves to the life of that One Being. Just as there are innumerable cells in the body, but each cell-life subordinate itself to the one life that pervades the whole body, so the life of every being is to be subordinated to the life of the Īshvara of the Universe. Different cells have different functions to perform, but each function is a part of the general function of the whole body.

As each cell has its fixed place in the body, so each being has a definite place in the Universe. There is one general life-current that pervades all beings, and the life of each individual has to conform to the One Life, the life of the One Self, Īshvara. This is the limitation under which we all work, and this limitation is the law of our very being; all beings are mutually linked to one another, and the links impose mutual relations and mutual sacrifices. All beings are dependent on one another, and they are all dependent on the one great Life. This law of interdependence, of mutual sacrifice, is known as yajna, and has already been explained in Parts I and II.

Whatever actions we do, we ought to do them for the sake of Yajna. Thus, only we can follow the Great Law. If a man lives for self, and makes an independent centre in himself, overlooking the one great centre of the Universe, he creates bonds for himself and suffers therefrom.

यज्ञार्थात्कर्मणोऽन्यत्र लोकोऽयं कर्मबंधनः ।
तदर्थं कर्म कौंतेय मुक्तसंगः समाचर ।।[1]

"The world is bound by action, other than action done for the sake of sacrifice; with such object, free from attachment, O son of Kunti, perform thou action."

We have seen that the different classes of beings linked together in this universe are five: - the Devas, the Pitṛis, the Ṛiṣhis, men and animals, and that sacrifices to these classes are a duty, which every man performing actions is bound to discharge. For when sacrifice is imposed by law, there is an obligation to perform it, and hence the performance becomes a duty.

In its exact ethical sense duty means an action which is due, which ought to be done, which is owed; it is an obligation to be discharged. Nature is ever restoring disturbed equilibrium, and the universal law of Karma, of action and re-action, is the full statement of this fact. She is always balancing her accounts. Duties are the debts a man owes to his fellows, paid to discharge the obligations under which he lies for benefits received.

While five duties are mentioned for the purposes of the five Daily Sacrifices, three of these are called the debts in a special and

---

1 *Bhagavad-Gītā*. iii. 9.

larger sense, as permeating the man's whole life. They are the Ancestors; the देवऋणम् Deva-Ṛiṇam, the debt to the Devas, the ऋषिऋणम्, Ṛiṣhi-Riṇam, the debt to the Ṛiṣhis; the पितृऋणम्, Pitṛi-Ṛiṇam, indebted by our efforts for heirs/heiress.

अधीत्य विधिवद्वेदान्पुत्रांश्चोत्पाद्य धर्मतः ।
इष्ट्वा च शक्तितो यज्ञैर्मनो मोक्षे निवेशयेत् ॥[2]

"Having studied the Vedas according to the rules, having begotten sons according to righteousness, having offered sacrifice according to his power, let him turn his mind to mokṣha."

The three twice-born castes were directed to pay these debts by passing through the three Āshramas, Brahmacharya, Gārhasthya and Vānaprastha, each of which, it will be seen, answers to one of the above three duties.

The debt to the Ṛiṣhis was paid by अध्ययनम्, adhyayanam (including अध्यापनम्) studying the Vedas, serving the teacher in the Brahmacharya-Āshrama and by teaching others; the debt to the Ancestors was paid by rearing a family and discharging the duties of Gārhasthya, including दानं, *dānam*, charitable gifts; the debt to the Devas was paid by यजनं, yajanam, sacrifice, chiefly in Vānaprastha. Sannyāsa, the fourth Āshrama, sums up the three others on the highest level. For the youngest caste, the Shūdra, only, शुश्रूषा, shushrūṣhā service, was prescribed as summing up all duties in a single word. Looked at truly, service of the world includes all duties for the highest Sannyāsī, for he has nothing left to gain for himself. Thus the duty of the youngest becomes also the duty of the eldest, but in the latter case on a much higher level.

2 *Manusmriti*, vi, 36.

We may illustrate the idea of duty by the relation of father and son. The father received in his childhood protection and care from his own parents, and thus incurred a debt; he pays this as parental duty to his son, to whom he, in turn, has given a physical body, which requires from him the fostering care bestowed on his own in his infancy and childhood. The son, having received his body from the father, has the duty of serving him with that body, and is also incurring a debt during his helpless years to be paid in time to his own children.

Now the quality which dictates the fulfilment of a duty is called a Virtue; that which prompts the non-fulfilment, or violation of it, is called a Vice. Happiness in any relation depends on the parties to the relation fulfilling their duties to each other; that is, on their practicing the virtues which are the fulfilment of the duties of the relation. Unhappiness in any relation results if one or both the parties do not fulfil their duties to each other that is, if they practise the vices which are the non-fulfilment of the duties of the relation. A father and son are happy with each other if the father shows the virtues of tenderness, protection, care for the well-being of the son, and the son shows the virtues of obedience, reverence and serviceableness. A father and son are unhappy if the father shows the vices of harshness, oppression, neglect, and the son shows the vices of disobedience, disrespect and careless disregard. If father and son love each other, the virtues of that relation will be practised; if they hate each other, the vices of that relation will appear. Virtues grow out of love regularised and controlled by the righteous intelligence that sees more the unity of the Self than the diversity of the Not-Self; vices grow out of hate strengthened and intensified by the unenlightened intelligence, that sees more the separateness of the bodies than the oneness of the Self.

Speaking of virtues and vices, of right and wrong, of good conduct and bad conduct, we must not forget that in whatever way they may find expressions in human conduct, they are all based on Truth, which embodies the Law itself. Sacrifice and duty follow the Law; the Law itself is an expression of Truth. In factĪshvara Himself is Truth. The Devas adoring the Divine Lord, when He appeared as Shrī Krishṇa, broke forth:

सत्यव्रतं सत्यपरं त्रिसत्यं सत्यस्य योनिं निहितं च सत्ये।
सत्यस्य सत्यमृतसत्यनेत्रं सत्यात्मकं त्वां शरणं प्रपन्नाः ॥[3]

"O True of promise, True of purpose, triply. True, the Fount of Truth and dwelling in the True, the Truth of Truth, the Eye of Right and Truth, Spirit of Truth, refuge we seek in Thee."

Thus Virtues have been called forms of Truth. Bhīṣhma describes them as follows:

सत्यं च समता चैव दमश्चैव न संशयः।
अमात्सर्यं क्षमाचैव ह्रीस्तितिक्षाऽनसूयता ॥
त्यागो ध्यानमथार्यत्वं धृतिश्च सततं दया।
अहिंसा चैव राजेंद्र सत्याकारास्त्रयोदश ॥[4]

"Truthfulness, equability, self-control, absence of self-display, forgiveness, modesty, endurance, absence of envy, charity, a noble well-wishing towards others, self-possession, compassion, and harmlessness—surely these are the thirteen forms of Truth."

Truth is that which is. As Bhīṣhma says:

3 *Viṣhṇu - Bhāgavata*, X. ii. 20.
4 *Mahābhārata*, Shānti Parva, clxii. 8,9.

......सत्यं ब्रह्म सनातनं।
........सर्वं सत्ये प्रतिष्टितं॥[5]

"Truth is the eternal Brahman..... Everything rests on Truth."

All the laws of nature are expressions of Truth, i.e., they are the methods, the expressions of the nature of That which is, of the Truth, Reality, Being, the Self or Puruṣha manifesting amidst the limitations of the Not-Self, Untruth, Non-Being, or Mūlaprakṛiti. They work therefore, with undeviating accuracy, with absolute justice and precision. To be true is to be in accord with these laws, and to have nature's constructive energies on our side and working with us. It is to be working with Īshvara. The intellect has the power of discerning what is from what is not, the power of discrimination, of seeing the Real and the Unreal. Recognising the Real as stable and permanent, it seeks to grasp it and thus cultivates the virtues which are the forms of truth.

Untruth is that which IS NOT.

All vices are forms of Untruth, even as all virtues are forms of Truth. Hence the overwhelming importance of Truth, which is thus the foundation and essential constituent of all virtues, rather than a separate virtue to be taken by itself.

Truthfulness was in ancient days, the leading characteristic of the Āryan, and is constantly alluded to as a constituent in the heroic character. Thus, when about to revive the dead child of Abhimanyu, Shrī Kriṣhṇa says:

न ब्रवीम्युत्तरे मिथ्या सत्यमेतद्भविष्यति।
एष संजीवयाम्येनं पश्यतां सर्वदेहिनां॥

5 Ibid, 5.

नोक्तपूर्वं मया मिथ्या स्वैरेष्वपि कदाचन।
न च युद्धात्परावृत्तस्तथा संजीवतामयं॥
यथाहं नाभिजानामि विजयेन कदाचन।
विरोधन्तेन सत्येन मृतोजीवत्वयं शिशुः॥
यथा सत्यं च धर्मश्च मयि नित्यं प्रतिष्ठितौ।
तथा मृतः शिशुरयं जीवतामभिमन्युजः॥[6]

"O Uttara! I speak not falsely, and this shall truly come about. Even now do I revive this child let all beings behold it.

"As I have never uttered an untruth, even in play, as I have never turned back from battle, so may this infant live.

"As I have never known dispute with Arjuna, so by that truth may this dead babe revive.

"As truth and Dharma ever dwell in Me, so may the dead child of Abhimanyu live."

Other heroes repeatedly make the same statement: "My lips have never uttered an untruth." Shrī Rāma goes into exile for fourteen years in order that his father's promise may remain unbroken. Yudhishthira refuses to struggle for his kingdom before due time, because he has promised to remain in exile.

The effect of these continually repeated precepts and examples was to work into the Āryan character a profound love of truth, and this has repeatedly been noticed as a predominating feature of Hindu character.

It must never be forgotten that no character can be virtuous which has not truth for its basis, and that no character can be base when truth is preserved unsullied. It is the root of all true

6 *Mahābhārata*, Ashvamedha Parva. lxix. 18, 19, 21, 22.

manliness, the glory of the hero, the crown of the virtuous, the preserver of the family, the protection of the State. Falsehood undermines alike the home and the nation, poisons the springs of virtue, degrades and pollutes the character. The liar is always weak and always despicable scorn and contempt follow him. For the building up of character, truth is the only sure foundation.

Here, again, we come back to our basis of morality, and see why Truth is so all important. For if it be carefully traced back, every untruth uttered will be found to be ultimately connected with the desire for a separate and exclusive existence, and hence to arise from repulsion, separateness, hate, while every truth uttered is ultimately connected with the desire for the common and united life of the one Self, the Real, whence all love proceeds.

BLISS AND EMOTIONS

THE life of Īshvara permeates all beings and expresses itself as consciousness and bliss, through the bodily limitation of these beings. The body becomes more and more complex, the organs become developed, so that the imprisoned life may assert itself more and more. It is the force of life that directs the development of all being. It is that force that breaks through the *tāmasic* inertia of the mineral form, and makes the mineral matter more and more plastic and capable of receiving impressions from the outside. It is that force which eventually makes a centre of Self in all beings, and develops faculties that digest the outside impressions and work them out into tendencies that form the character of man. Ideas of virtues and vices thus arise, ideas of right and wrong, of good and bad.

The life force works itself out by *impulses* seeking bliss, and by the *direction* of the guiding intelligence. We need not, in this treatise, go further back than the human stage of development. The impulses of man lead him indiscriminately to various objects in pursuit of pleasure. But the rebuffs of pain make him stop and think. Over and over this happens in life. Over and over again the impulses propel; over and over again intelligence checks. The impulses are thus restrained, directed and refined. Bliss and intelligence act and react on each other and constantly press man onward. One becomes known as Emotion, the other as Intellect. A man may progress continually: he may no longer require a brain, he may no longer require the help of propelling emotions, he may no longer require some particular forms of intelligence and bliss; but intelligence and bliss themselves form part of his life; they are aspects of the Īshvaric life, which he assimilates and calls his own, and they are inseparable from him.

Emotions lead a man outwards and make him identify himself with the things he sees around him. But intellect forms a centre of I-ness, the centre of a small circle of personality, forces all experiences to that centre, and judges all things from the standpoint of that centre. Intellect forms the barrier of selfishness, which separates man from man, till at last by wider and wider knowledge, by knowledge embracing the whole universe, the barrier is swept away, all mankind, nay all beings, form one field, one circle; but the centre is then removed, and becomes the great centre of the Universe, the centre of Īshvaric existence; man rises above the Ahamkāra tattva, the tattva that causes the limited sense of I-ness. He plunges into Mahat, or the great tattva, and becomes the possessor of universal knowledge.

The emotions of a man, bound down to the personal self, find expression through the *indriyas* (senses). The *indriyas* rush out and bring back their experiences to the intellect of man. The experiences that cause harmonious vibrations are recorded by the intellect as pleasurable, and those that produce opposite vibrations are recorded as painful. The register is made in the memory of man, and intellect proceeds to discriminate between what is pleasurable and what is painful in the long run. Emotions thus become trained. Likes and dislikes become the natural expressions of the emotions, under the guidance of intellect which has developed Discrimination.

The senses become thus indissolubly wedded to the mind, the emotions to the intellect, the *indriyas* to Mahat, and man becomes normally Emotional-Intellectual, or Kāma-Mānasic. This is essentially necessary at this stage of his progress.

Thus man likes in the beginning whatever is sweet, and dislikes whatever is bitter. But experience tells him that too much of a sweet thing is as bad as a bitter thing. Temperance in time becomes a normal emotion in a developed man.

What is sweet in the beginning becomes sometimes bitter in the end; what is apparently sweet is sometimes really bitter.

यत्तदग्रे विषमिव परिणामेऽमृतोपमम् ।
तत्सुखं सात्विकम्प्रोक्तमात्मबुद्धिप्रसादजम् ॥
विषयेंद्रियसंयोगाद्यत्तदग्रेऽमृतोपमम् ।
परिणामे विषमिव तत्सुखं राजसं स्मृतम् ॥[1]

"That which at first is as venom, but in the end is as nectar; that pleasure is said to be *sāttvic*, born of the blissful knowledge of the Self.

"That which from the union of the senses with their objects at first is as nectar, but in the end is like venom, that pleasure is accounted *rājasic*."

As these experiences are repeated, man learns prudence, and prudence becomes a normal emotion in man.

To rush out to do a thing on the first impulse sometimes

1 *Bhagavad Gītā*. xviii. 37, 38.

brings on disastrous results. To lose temper brings more disharmonious than harmonious experiences. Forbearance, Toleration, become thus normal emotions in man.

Emotions, rightly directed by the intelligence, are virtues. In the culture of emotions lies the formation of a man's character, his ethical development. Emotional culture is the highest culture of man, and the training of likes and dislikes is his best evolution. The man of cultured emotions is propelled by them to do what he thinks right; he becomes patriotic, he becomes philanthropic, he becomes compassionate, he becomes friendly to all beings. His emotions become predominantly those of Love, and he takes an ever wider and wider range in the manifestation of that Love. And when the barrier of personality is swept away, when the *ahamkāric* mind becomes Mānas, or the reflection of the Universal Mind, the emotions also break through the barrier of *indriyas* and ascend to Buddhi, and reflect the life of Īshvara within, Verily then the Trinity of Ātmā, Buddhi and Mānas, becomes a Unity, and the man a Jīvānmukta.

We now understand why Ethical Science is particularly concerned with the emotions and hence with the bliss aspect of Īshvara. There are many ways of showing why happiness should follow right conduct, and unhappiness wrong conduct, but they are all modifications of the one essential reason, that, as there is but One Self in all, to hurt or help another is virtually to hurt or help oneself.

It is written in the Shruti:

विज्ञानमानन्दं ब्रह्म ।[2]

"Brahman is knowledge and bliss."

---

2 *Brihadāraṇyakop*. V. ix 28.

Over and over again the bliss of Brahman is spoken of, and bliss is said to be His nature. In fact the threefold nature of Īshvara, of the Saguṇa Brahman, is expressed in the epithet, Sat-Chit-Ānanda: Bliss is thus the very nature of the Jīvātmā, since his-nature is that of Brahman; he, too, is bliss. But we learn further that the Saguṇa Brahman is विरजंspotless, and शुभ्रं, pure.[3] Therefore, only the pure, the good, is of His nature, and is compatible with His bliss. So then must the essence of the Jīvātmā be purity, and it is written of it:

तं विद्याच्छुक्रममृतम् ।[4]

"Let him know it, pure and immortal."

Thus purity and bliss are of the nature of the Jīvātmā and are inseparable, for unity is purity, and the feeling of unity is the feeling of bliss.

Each Jīvātmā being of the nature of the one Self it is ever, when embodied in a separate form, seeking union with the Self in other forms. This search for unity, for the bliss of union, is instinctive, and results, when the union is found, in perfect happiness. In this everyone is alike. Men differ in most things, but in their longing for happiness they are all alike. Every man, woman, boy and girl wants to be happy. They seek happiness in many different ways, but they all seek happiness. The Jīvātmā, blinded by his body, chooses the wrong things very often, but the motive of his choice is always the same, the desire to be happy. It is his nature to be happy, and he is always trying to express that nature. Through the whole of his long pilgrimage, he is searching

---

3 *Muṇḍakop.*, II. ii. 9. The statement is repeated over and over again.

4 *Kaṭhop.*, II. vi. 7.

for happiness. This is his root-motive, the object at which he invariably aims. If he does a painful thing, it is in order to gain a greater happiness. If he endures toil and discomfort, it is because the result of the toil and discomfort will be happiness. Happiness is his end; everything else is only means to that end. A life of austerity and continued self-denial and suffering is embraced in the belief that it will lead to supreme bliss. The whole of evolution may be described in the words; "A search for happiness." Continually disappointed, with unwearying perseverance man returns again and again to the search, until at last he recognises that purity, wisdom, bliss, are one and indivisible. Then he goes to Peace.

For purity, wisdom and bliss, Sat, Chit and Ānanda, are the very nature of Īshvara, His own Self.

Thus Ethics leads us to the highest religion, to the realisation of the highest truths, and when Ethics reaches its goal, the barrier between Ethics and Religion vanishes away, Ethics becomes Religion and Religion, Ethics. The goal of both is Īshvara and Ishvaric life. This is why the Hindu ethical system is a branch of the Hindu Religion, and why one cannot be separated from the other.

"SELF-REGARDING" VIRTUES

WE have already seen that Ethics has as its object the establishment of harmonious relations. These relations are concerned with the surroundings of a man-his home, city, nation, etc.—and also with his own body. Now the body of a man, according to the scriptural teachings, is, as we have seen, a complex one, consisting of several sheaths, or koṣhas. It is enough to remember here that we have the physical sheath, in which Prāṇa functions, the sheath of the indriyas or senses (the sensuous or kāmic sheath), the mental sheath and the buddhic sheath. Ethics concerns itself at present with the physical, the kāmic, and the mental sheaths. For when the buddhic sheath is reached, man becomes divine, and the present limit of ethical teachings is crossed.

Ethical teachings have therefore reference to the lower sheaths of a man's body, and to the different classes of beings, who form his surroundings. The different classes of beings, as we have already seen, are the Devas, the Pitṛis, the Ṛiṣhis, men in general, and the lower animals, i. e., beings both higher and lower than man, as well as the whole of mankind.

We have thus, in the first place, duties which we owe to the sheaths of our own body, and in the next place, duties that we owe to Devas, Pitris, Ṛiṣhis, mankind and the lower animals.

When the body becomes entirely harmonious with the Self within, it becomes a true and subdued vehicle of the life of Ātmā, which is an aspect of the vara.

When the surrounding universe becomes harmonious with the Self within, the life of Īshvara flows out to the universe from the centre of the Self. Man, then becomes fully an expression of the Law, the voice of Īshvara, the sacred word Praṇava. Towards that goal we should all strive, and to that goal ethics must lead us.

Now let us turn to our body, or bodies, if the term be preferred.

First, the Sthūla Sharīra. The physical body must be kept clean and healthy. Cleanliness and health mean harmony and order. Man is better able to do work with a clean and healthy body. He remains cheerful and bright. The diseased man cannot give attention to work. He is uneasy in mind.

The disharmony and disorder of one sheath also react on the other sheaths of the man.

The body should be kept up by means of sāttvic food. For the food retains its essential magnetic properties after its conversion into blood, and produces corresponding effects on the indriyas and the mind. The Bhagavad-Gītā says:

आयुः सत्त्वबलारोग्यसुखप्रीतिविवर्धनाः ।
रस्याः स्निग्धाः स्थिरा हृद्या आहाराः सात्त्विकप्रियाः ॥
कट्वम्ललवणात्युष्णतीक्ष्णरूक्षविदाहिनः ।
आहारा राजसस्येष्टा दुःखशोकामयप्रदाः ॥
यातयाम गतरसं पूतिपर्युषितं च यत् ।
उचिष्टमपि चामेध्यं भोजनं तामसप्रियम् ॥[1] ***

"The foods dear to the Sāttvic, increasing life, energy, strength,

1 *Loc cit.*,xvii.8,9,10.

health, joy and cheerfulness, are those that are full of juice, oleaginous, non-volatile and heart-strengthening.

"Those dear to the Rājasic, causing pain, depression and sickness, are the bitter, acid, saline, over-hot, pungent, dry and burning.

"Stale and flat, putrid and corrupt, leavings and unclean (things), are the food loved by the Tāmasic."

We have already seen that the higher evolution is brought about by the predominance of Sattva, and that Sattva means harmony.

Secondly, the Sūkṣhma Sharīra. The indriyas, through the heredity of our past existence, are largely guided by animal appetites, which are distinctly rājasic. We should therefore subdue our indriyas. We may see, hear, smell, taste and touch, but we should not ascribe our likes and dislikes to the object of the senses. We must *sense* as a matter of course, but the sensing must not be vitiated by personal likes and dislikes, which form a barrier between ourselves and the external world and make harmonious relations impossible. Every man makes a world to himself, by means of his likes and dislikes. Thus many worlds are formed, each different from the other, and all different from the world as it is, the world of Īshvara. Men are jaundiced by the tint and taint of their personalities and, blinded by the distractions of Rajas, they do not see the Law, the word of Īshvara.

Therefore our mind should not be guided by the indriyas, but the mind should be guided by its own discriminative faculty, and should then subdue the senses.

The indriyas are divided into organs of perception and organs of action (the latter belonging to the Sthūla Sharīra). There is no harm done by the perception of objects, if the perception be not followed by likes and dislikes. Rāga and Dvesha drive us helplessly along, using the karmendriyas for their own satisfaction.

इन्द्रियस्येन्द्रियस्यार्थे रागद्वेषा व्यवस्थितौ ।
तयोर्न वशमागच्छेत्तौ ह्यस्य परिपंथिनौ ॥[2]

"Affection and aversion for the objects of sense abide in the senses; let none come under the dominion of these two; they are the obstructors of his way."

Affection and aversion, Rāga and Dvesha, form the desire-nature of man. This, emotion in its origin, has to be controlled. The emotional nature has to be purified. Raga is to expand into universal love. Dvesha is to be eliminated entirely in personal relations, in relations between man and man, between one being and another being, and is to be retained only as an abstract dislike for anything that goes against the law, against the will of Īshvara. But this abstract dislike is not at all to interfere with the universal love of all beings. It is only to make a man strong in his purity, in his rejection of all that is evil. He should dislike evil ways, but not evil men.

The mind, when wedded to the indriyas, becomes rājasic. When wedded to Buddhi, it becomes sāttvic. The mind of an average man is normally rājasic at the present day. He should make efforts to change it to sāttvic.

We have already said that the mind should give up personal likes and dislikes, Rāga and Dvesha. Rāga and Dvesha form the impurities of the mind, and when they are given up the mind becomes purified.

There is another doṣha, or fault, of the mind. It gets distracted.

---

2 *Bhagavad-Gītā*, iii, 34

It applies itself to a number of outside objects. It runs away from this matter to that matter, and it can with very great difficulty be tied down to one. The mind is compared to a chariot, which is constantly being drawn away in ten different directions by ten horses, which are the ten indriyas. This Vikṣhepa, or distraction of the mind, has to be checked. The mind has to be concentrated, to be made one-pointed.

When the impurities and distraction of the mind are removed, it becomes sattvic. Then it reflects the Self within, and causes harmony and bliss. This is harmony with the Universe, or harmony with the Divine Law as manifested in the Universe.

The first step towards removing distraction is to deal with abstractions more than with concrete objects; we must generalise truths, and come at last to the highest Truth, the one Reality, Īshvara, and grasp Him firmly. Then all the universe appears as His manifestation, all works as His action, all laws as His law. Varieties disappear. Diversities fade away. Harmony prevails.

The training of the mind is man's most important duty, and next to this follows the control of speech and actions. At the same time he must not neglect his physical body. All the vehicles forming his body must be controlled and made harmonious with each other.

The tenfold law, as laid down by Manu, gives some of the characteristics needed:

धृतिः क्षमा दमोऽस्तेयं शौचमिन्द्रियनिग्रहः ।
धीर्विद्या सत्यमक्रोधो दशकं धर्मलक्षणम् ॥[3]

"Endurance, patience, self-control, integrity, purity, restraint

3 *Manusmriti*, vi. 92.

of the senses, wisdom, learning, truth, absence of anger, are the ten signs of virtue."

In briefer form:

अहिंसा सत्यमस्तेयं शौचमिन्द्रियनिग्रहः ।
एतं सामासिकं धर्मं चार्तुवणर्येऽब्रवीन्मनुः ॥[4]

"Harmlessness, truth, integrity, purity, control of the senses, saith Manu, is the summarised law for the four castes."

In the Bhagavad Gītā, an exhaustive list of these general characteristics is given:

अभयं सत्त्वसंशुद्धिर्ज्ञानयोगव्यवस्थितिः ।
दानं दमश्च यज्ञश्च स्वाध्यायस्तप आर्जवम् ॥
अहिंसा सत्यमक्रोधस्त्यागः शांतिरपैशुनम् ।
दया भूतेष्वलालुप्त्वं मार्दवं ह्रीरचापलम् ॥***
तेजः क्षमा धृतिः शौचमद्रोहो नातिमानिता ।
भवंति संपदं दैवीमभिजातस्य भारत ॥[5]

"Fearlessness, clean-living, steadfastness in the Yoga of wisdom, almsgiving, self-restraint, sacrifice, study of the Shāstras, austerity, straight forwardness,

"Harmlessness, truth, absence of wrath, renunciation, peacefulness, absence of crookedness, compassion to living beings, uncovetousness, mildness, modesty, steadfastness,

"Energy, patience, fortitude, purity, absence of envy and pride-these are his who is born with the divine qualities, O Bhārata."

Some of these virtues would fall into one or other of the three

---

4 Ibid, x. 63.

5 *Bhagavad-Gītā*, xvi. 1—3.

classes already spoken of, but for the most part they belong to the JīvāJīvātmā as his general expression of the love-emotion, and as the balance of his own nature, the due control of his energies.

The essential importance of Truth has already been dwelt upon. As a general virtue it appears as Truthfulness, Honesty, Integrity, Uprightness. Its utter indispensability is concentrated by the wisdom and experience of ages into short sayings, such as: "Honesty is the best policy," "सत्यमेवजयते नानृतं" "Truth alone prevails, not falsehood."

The virtue of *Self-control*, or *Self-restraint*, mentioned in each of the above quotations, is the general reining-in of all the energies of the mind, desire-nature, and physical body, the holding of them all in due submission, so that each is allowed or refused exercise at the will of the man. It implies that the man is conscious of the difference between himself and his lower upādhis, and no more indentifies himself with his lower nature than a rider identifies himself with the horse on which he is sitting. The contrast between an uncontrolled man and a self-controlled man is very much like the contrast between a bad rider on an unbroken horse, and a good rider on a well broken horse. In the first case, the horse rushes about, carrying his helpless rider, plunges violently, and gives his rider a bad fall; in the other case, the man sits easily, guiding the docile steed in any direction, galloping or standing still, leaping or walking, every motion of the rider obeyed by the horse.

So necessary is self-control, that the teachers of morality are continually recurring to it, and enforcing it. Manu dwells on its necessity, and explains that action has three roots, and that control of each generator of action must be gained.

कर्म मनोवाग्देहसंभवम् ।[6]

"Action is born of mind, speech and body."

Each of these, mind, speech, and body, must be brought under complete control, and then success is sure.

वाग्दण्डोऽथ मनोदण्डः कायदण्डस्तथैवच ।
यस्यैते निहिताबुद्धौ त्रिदण्डीति स उच्यते ॥
त्रिदण्डमेतन्निक्षिप्य सर्वभूतेषु मानवः ।
कामक्रोधौ तु संयम्य ततः सिद्धिं निगच्छति ॥[7]

"He is called the holder of the Tri-daṇḍa in whose reason these are fixed-control of speech, control of mind, control of body."

"The man who lays this triple rule (over himself) amidst all creatures, he verily dominates desire and wrath, and goes to perfection."

Of these three, control of the mind is the most important, as speech and action alike depend on the mind. Manu says again:

मनो विद्यात्प्रवर्तकम् ।[8]

"Let the mind be known as the instigator."

Once let the mind be brought under control, and all else follows, but here lies the great difficulty, owing to the extreme restlessness of the mind. Arjuna placed this difficulty before Shrī Kṛiṣhṇa 5,000 years ago:

चंचलं हि मनः कृष्ण प्रमाथि बलवद्दृढम् ।
तस्याहं निग्रहं मन्ये वायोरिव सुदुष्करम् ॥[9]

---

6 *Manusmriti*, xii. 3.

7 Ibid. 10. 11.

8 Ibid. 4.

9 *Bhagavad Gītā*. vi. 34.

"Verily the mind is restless, O Kṛishṇa, impetuous, strong, difficult to bend; I deem it very hard to curb, like the wind."

And no answer can be given to this, save the answer given by the Divine Teacher:

असंशयं महाबाहो मनो दुर्निग्रहं चलम्।
अभ्यासेन तु कौंतेय वैराग्येण च गृह्यते ॥[10]

"Without doubt, O mighty-armed, the mind is hard to curb and restless; yet verily, O son of Kuntī, it may be curbed by constant practice and dispassion."

Only long-continued effort and perseverance can bring under control this restless vigorous mind, and yet without this control man can never be happy.

यतो यतो निश्चरति मनश्चंचलमास्थिरम्।
नतस्ततो नियम्यैतदात्मन्येव वशं नयेत् ॥[11]

"As often as the restless and unstable mind goeth forth, so often reining it in, let him place it under the control of the Self."

If this be done, then happiness is secured, so much so that Shrī Kṛishṇa makes happiness part of the successful austerity of the mind:

मनःप्रसादः सौम्यत्वं मौनमात्मविनिग्रहः।
भावसंशुद्धिरित्येतत्तपो मानसमुच्यते ॥[12]

"Mental happiness, equanimity, silence, self-control, purity of nature—this is called the austerity of the mind."

10 Ibid. 35.
11 *Bhagavad-Gītā*. vi. 26.
12 Ibid. xvii. 16.

But the most disturbing part of man's nature is his desires, ever-craving, never satisfied. In fact the more they are gratified, the fiercer they grow.

न जातु कामः कामानामुपभोगेन शाम्यति।
हविषा कृष्णवर्त्मेव भूय एवाभिवर्धते ॥[13]

"Desire is verily never quenched by the enjoyment of objects of desire; it only increases further as fire with butter."

To bring the senses under control the mind must be used, else will a man ever be restless and uneasy.

He must learn to use his mind to control his senses, for through the senses come his chief temptations.

And every sense must be brought under control; for one uncontrolled sense may play havoc with the mind:

इन्द्रियाणां हि चरतां यन्मनोऽनुविधीयते।
तदस्य हरति प्रज्ञां वायुर्नावमिवांभसि ॥[14]

"That one of the roving senses which the mind yieldeth to, that hurries way the understanding, as a gale (hurries away) a ship on the waters."

Manu also lays stress on the danger of allowing even one sense to slip away from control, using a very graphic symbol:

इन्द्रियाणां तु सर्वेषां यद्येकं क्षरतीन्द्रियम्।
ततोऽस्य क्षरति प्रज्ञा हृतेः पादादिवोदकम् ॥[15]

"If one sense of all the senses leaks, then understanding leaks through it, as water from the leg of the water-skin."

13 *Manusmriti* ii 94.

14 *Bhagavad-Gītā* ii. 67.

15 *Manusmriti.* ii. 99.

One open passage is enough to allow all the water to pour out from the water-skin of the water-carrier; and so one uncontrolled sense is opening enough for man's understanding to flow away from him.

The mind, then, is to be brought under control, and is to be used to control the senses. In the *Kaṭhopaniṣhat*, the mind is therefore compared to the reins with which a driver pulls in, guides and controls his horses, the horses being compared to the senses, which run away with the body and the JīvāJīvātmā, who dwells in the body:

आत्मानं रथिनं विद्धि शरीरं रथमेव तु।
बुद्धिं तु सारथिं विद्धि मनः प्रग्रहमेव च॥
इन्द्रियाणि हयानाहुर्विषयांस्तेषु गोचरान्।
आत्मेन्द्रियमनोयुक्तं भोक्तेत्याहुर्मनीषिणः॥
यस्त्वविज्ञानवान्भवत्ययुक्तेन मनसा सदा।
तस्येन्द्रियाण्यवश्यानि दुष्टाश्वा इव सारथेः॥
यस्तु विज्ञानवान्भवति युक्तेन मनसा सदा।
तस्येन्द्रियाणि वश्यानि सदश्वा इव सारथेः॥
विज्ञानसारथिर्यस्तु मनःप्रग्रहवान्नरः।
सोऽध्वनः पारमाप्नोति तद्विष्णोः परमं पदम्॥[16]

"Know the Self as the occupant of the car, the body verily as the car. Know indeed the reason as the charioteer, the mind as the reins.

"The senses are said to be the horses, the objects of the senses the field for them. The Self, joined to the senses and the mind, is the enjoyer—so say the wise.

16 *Kaṭhop.* iii.3—6, 9.

"He who is unwise, with the mind ever unapplied, of him the senses are uncontrolled, like the bad horses of the charioteer.

"He who is wise, with the mind ever applied, of him the senses are controlled, like the good horses of the charioteer.

"The man whose charioteer is wise, whose mind-reins are used, he only travels to the end of the road, to the highest abode of Vishṇu."

Manu uses the same imagery:

इन्द्रियाणां विचरतां विषयेष्वपहारिषु ।
संयमे यत्नमातिष्ठेद्विद्वान्यन्तेव वाजिनाम् ॥[17]

"The wise man should make effort to control the senses running amid the alluring objects of sense, as the driver the horses."

Recounting the five organs of sense and the five organs of action, Manu declares that the control of the mind includes the control of these:

एकादशं मनो ज्ञेयं स्वगुणेनोभयात्मकम् ।
यस्मिञ्जिते जितावेतौ भवतः पञ्चकौ गणौ ॥[18]

"Mind is to be known as the eleventh, belonging by its nature to both; in conquering this, the two sets of five become conquered."

The control of speech consists in making it respectful to superiors, courteous to equals, gentle to inferiors, and we shall return to this in studying the special virtues. For the moment we may leave it with the general description of right speech:

अनुद्वेगकरं वाक्यं सत्यं प्रियहितं च यत् ।
स्वाध्यायाभ्यसनं चैव वाङ्मयं तप उच्यते ॥[19]

---

17 *Manusmriti*, ii. 88.

18 Ibid. 92.

19 *Bhagavad-Gītā*. xvii. 15.

"Speech causing no annoyance, truthful, pleasant and beneficial, and the repetition of the Vedas, this is called the austerity-of speech."

And Manu remarks:

वाच्यर्था नियताः सर्वे वाङ्मूला वाग्विनिःसृताः ।
तां तु यः स्तेनयेद्वाचं स सर्वस्तेयकृन्नरः ॥[20]

"All things are governed by speech: speech is the root, from speech they originate; that man verily who is dishonest in speech, he is dishonest in all."

Thus speech is said to be important.

The control of the body is similarly summed up by Shrī Kṛiṣhṇa:

देवद्विजगुरुप्राज्ञपूजनंशौचमार्जवम् ।
ब्रह्मचर्यमहिंसाचशारीरंतपउच्यते ॥[21]

"Worship of the Devas, the twice-born, the gurus and the wise, purity, straightforwardness, chastity, and harmlessness, are called the austerity of the body."

Control such as this produces a balancing of the mind, calmness, quiet and contentment.

The secret of self-control is through be Abhyāsa and Vairāgya, "constant practice and dispassion." The second word is especially significant, and the whole statement should be studied in the light of the shlokas quoted from the Kaṭhopaniṣhat. Buddhi, the Pure Reason, is there said to be the charioteer, in whose one hand are grasped the many-branching reins of Mānas. Buddhi is, as has

20 *Manusmriti*. iv. 256.
21 *Bhagavad-Gītā*. xvii. 14.

been said, the faculty which recognises and realises the Unity of the Self, as Mānas is that which cognises the many-ness of sense-objects. The owner of the car, the JīvāJīvātmā, should make sure that Buddhi drives his car, and then the reins and the horses will be well managed.

Now the student who wishes that Buddhi should thus drive his car, should constantly dwell on the fact of the Unity of the Self.

शनैः शनैरुपरमेदबुद्ध्या धृतिगृहीतया।
आत्मसंस्थं मनः कृत्वा न किंचिदपि चिंतयेत्॥
यतो यतो निश्चरति मनश्चंचलमस्थिरम्।
ततस्ततो नियम्यैतदात्मन्येव वशं नयेत्॥[22]

"Little by little let him gain tranquillity by means of Buddhi controlled by steadiness, having made Mānas abide in the Self, let him not think of anything.

"As often as the wavering and unsteady Mānas goeth forth, so often, reining it in, let him bring it under the control of the Self."

This is the Abhyāsa that he needs. This Abhyāsa will naturally strengthen Vairāgya, the absence of desire for personal and selfish ends. Whenever he sees a desire for such personal and selfish ends rising up within himself, he should at once call up before his mental view the injury that he is likely to inflict on others by its indulgence, the evil consequences to himself in increasing selfishness, and the whole series of disturbances which will flow from his selfishness to the common life of the society to which he belongs. By picturing to himself the consequences of selfishness

---

22 *Bhagavad-Gītā*. vi. 25, 26.

in his own life and in those of others, and by studying the illustrations of them given in the Purāṇas, he will gradually strengthen his power of self-control, and will establish himself in that constant mood of righteousness and performance of duty so unceasingly inculcated in the sacred books.

For that Righteousness, and righteousness only, should be followed is reiterated again and again:

अधार्मिको नरो यो हि यस्य चाप्यनृतं धनम्।
हिंसारतश्च यो नित्यं नेहासौ सुखमेधते।।
न सीदन्नपि धर्मेण मनोऽधर्मेनिवेशयेत्।
अधार्मिकाणां पापानामाशु पश्यन्विपर्ययम्||
नाधर्मश्चरितो लोके सद्यः फलति गौरिव।
शनैरावर्तमानस्तु कर्तुर्मूलानि कृन्तति॥[23]

"The man who is unrighteous, or he who (gains) wealth by falsehood, or he who ever delights in injuring, never obtains happiness in this world.

"Although suffering by righteousness, let him not turn his mind to unrighteousness; he will behold the speedy overthrow of the unrighteous, of the sinners."

"Unrighteousness, practised in this world, does not bear fruit at once like a cow; slowly re-acting, it cuts off the very roots of the doer."

In a sense, righteousness is truth; its special significance may be said to be the desire to do what is right, the desire to give everyone his due, the desire always to find out the truth and act according to it rather than according to anything else.

To do righteousness is to gain a companion that never fails a

---

23 *Manusmriti* iv. 170—172

man, and when all else deserts him this faithful companion will remain, will cling to him through death, and clothe him with glory in the world beyond the grave. Manu writes hereon as follows:

धर्मं शनैः संचिनुयाद्वल्मीकमिव पुत्तिकाः ।
परलोकसहायार्थं सर्वभूतान्यपीडयन् ॥
नामुत्र हि सहायार्थं पिता माता च तिष्ठतः ।
न पुत्रदारा न ज्ञातिर्धर्मस्तिष्ठति केवलः ॥
एकः प्रजायते जन्तुरेक एव प्रलीयते ।
एकोऽनुभुङ्क्ते सुकृतमेक एव च दुष्कृतम् ॥
मृतम्शरीरमुत्सृज्य काष्ठलोष्टसमं क्षितौ ।
विमुखा बान्धवा यान्ति धर्मस्तमनुगच्छति ॥
तस्माद्धर्मं सहायार्थं नित्यं संचिनुयाच्छनैः ।
धर्मेण हि सहायेन तमस्तरति दुस्तरम् ॥
धर्मप्रधानं पुरुषं तपसा हतकिल्बिषम् ।
परलोकं नयत्याशु भास्वंतं स्वशरीरिणम् ॥[24]

"Giving no pain to any creatures, let him slowly build up righteousness like white ants their hill, that it be to him a companion in the world beyond.

"Nor father, nor mother, nor son, nor wife, nor kinsfolk remain to accompany him to the next world; righteousness alone remaineth.

"Alone each being is born; alone verily he dies; alone he enjoys good deeds; alone also the evil.

"Leaving the dead body on the ground like a log or a clod of earth, the relatives depart, with averted faces; righteousness alone followeth him.

"Therefore, to gain an unfailing friend let him ever gather

24 *Manusmriti*, iv. 238—243,

righteousness; with righteousness as companion be will cross over the darkness, difficult to cross.

"It rapidly leadeth the man who is devoted to righteousness and has destroyed his sins by austerity, to the world beyond, radiant and clad in a celestial body."

This insistence on righteousness as the only way to happiness in this world or in any other is characteristic of the Sanātana Dharma, whose very heart is duty, as justice is its key-note and unalterable law its life-breath. A man obtains everything that he has duly earned, neither more nor less; every debt must be paid; every cause must be followed by its effect.

The virtue of *Content* springs from a full recognition of this fact, and it is itself the root of happiness, a virtue which every student should endeavour to work into his character:

संतोषं परमास्थाय सुखार्थी संयतो भवेत् ।
संतापमूलं हि सुखं दुःखमूलं विपर्ययः ॥[25]

"Let one who desires happiness be controlled and take refuge in perfect content; content is verily the root of happiness, the opposite is the root of sorrow."

The contented man is happy under the most unfavourable circumstances, the root of his happiness being in himself; whereas the discontented man finds food for his discontent, however favourable his circumstances may be. There are always some who are superior in position to more wealthy, more fortunate than ourselves, and hence reasons for discontent may ever be found by the unwise. To be satisfied with what we have because we have our due is true wisdom, and all dissatisfaction is folly.

We have spoken of virtues as bringing about harmonious

25 *Manusmriti*, iv. 12.

relations between JīvāJīvātmās, but it must not be thought that this excludes the above virtues which at the first glance seem chiefly to concern their possessor, and to aid his own general evolution. For when carefully considered, it will be found that these so-called personal virtues react upon the happiness of others, though in a way not immediately apparent. Life, evolution, virtue and vice, duty—all these things would be impossible with only a single JīvāJīvātmā in existence. The idea of a community is inseparable from the ideas of these. A so-called duty to self, or a personal virtue, is also ultimately a duty to another, a giving of some help or a saving of some inconvenience to others. For instance if we are unclean, we inevitably make our neighbours uncomfortable when we come into contact with them. When a man sways to another You owe it to yourself to do so and so."

He really and instinctively means: "You owe this to the evolution of humanity generally as connected, by the unity of the Self, with the evolution of your individual self," for the evolution of one Jīvā is inseparable from that of other Jīvās, and helping or hindering our own progress is also directly or indirectly helping or hindering the progress of others. An unclean or slovenly man injures himself primarily and his fellows secondarily, by lowering the general ideal and influencing their lives indirectly if not actively.

The duties to Devas, Pitṛis, Ṛiṣhis, men and animals were mentioned in Parts I and II, and we need only add, ere turning to our duties to human beings, that our general attitude should be that of Harmlessness.

अहिंसा परमो धर्मः[26]

"Harmlessness is the highest duty," taught Bhīṣhma.

---

26 *Mahābhārata*. Anushāsana Parva, cxiv

Manu also says:

यस्मादण्वपि भूतानां द्विजान्नोत्पद्यते भयम् ।
तस्य देहाद्विमुक्तस्य भयं नास्ति कुतश्चन ॥[27]

"For the twice-born man from whom no fear arises to any living creatures, for him, freed from the body, there will be no fear from any."

Īshvara is just, and the harmless man is harmed by none. The Yogī can wander without danger among wild animals, because his heart is full of love and he is a source of danger to none. Once again says Bhishma: "The slayer is slain," but the man who slays none will himself be slain of none. For the harmless man, full of love to all creatures, sees the Self in each and regards each as part of his own body, and such a man is the friend of all creatures, and is safe wherever he goes.

We have seen that by sacrifice only we can establish harmonious relations amongst all beings, and the establishment of harmonious relations, as we have seen, is the very essence of our evolution. Man cannot be selfish. The world is not for one man alone. He may think in his own way and act in his own way. But if he does not conform himself to the Lord, the word of Īshvara, the sacred Praṇava, woe falls on him and misery becomes his lot, firmly and steadfastly, his obstinate selfishness is removed, and he becomes harmonised with the whole universe.

Let the student bear this principle in mind firmly and steadfastly, and he will easily understand what is said in the next chapter.

27 *Manusmriti*. vi. 40.

VIRTUES AND VICES IN HUMAN RELATIONS TO THOSE IN RELATION TO SUPERIORS

WE may study the virtues and vices as the outgrowths from love and hate. Love prompts us to make sacrifices, to limit, to restrict ourselves, to subordinate ourselves to the common well-being. This love emanates from the Self within, is an aspect of Bliss, and makes our duty a work of love, our sacrifice a pleasure.

Emotions in their early rushings forth transgress the law, for the law is not known. But when the law is known and realised, when Chit and Ananda combine, when the emotion proceeds from a discriminating Self-centre, when still later, the Self-centre becomes a universal centre, every emotion becomes a virtue, every emotion becomes a voice of the divine.

As love underlies every virtue, so hate underlies every vice. For union is law, separation is against the law; harmony is evolution, disharmony is the opposite of evolution.

If love prompts our mutual relations, we naturally and readily make sacrifices to render those relations harmonious and blissful.

Now in considering virtues and vices in human relations, we may classify them as those called out in relation to Superiors, in relation to Equals, and in relation to Inferiors.

The natural superiors of a man are: God; the Sovereign; Parents; Teachers; the Aged.[1]

There may be what may be called "accidental superiors"—persons who are on a level with a man's parents and teachers, and persons above him in intelligence and morality, towards whom he would exercise modified forms of the virtues now to be considered. But such adaptations are readily made, and need not change our classification.

The love-emotion directed to God will show itself as the virtue of *Reverence*, carried to its highest degree. This will primarily express itself in worship, and secondarily in treating with respect all ideas about God, all things connected with his worship, sacred places and sacred objects. Reverence being due to a sense of His infinite superiority, attracting love by virtue of His supreme wisdom and compassion, it will naturally be accompanied by *Humility*, the willing recognition of comparative littleness, unassociated with pain and coupled with the readiness to submit to guidance; by *Faith* in and therefore *Submission*, to His wisdom; and by *Devotion* and *Gratitude* responding to His compassion, leading to complete *Self-Sacrifice* in His service. The steady cultivation of these virtues, the fruits of love directed to God, comprise our duty to Him: Reverence, Humility, Faith, Submission, Devotion, Gratitude, Self-Sacrifice.

There are many examples of great devotees in the Hindu books, men who showed out these virtues to the fullest extent, and have set examples of love to God which should be studied in order that they may be imitated. Bhīṣhma's noble hymn to Shrī Kṛiṣhṇa, uttered as he lay wounded on the battle-field, and which

1 There is no order of superiority intended here; the shāstras give different orders.

drew Shrī Kṛiṣhṇa to his side, should be carefully read and thought over.[2]

Prahlāda, triumphant by devotion over all attacks, prayed: "In all the thousand births through which I may be doomed to pass, may my faith in Thee, Achyuta, never know decay. May passion, as fixed as that which the worldly-minded feel for sensual pleasures, ever animate my heart, always devoted unto Thee."[3]

Of such devotees Shrī Kṛiṣhṇa says:

महात्मानस्तु मां पार्थ दैवीं प्रकृतिमाश्रिताः ।
भजंत्यनन्यमनसो ज्ञात्वा भूतादिमव्ययम् ॥
सततं कीर्तयन्तो मां यतंतश्च दृढव्रताः ।
नमस्यंतश्च मां भक्तया नित्ययुक्ता उपासते ॥
ज्ञानयज्ञेनचाप्यन्येयजतोमामुपासते ।
एकत्वेनपृथक्त्वेनबहुधाविश्वतोमुखम् ॥[4]"

"Verily the Mahātmās, O Pārtha, sheltered in My divine Prakṛiti, worship with unwavering mind having known Me, the imperishable source of beings.

"Always glorifying Me, strenuous, firm in vows, bowing unto Me, they worship Me with devotion, ever harmonised.

"Others also, sacrificing with the sacrifice of wisdom, worship Me as the one and the Manifold everywhere present."

And again:

अहं सर्वस्य प्रभवो मत्तः सर्वं प्रवर्तते ।
इति मत्वा भजंते मां बुधा भावसमन्विताः ॥
मच्चित्ता मद्गतप्राणा बोधयंतः परस्परम् ।

---

2 Mahābhārata. Shānti Parva, xlvii.

3 Viṣhṇu Purāṇa. I. xx.

4 Bhagavad-Gītā. ix. 13—15.

कथयंतश्च मां नित्यं तुष्यंति च रमंति च ॥
तेषां सतत युक्तानां भजतां प्रीतिपूर्वकम् ।
ददामि बुद्धियोगं तं येनमामुपयांतिते ॥[5]

"I am the Generator of all; all evolves from Me; understanding thus, the wise adore Me in rapt devotion,

"Mindful of Me, their life hidden in me, illumining each other, ever conversing about Me, they are content and joyful.

"To these, ever harmonious, worshipping in love, I give the Buddhi-Yoga by which they come unto Me."

The cultivation of devotion is by meditating on the Object of devotion, by worshipping Him, by reading about Him, and by listening to, talking to and associating with those who are superior in devotion. In this way devotion increases.

ये तु सर्वाणि कर्माणि मयि संन्यस्य मत्पराः ।
अनन्येनैव योगेन मां ध्यायंत उपासते ॥
तेषामहं समुद्धर्ता मृत्युसंसारसागरात् ।
भवामि न चिरात्पार्थ मय्यावेशितचेतसाम् ॥[6]

"Those verily who, renouncing all actions in Me, and intent on Me, worship meditating on me with whole hearted Yoga,

"These I speedily lift up from the ocean of death and existence, O Pārtha, their minds being fixed on Me."

Submission to the divine Will grows easily out of devotion, for we always readily desire to yield where we recognise and love the superior. Wisdom and, compassion invite submission, for the wisdom will choose the best, and the compassion the least painful

5 Bhagavad-Gītā. x. 8—10.
6 Bhagavad-Gītā xii. 6—7.

path for us. Where wisdom and compassion are perfect, as in God, complete submission is the natural answer; and when all the events of life are seen as under His guidance, they can be accepted cheerfully and contentedly. The attitude of man in this respect to God should be that of a loving child to a wise and tender Father, carried to a far higher degree.

पिताह्मस्यजगतोमाताधातापितामहः ।
...भर्ता......निवासः शरणं सुहृत् ॥[7]

"I am the Father of this universe, the Mother, the Supporter, the Grandsire, the Husband, Home, Shelter, Lover."

Towards such a One, gratitude springs up, ever increasing with increasing knowledge; and self-surrender, self-sacrifice, is but the culmination of reverence. By daily offering of all our acts to God, the spirit of self-sacrifice is cultivated, and as it becomes perfect the lower self is conquered and the Supreme Self is seen.

यत्करोषि यदश्नासि यज्जुहोषि ददासियत् ।
यत्तपस्यसि कौंतेय तत्कुरुष्व मदर्पणम् ॥[8]

"Whatsoever thou doest, whatsoever thou eatest, whatsoever thou offerest, whatsoever thou givest, whatsoever thou doest of austerity, O Kaunteya, do thou that as an offering unto Me."

As these virtues are the branches of Reverence springing from love, so do corresponding branches of vices grow out of Fear, which springs from hate in the presence of a superior. A constant attempt is made to belittle the superior, to pull him down to our own level, so that we may no longer have reason to

7 Bhagavad-Gītā, ix. 17—18.
8 Bhagavad Gītā ix. 27.

fear him. For when we are in face of a superior whom we regard as an enemy, we are naturally inclined to dread the exercise of his power, which we feel ourselves unable to resist, and we long to lessen this hostile power or to escape from its reach.

The hate-emotion directed to God shows itself in attempts to lesson the feeling of His greatness, to diminish the recognition of His powers. *Irreverence* is the commonest vice of this class, flippant careless speech and manner about sacred objects and sacred places, foolish jokes and idle laughter in speaking of the religious beliefs of others. This passes on into the vice of *Profanity* in coarse natures, and both are destructive of the finer emotions and should be sedulously guarded against. This dulling of the finer emotions leads on to complete alienation from religion, for God can be reached only through these finer emotions and by the virtues we have seen to be the offspring of love and as a man is driven further and further away by the repellent action of hate, he loses all sense of the divine Presence, and often lapses into entire ethical unbelief, which leads to evil living.

असत्यमप्रतिष्ठं ते जगदाहुरनीश्वरम् ।[9]

"The universe is without truth, without basis, without God, they say."

Reverence to the Sovereign, the head of the State, comes naturally after Reverence to God, the representative of whose power, justice, and protection he is on earth, if he be a true King, intent on the welfare of his subjects, always subordinating and sacrificing his own personal comforts and interests to those of his

9 Bhagavad Gītā. xvi, 8.

people, as did the ancient divine Kings, who give us the ideal of Kingship. The virtues spoken of above should be repeated in a lesser degree, in a subject's relation to his King. The virtues of *Loyalty, Fidelity* and *Obedience* are those which make a good subject, and the necessity of these for the prosperity of a nation is strongly insisted on. Manu says that the King was made by God to protect the world, and was made of particles taken from Indra, Vāyu, Yama, Sūrya, Agni, Varuṇa, Soma and Kubera.

As Indra, he is to shower benefits on his kingdom; as Vāyu, to know all that goes on; as Yama, to control his subjects; as Sūrya, to take taxes; as Agni, to be full of brilliant energy; as Varuṇa, to punish the wicked; as Soma, to give joy to his subjects; as Kubera, to support his people.[10] Bhīṣhma's discourse on the duties of King and subjects is most instructive; the King is to stand as God to his people, he being their protector and the guardian of all.[11]

The Itihāsa are full of statements as to the blessings enjoyed by a loyal people ruled over by a good King. As loyalty is insisted on, so are the corresponding vices of *Disloyalty, Treason* and *Rebellion* condemned, and the miseries are described of kingdoms that are a prey to anarchy.

Closely attached to the virtue of loyalty is that of *Patriotism*, in which the country is thought of as a collective whole, a living individual, to whom service is due. The King, in fact, is the embodied Majesty of the Nation, and loyalty to him grew out of patriotism of the purest kind.

Patriotism is a virtue that has its roots in several emotions; it grows out of veneration for the past of the country, admiration of

10 *Manusmriti*,vii.3,4.andix. 303-311.
11 *Mahābhārata*, Shānti Parva. lvi-xci.

its saints, heroes and warriors, its great men of every kind, of its strength, power and splendour; it identifies itself with the country by sympathy, feeling its joys and sorrows, its successes and reverses, its prosperity and adversity, as its own; it loves its natural beauties, and rejoices in its artistic and mechanical triumphs. The motherland, the country as a whole, is looked up to as an ideal, as an object of reverence, to be served and worked for above and beyond all else. Though, as a whole, the country is greater than the patriot, the patriot has the power of helping his country by his service; he gladly sacrifices ease, comfort, wealth, life itself, on the altar of his country. As a tender father seeks the good of his family so the patriot seeks the good of his land, and puts its interests before his own. The virtue of Public Spirit is but another name for patriotism, and the public-spirited man is the man who will exert himself for a public object even more earnestly and diligently than for a private one. The very expression "public spirit" instinctively embodies the truth that has been referred to so often as the very basis of morality—the Unity of all. Public spirit is the common spirit, the spirit of all the public, the spirit which is one in all the public; and the public-spirited man is he who—consciously or unconsciously—realises the oneness of the Self in all the members of that public to which he belongs; who feels that the good and the evil of each are the good and the evil of all the members of that public, and who acts accordingly, endeavouring to ameliorate the conditions of life for all.

As in the case of virtues and vices towards God, so in the case of virtues and vices to the State and its Ruler, it must be borne in mind that no man can free himself from the duty of incessantly endeavouring to base his mental attitude and his outer actions on the best reason he can reach up to, nor can he free himself from responsibility for acquiescence in flagrant injustice, or for allowing himself to be carried away by any mere public opinion which he knows to be wrong, or has not taken the trouble to test, although feeling that its accuracy is doubtful. There is a false loyalty—the lip-loyalty of the flatterer—which is far more dangerous and sinful than the apparent opposition of the honest counsellor, who gives unpleasant but wholesome advice, and there is a false patriotism that merely truckles to the prejudices of the ignorant.

सुलभाः पुरुषा राजन्सततं प्रियवादिनः ।
अप्रियस्य च पथ्यस्य वक्ता श्रोता च दुर्लभः ॥[12]

"Easy to find, O King! are the men that always speak the words that please. Difficult to find are the men, both those that hear and those that speak (gently), the words that are not pleasant but wholesome."

These virtues of patriotism and public spirit, directing the mind to ends beyond those of the personal separated self, are enlarging and ennobling to the character, and train the man to see a larger Self, and so to make some progress towards the recognition of the ONE. The public-spirited patriotic man is nearer to God than the man whose interests are restricted within a narrower area, and gradually he will widen out from love of country to love of humanity. Happy is the land whose sons are patriotic; she is sure to rise high amid the nations of the earth.

We have now to consider the duties owed to Parents and Teachers, who also stand as Superiors. These will include those that are shown to God and the King, and we may add to them the

12 Rāmāyaṇa, VI. xvi. 21.

virtues of *Gentleness, Trustfulness* and *Teachableness.* Perhaps no virtues are more strongly insisted on than those that a child owes to his parents and teachers, and down to the present time none are more characteristic of the true Āryan.

यं मातापितरौ क्लेशं सहेते संभवे नृणाम्।
न तस्य निष्कृतिः शक्या कर्तुं वर्ष शतैरपि॥
तयोर्नित्यं प्रियं कुर्यादाचार्यस्य च सर्वदा।
तेष्वेव त्रिषु तुष्टेषु तपः सर्वं समाप्यते॥
तेषां त्रयाणां शुश्रूषा परमं तप उच्यते।
न तैरनभ्यनुज्ञातो धर्ममन्यं समाचरेत्॥
त एव हि त्रयो लोकास्त एव त्रय आश्रमाः।
त एव हि त्रयो वेदास्त एवोक्तास्त्रयोऽग्नयः॥
त्रिष्वप्रमाद्यन्नेतेषु त्रींल्लोकान्विजयेद्गृही।
दीप्यमानः स्ववपुषा देववद्दिवि मोदते॥
सर्वे तस्यादृता धर्मा यस्यैते त्रय आदृताः।
अनादृतास्तु यस्यैते सर्वास्तस्याफलाः क्रियाः॥
यावच्चयस्ते जीवेयुस्तावन्नान्यं समाचरेत्।
तेष्वेव नित्यं शुश्रूषां कुर्यात्प्रियहिते रतः॥
त्रिष्वेतेष्विति कृत्यं हि पुरुषस्य समाप्यते।
एष धर्मः परः साक्षादुपधर्मोऽन्य उच्यते॥[13]

"The suffering which the mother and father endure in the birth of children cannot be compensated, even in a hundred years. Let him do always what is pleasant to these two, and also to the āchārya; in the satisfaction of these three all (the fruit of) austerity is obtained.

"The service of these three is called the highest austerity; without the permission of these let him not perform other duties.

---

13 *Manusmriti* ii. 227- 230, 232, 234, 235, 237.

"For verily these are the three worlds and the three Āshramas; these also are said to be the three Vedas and the three fires.

"The householder who neglects not these three, will conquer the three worlds, and in a shining body he will rejoice, as a Deva, in heaven.

"All duties are honoured by him who honours these three; for him who does not honour these, all rites are fruitless.

"As long as these three live, so long let him not do ought else; let him ever do service to them, intent on what is pleasant and beneficial.

"In (honouring) these three all is achieved that should be done by man; this is plainly the highest duty; all other is called a lesser duty."

Teachableness and obedience to the teacher are insisted on, and many rules were given intended to impress on the student the duty he owned to his preceptor. He was to be ever serviceable and careful not to offend, regarding the guru as his father in the highest sense.

उत्पादकब्रह्मदात्रोर्गरीयान्ब्रह्मदः पिता।
ब्रह्मजन्म हि विप्रस्य प्रेत्य चेह च शाश्वतम्॥

"Of the progenitor and the giver of the knowledge of Brahman, the giver of the knowledge of Brahman is the more venerable father; for the birth of the Brahman in the Brahmana is verily eternal, both here and after death."

Only to the dutiful pupil was knowledge given:

यथा खनन्खनित्रेण नरो वार्यधिगच्छति।
तथा गुरुगतां विद्यां शुश्रूषुरधिगच्छति॥[14]

---

14 *Manusmriti*. ii. 206, 207.

"As a man by digging with a spade obtains water, so he who does service obtains the wisdom enshrined in his guru."

The vices which grow out of hate in relation to parents and teachers include, as do the virtues, those named under the relation to God and the King, and we may add to them those of *Suspiciousness*, *Cowardice*, *Falsehood*, and *Insolence*. Where there is fear of one stronger than ourselves, suspicion inevitably arises, the expectation that he will use his power for our injury and not for our benefit. There is perhaps no greater poisoner of human relations than constant suspiciousness—the suspicious nature—for it casts a false appearance over everything, distorts and exaggerates actions, and supplies evil motives to the most harmless acts.

A suspicious nature sees hidden malevolence everywhere, and is always miserable because it is always afraid. Cowardice engenders falsehood, the putting on of a false appearance for the sake of protection against a dreaded exercise of hostile power.

When we come to study the reaction of the emotions of one person on those of another, we shall see that oppression, the part of the strong leads to the growth of these vices in the weak, and that these are the vices characteristic of the slave and the downtrodden.

Arrogance and superciliousness are attempts of the inferior to diminish the distance between himself and the superior, and are the reverse of the virtues of humility and teachableness. They render impossible any happy and mutually beneficial relation between parents and children, between teachers and pupils. The sweet natural ties which grow out of the love-emotion are violently disrupted by these evil growths of the emotion of hate, and they destroy the peace and happiness of families, as, when carried to a higher degree, they destroy the prosperity of States and the influence of religion.

The general attitude of the inferior to the superior is summed up by Manu as being that which is shown to the teacher:

विद्यागुरुष्वेतदेव नित्या वृत्तिः स्वयोनिषु ।
प्रतिषेधत्सु चाधर्माद्धितं चोपदिशत्स्वपि ॥
श्रेयःसु गुरुवद्वृत्तिं नित्यमेव समाचरेत् ॥[15]

"Such also constantly his conduct among teachers of learning, relatives, among those who hold him back from unrighteousness and give him counsel.

"Among his superiors let him ever follow the same behaviour as with his teacher."

In cultivating the virtues and weeding out the vices above mentioned, the young man should not forget one important consideration. His parents are given to him by his prārabdha karma, while this is not completely the case with his teacher, the element of present choice also entering into the latter relation for the most part. While therefore the duty of reverence and trust and submission without reserve, short of what involves the commission of a positive sin, is desirable towards parents, even if they are not as loving and considerate as parents ought to be, that duty is influenced by certain other considerations in the case of the teacher. The teacher is chosen either by the parents for the student in the days of youth, or by himself when he reaches years of discretion. In the first case, the authority of the teacher is the authority of the parents, delegated to him by them.

15 *Manusmriti*, ii, 206, 207.

If any doubt arises in the mind of the student as to whether that authority has been duly exercised, the student should at once consult his parents and abide by their decision. In the second case, should such a doubt arise, he must exercise his own judgment, as he did when first he chose the teacher, and if teacher and student duly understand their respective duties then the wisest and most useful course is for the student to say clearly and respectfully to his teacher: "Sir, there is such and such a doubt in my mind; kindly remove it;" and for the teacher to remove the doubt either by convincing the student of the rightness of the course adopted, or by altering that course, if indefensible.

The above is important to bear in mind, as the abuse of authority and the misplacing of trust are unfortunately but too common in the world. In India especially, where the spirit of devotion to teachers is strong, having come down from the time when the teacher was a true teacher, there is exceptional danger of the misplacing of faith, and consequently there is exceptional need for preserving a balance of mind and for rejecting false claims.

To the aged, *Respect* is the virtue which should ever be shown by the young, and they should ever be regarded and treated as superiors.

शय्यासनेऽध्याचरिते श्रेयसा न समाविशेत् ।
शय्यासनस्थश्चैवैनं प्रत्युत्थायाभिवादयेत् ॥
ऊर्ध्वं प्राणा ह्युत्क्रामन्ति यूनः स्थविर आयति ।
प्रत्त्युत्थानाभिवादाभ्यां पुनस्तान्प्रतिपद्यते ॥
अभिवादनशीलस्य नित्यं वृद्धोपसेविनः ।
चत्वारि तस्य वर्धन्त आयुः प्रज्ञा यशो बलम् ॥[16]

16 *Manusmriti*, ii. 119—121.

"He should not take the bed or the seat belonging to a superior; and he who is occupying a bed or seat should rise and salute him.

"A young man's prāṇas rise upwards when an old man approaches; rising, and saluting, he again recovers them.

"He who ever salutes and shows reverence to the aged, obtains an increase of four things: life, intelligence, fame and strength."

And so again:

अभिवादयेद्वृद्धांश्च दद्याच्चैवासनं स्वकम्।
कृताञ्जलिरुपासीतगच्छतः पृष्ठतोऽन्वियात्॥[17]

"Let him salute the aged, let him give them his own seat, let him sit by them with folded hands, let him walk behind when they leave."

This reverence to the aged is one of the most gracious virtues of youth and manhood, and one who shows it wins love and approval from all.

It is naturally accompanied with *Modesty*, a virtue which is a lesser degree of humility.

That obeisance to the aged is even physically beneficial to the young man is hinted in the second of the shlokas above quoted. By one of the laws of nature there is always a tendency towards equilibrium; as heat radiates from the warmer to the cooler, so strength and vitality go out from the stronger to the weaker. It has been proved by ordinary medical Science that invalids draw vitality from the vigorous, the feeble draw life from the healthier and stronger, and a large portion of the cures effected by

17 *Manusmriti*, iv. 154.

magnetism are due to this fact. In accordance with this law, the prāṇas of the young move out towards the old and the feeble but when the young man rises and makes obeisance, he at once creates in the mind of the elder the mood of benevolence and of giving instead of taking, and this mood sends back those prāṇas to the younger man.

Good manners to a superior involve respect, modesty, truthfulness, readiness to render service, an absence of fear, suspicion and conceit. A youth, who shows those virtues will always meet with favour, and will enjoy many opportunities of improvement in the company of his elders and superiors Such a youth is always welcome, and his elders will take pleasure in helping and guiding him, and giving him the benefit of their experience.

The vices which show themselves in relation to the aged include those noted in connection with the other classes of superiors, and *Disrespect* and *Conceit* may be added. The latter vice is peculiarly likely to arise, because the strength and vigour of the youthful body give it a physical superiority over the body of the aged, more obvious than the inferiority in experience and ripeness of judgment. *Impatience* is another vice that shows itself in this connection, the swift activity of youth being apt to chafe against the slowness of the aged.

No virtues need cultivation more in modern life than those dealt with in this chapter, for in the rush and hurry of the present day, and the self-assertiveness that flourishes in a competitive civilisation, these are the virtues most likely to disappear.

Religious virtues have decayed with the growth of misunderstood scientific facts, and reverence and faith towards God have been depreciated as weakness and credulity. But religious virtues are the foundation-stones of a strong and manly character, and are found in history in heroes and not in base and degenerate men.

Still more, perhaps, is visible the decay of a high-minded loyalty to the Monarch, and a patriotic fidelity to the State. This, as the student will learn from the careful study of history, is due to internal organic reasons, mainly the failure in duty to each other first of Rulers and then of the Ruled, after the divine dynasties of Kings were withdrawn, in order that humanity might be left to learn by painful experience how to stand on its own feet, with many falls and struggles, like an infant. The spread of general though superficial knowledge, the growth through bitter conflicts of democratic institutions, and the passing of authority into the hands of a majority – in the absence of the wise and experienced, or because of their inability to take up their duties—have hidden the true rights and duties of the Sovereign from careless eyes and minds. The one-sided exaggeration of the instruments of administration—cabinets, councils, parliaments, republican senates and congresses—has veiled the Governor, the King himself. In the course of these experiments of humanity, there have arisen, in consequence of the mistakes due to inexperience and selfishness, increasing poverty and distress, the strife of labour and capital, the growing disorganisation of society. The remedy for these lies in restoring right feeling between King and Ministers and Sabhā and people, in restoring right feeling between all the limbs and organs of the State, and in each and all performing their respective duties of protecting and ruling, advising, administering, and helping with loyalty, fidelity and obedience; in restoring, in fact, the ancient system on a higher level, with fuller knowledge, according to the law of cyclic growth. Perhaps it may be for Āryan youths, trained up in the ancient virtues, to restore to modern life the ideal of the true citizen, and to set again the example of the true gentleman, pious to his God and loyal to his King and Country.

That this may be so, it will be well to begin with the cultivation of these virtues in the family, where the Father and the Mother represent the superiors. The decay of reverence, obedience, respect and serviceableness to them is only too patent in modern Indian life. Here every youth can at once begin to copy the old ideals, and to restore in his own home the ideal of the perfect son. Eager attention to their wants, prompt and cheerful obedience to their wishes, frank confidence in their goodwill, trustful reliance on their deliberate judgment—these virtues will lay the foundation of the strong, dutiful, orderly character that will make a good citizen and a patriot.

In his relations to his teachers also, the student should strive to practise the appropriate virtues; and different as are the modern conditions between teacher and pupil from the ancient ones, yet the appropriate virtues might be cultivated, and the relation would then gradually again take on the affectionate intimacy of the older time.

To the aged also, the Indian youth should show unvarying respect, consideration and readiness to serve, utilising his physical advantages to supply their weaknesses, looking on aged men as his fathers, on aged women as his mothers, and showing ever to them the loving duty of a son.

Let, then, the young man study these virtues, and build them into his own character by repeated effort, earnest, deliberate and well-reasoned thought, and with reliance on the Divine Self. Then shall his own life be useful and honourable, and his motherland the better for his work.

VIRTUES AND VICES IN RELATION TO EQUALS

WE have now to consider how love and hate work out in the relations that arise between equals in the family and in society, binding them together or driving them apart accordingly as love or hate prevails. The relations between husband and wife, brothers and sisters, and between relatives of the same generation, those between friends, acquaintances and members of a society of similar age and standing, give rise to emotions which are rendered permanent as virtues and vices, constantly active in the family and in the community.

The virtues belonging to the family among those of the same generation are those which gradually lead the JīvāJīvātmā to recognise his unity with others, and so prepare him for the recognition of the One Self in all He finds himself surrounded by a small band of JīvāJīvātmās whose conditions, interests, hopes and fears are much the same as his own, with whom he enjoys and suffers, rises and falls, is prosperous and unsuccessful, from whom his own interests cannot be disjoined. As he practises the family virtues and sees the happiness ensured by the practice, or as he falls into the family vices and sees the sorrow and discomfort arising from them, he gradually learns that to bring about general happiness he must treat all men as his brothers, as members of one family, and that the miseries that afflict humanity all have their root in the neglect of the practice of brotherliness.

Affection, or love between equals, is the form of the love-emotion here to be cultivated. It will show itself in *Kindness* of thought, speech and action. Kindness of thought is at the root of kindness of speech and of action, and one who guards himself against all harshness of thought will not err in speech or in act. We have already seen what great stress Manu lays on control of speech, and sweetness, gentleness of speech should be cultivated in all family relations as well as in those of the outer world:

यस्य वाङ्मनसी शुद्धे सम्यग्गुप्ते च सर्वदा।
स वै सर्वमवाप्नोति वेदान्तोपगतं फलम्॥
नारुन्तुदः स्यादार्तोऽपि न परद्रोहकर्मधीः।
ययास्यो द्विजते वाचा नालोक्यां तामुदीरयेत्॥[1]

"He whose speech and mind are pure and ever carefully guarded, he obtains all the fruit that is obtained by means of the Vedānta.

"Let him not, even though distressed, cut another to the quick (by his speech), nor meditate acts of hostility to others; let him never utter the malignant word that disturbs (the mind of the hearer)."

This injunction, addressed primarily to superiors in their intercourse with inferiors, covers all human intercourse, and is, perhaps, nowhere more needed than in family relations, where close knowledge of the weakness of each is apt to barb the tongue to cutting speech. Again, the right family relations are well sketched in the following:

---

1 *Manusmriti*, ii. 160, 161.

न पाणिपादचपलो न नेत्रचपलोऽनृजुः ।
न स्याद्वाक्चपलश्चैव न परद्रोहकर्मधीः ॥
ऋत्विक्पुरोहिताचार्यैर्मातुलातिथिसंश्रितैः ।
बालवृद्धातुरैर्वैद्यैर्ज्ञातिसंबन्धिबान्धवैः ॥
मातापितृभ्यांयामीभिर्भ्रात्रा पुत्रेण भार्यया ।
दुहित्रा दासवर्गेण विवादं न समाचरेत् ॥[2]

"Let him not be aimlessly restless with his hands and feet, nor with his eyes, nor crooked (in his conduct), nor aimlessly restless with his tongue, nor meditate acts of hostility to others.

"With the Ṛitvik, Purohita, Āchārya, maternal uncle, guest, dependent, children, the aged, sick, physician, kinsfolk, connexions by marriage, relatives,

"Mother, father, female relative, brother, son, wife, daughter, servant-folk, let him not enter into altercation."

And, after recounting the different worlds with which the persons above-named are connected, as representing in the organisation of human society, the position of the worlds in the organisation of the Brahmāṇḍa, so that if a man be at peace with them, he is at peace with these worlds, Manu concludes:

भ्राता ज्येष्ठः समः पित्रा भार्या पुत्रः स्वका तनुः ॥
छाया स्वा दासवर्गश्च दुहिता कृपणं परम् ।
तस्मादेतैरधिक्षिप्तः सहेतासंज्वरः सदा ॥[3]

"The elder brother is the same as the father; the wife and the son are one's own body.

---

2 *Manusmriti*, vi. 177, 179, 180.

3 *Manusmriti*, iv. 184, 185.

"The servant-folk are one's shadow, the daughter is most deserving of compassion; therefore, though slighted by these, let a man bear it ever undisturbed."

The right relation between husband and wife, between father and sons, and between brothers, is beautifully shown in the *Rāmāyaṇa* in Shrī Rāma and Sītā, the four divine sons and Dasharatha, and the four brothers, Shrī Rāma, Lakṣhmaṇa, Bharata and Shatrughna. These are the models a youth should set before himself, and he should shape his conduct on these.

Of the good wife, Manu says:

प्रजनार्थं महाभागाः पूजार्हा गृहदीप्तयः ।
स्त्रियः श्रियश्च गेहेषु न विशेषोऽस्ति कश्चन ॥
उत्पादनमपत्यस्य जातस्य परिपालनम् ।
प्रत्यहं लोकयात्रायाः प्रत्यक्षं स्त्रीनिर्बन्धनम् ॥
अपत्यं धर्मकार्याणि शुश्रूषा रतिरुत्तमा ।
दाराधीनस्तथा स्वर्गः पितृणामात्मनश्च ह ॥
पतिं या नाभिचरति मनोवाग्देहसंयता ।
सा भर्तृलोकानाप्नोति सद्भिः साध्वीति चोच्यते ॥[4]

"There is no difference whatsoever between Shrī (the Devī of Prosperity) and the wife in the house, who is the mother of the children, who brings good fortune, who is worthy of worship, the light of the home.

"Of the bearing of children, the protection of those born, the continuance of the world-process, woman is evidently the only source.

"Children, religious ceremonies, service, marital happiness, heaven for one's ancestors and oneself, depend on the wife.

---

4 *Manusmriti* xi. 26—29.

"She who, ruling her mind, speech and body, wrongs not her husband, she obtains the heavenly world with her husband and is called by the virtuous a Sādhvī."

एतावानेव पुरुषो यज्जायात्मा प्रजेति ह ।
विप्राः प्राहुस्तथा चैतद्यो भर्ता सा स्मृताङ्गना ॥[5]

"This is the extent of the man, his wife, himself and his children; Brāhmaṇas thus declare that the husband and wife are known as the same."

This view of a family as a unit, as really one life, is the view which alone gives a sure foundation for the family virtues, and the indissolubility of the marriage tie among Āryans grows out of this idea. Father, mother and children are one, and each should love the other as himself; what pleases one should please all: what saddens one should sadden all. All the virtues can be practised in the family, which is a little world in itself; the parents represent the superiors, the children among each other the equals, the children to the parents the inferiors. A youth who cultivates the virtues in his home will be ready to show them out in the wider field of the world, and will be equipped for the duties of a good citizen. He can practise there all that he will require in his manhood, and develop all the qualities which will make him a faithful friend, an honourable, courteous and upright gentleman, a brave and unselfish patriot.

Tender affection between brothers and sisters lies at the root of family prosperity, and we may see in the story of the Pāṇḍavas how this consoled them in adversity and raised them finally to the height of prosperity.

---

5 *Manusmriti*. ix. 45.

Courtesy and Consideration for the feelings of others are enjoined as general principles of conduct, and noble bearing and manners have ever been held to be characteristic of the true Āryan.

Thus speech must be true, but also pleasing:

सत्यं ब्रूयात्प्रियंब्रूयान्न ब्रूयात्सत्यमप्रियम् ।
प्रियं च नानृतं ब्रूयादेषधर्मः सनातनः ॥[6]

"Let him speak the true, let him speak the pleasing, let him not speak an unpleasing truth, nor speak a pleasing falsehood; this is the ancient law."

Of course, there are occasions when it is the plain and positive duty of the person concerned to tell the truth even though it be unpleasant, as when a person in authority rebukes or corrects a subordinate. But even in such cases he should speak gently, and such instances of special duty do not justify uncalled-for and rude language or sharpness, which only mar the due effect of the rebuke and prevent its entering into the heart of the reproved.

Good manners are very apt to be undervalued in modern times, partly because of the hurry and rush of modern civilisation, and partly from ignorance. But this undervaluing is a mistake. Good manners spring from a good heart and a gentle nature, and show kindness and refinement of character. They imply self-control and a sense of self-respect and dignity, and many difficult social situations, which cause quarrels among ill-mannered people, are passed through without any trouble or ruffle by the nobly mannered. Soft words, courteous gestures, pleasant smiles, dignified bearing, make social intercourse refreshing and a source

6 *Manusmriti*. ii. 138.

of enjoyment, and the young Hindu should sedulously cultivate the noble manners of the elder generation, and thus sweeten the tone of modern society. Even gold becomes more beautiful by being refined and a noble and strong character is beautified by courtly bearing.

Hospitality is a virtue on which great stress is laid, and the guest must ever be honoured as a Deva.

संप्राप्ताय त्वतिथये प्रदद्यादासनोदके।
अन्नं चैव यथाशक्ति सत्कृत्या विधिपूर्वकम्॥
तृणानि भूमिरुदकं वाक्चतुर्थी च सूनृता।
एतान्यपि सतां गेहे नोच्छिद्यन्ते कदाचन॥
अप्रणोद्योऽतिथिः सायं सूर्योढो गृहमेधिना।
काले प्राप्तस्त्वकाले वा नास्यानश्नन्गृहे वसेत्॥[7]

"Let him offer to the guest who has come a seat, water and food, hospitably according to his power, in accordance with rule.

"Grass (for seat), room, water, and, fourthly, a kind word—these are never wanting in the houses of the good.

"The guest sent in the evening by the (setting) sun must not be sent away by the householder; whether arrived at a convenient or inconvenient time, he must not remain in the house unentertained."

That there was as much travel, with its beneficent results, in ancient India as there is now, when the means of locomotion were not so easy and rapid as they are to-day, was due solely to the general prevalence of this virtue, and the regarding of hospitality as an essential part of religion. The continuous pilgrimages from shrine to shrine and from city to city with all

7 *Manusmriti*. iii. 99, 101, 105.

their educative effects in broadening men's minds and experience, and in promoting affection and good-will between different and distant communities, by bringing them into familiar intercourse with each other—were only made possible by the generous provision of houses of rest, and of food and clothing, on an immense scale, by the voluntary hospitality and charity of the well-to-do.

Uprightness, Fair Dealing, Trust, Honour, Straightforwardness, Urbanity, Fidelity, Fortitude, Endurance, Co-operation—these are virtues which are necessary for happy and prosperous social life. Where these are found, the life of a community or of a nation is peaceful and contented, and men who show out these virtues in their characters make good citizens and lead happy lives.

Readiness to forgive injuries is a virtue necessary for peaceful living, for all, at times, do some wrong to another, moved by passion, or envy, or some other evil emotion. Readiness to forgive such wrong is a sign of a noble disposition, and *Magnanimity* includes this readiness, as well as the large-heartedness which makes allowance for the weaknesses of others, and takes a generous view of their motives and actions.

Toleration is an allied virtue that may be practised towards equals or towards inferiors—the recognition that the Self expresses itself in many ways, and that none should seek to force on another his own views or his own methods. Tolerance has always been a characteristic of Hinduism, which has never sought to convert men from their own faith, nor to impose on those within its own pale any special form of intellectual belief. The variety of philosophic views embraced within its Circle, as shown in the six Darshanas, testifies to the tolerance and wide-mindedness which have ever marked it. This tolerance is based on the belief in the One Self, and the reverent acceptance of the infinite variety of Its intellectual manifestations. Hence Hinduism has ever been permeated by the large-hearted toleration which is the very spirit of Īshvara; all are His; all paths by which men seek God lead to Him; as men walking from opposite quarters reach the same city, though walking in opposite directions, so men from all quarters, seeking God, meet in Him at last. It is foolish and childish, then, to quarrel about the ways.

ये यथा मां प्रपद्यन्ते तांस्तथैव भजाम्यहम्।
मम वर्त्मानुवर्तन्ते मनुष्याः पार्थ सर्वशः।[8]

"However men approach Me even so do I accept them, for the path men take from every side is Mine, O Pārtha."

Even when want of sufficient growth and knowledge keeps men away from the higher and attached to the lower manifestations of Deity, even then it is the One Īshvara who inspires their faith in the lower forms suited to their undeveloped intelligence, and it is He who gives the perishable fruit on which their desires are fixed.

कामैस्तेस्तैर्हृतज्ञानाः प्रपद्यन्तेऽन्य देवताः।
तं तं नियममास्थाय प्रकृत्या नियताःस्वया॥
यो यो यां यां तनुं भक्तः श्रद्धयार्चितुमिच्छति
तस्य तस्याचलां श्रद्धां तामेव विदधाम्यहम्॥
स तया श्रद्धयायुक्तस्तस्याराधनमीहते।
लभते च ततः कामान्मयैव विहितान्हितान्।।
अन्तवत्तु फलं तेषां तद्भवत्यल्पमेधसाम्।[9]

8 *Bhagavad-Gītā*. iv. II.

9 *Bhagavad-Gītā*. vii. 20—23.

"They whose wisdom hath been rent away by desires go forth to other Devas resorting to various external observances, compelled by their own natures.

"Any devotee who seeketh to worship with faith any such aspect, I verily bestow the unswerving faith of that man.

"He, endowed with that faith, seeketh the worship of such a one and from him he obtaineth his desires, I verily decreeing the benefits.

"Finite indeed the fruit; that belongeth to those who are of small intelligence."

येऽप्यन्यदेवताभक्ता यजंते श्रद्धयान्विताः ।
तेऽपि मामेव कौंतेय यजन्त्यविधिपूर्वकम् ।।
अहं हि सर्वयज्ञानां भोक्ता च प्रभुरवेच ।
न तु मामभिजानन्ति तत्त्वेनातश्च्यवन्ति ते ॥[10]

"Even the devotees of other Devas who worship, full of faith, they also worship Me, O son of Kuntī, though contrary to the ancient rule.

"I verily am the enjoyer of all sacrifices, and also the Lord, but they know Me not in essence, and hence they slip."

Such is the noble and liberal teaching of Hinduism, and it should shape the thoughts of every true Āryan, so that he may never fall into the error of trying to belittle or injure any of the religions of the world. Let him be tolerant even to the intolerant, and thus set a good example.

This tolerance of the religious beliefs, views, and *bona fide* opinions of others should not be misunderstood to mean

---

10 *Bhagavad-Gītā*. ix. 23—24.

toleration of and acquiescence in the active infliction of wrong by the wicked on the righteous and the innocent.

A good man, while forgiving as far as possible wrong done to himself, should endeavour to set right—by gentle means at first, and, if these do not succeed, then by stern ones in accordance with the law of the land—all wrong inflicted on others. Such is the duty that Shrī Kṛiṣhṇa expressly laid upon Arjuna, with the whole weight of the wisdom embodied in the *Bhagavad-Gītā*. Nor should any action be mistaken for intolerance which is only of the nature of counselling or education, even though it be the education of public opinion, or constitutional and sober endeavour to wean men from injurious ways, or a thoughtful discussion with the express object of eliciting truth. What is condemned is only the bigoted pride which imagines itself to be in sole possession of Truth, and would visit with punishment the slightest deviation from the course laid down by itself.

The vices which grow out of the hate-emotion when it prevails among equals correspond on the side of evil to the virtues we have been studying on the side of good. It may almost shock the student to see very common faults of character classed as the fruits of the hate-emotion, and yet if he thinks a little he will see that they have the marks of that emotion, as they drive men apart from each other, separating them and setting them in antagonism to each other, and that is clearly the result of the repellent force, which is Hate and not Love.

The opposite of *Kindness* is *Harshness*, which shows itself but too often in the family as *Moroseness*, *Sullenness*, *Irritability*, and *Peevishness*—very common failings, and the destroyers of family affection and peace. These faults bring dark shadows into the family circle, in strong contrast to the light spread by the kind and sunny temper, and are but forms of *Anger*, one of the root manifestations of the hate-emotion. Manu classes anger and harshness among the sins which are to be specially avoided:

नास्तिक्यं वेदनिन्दां च देवतानां च कुत्सनम्।
द्वेषं स्तम्भं च मानं च क्रोध तैक्ष्ण्ये च वर्जयेत्॥[11]

"Let him avoid unbelief, censure of the Vedas, and slighting of the Devas, hatred, obstinacy, pride, anger, and harshness."

And this is natural, for these are sins which are especially productive of misery, and probably most of the daily troubles of life which cause harassment and worry are due to anger in one form or another. It is classed by Shrī Kṛiṣhṇa[12] with lust and greed as forming part of the triple gate of hell and as one of the āsuric characteristics.[13] The mind confused by anger is easily hurried into other sins, and it is one of the chief roots of crime. *Impatience* is one of its smaller manifestations, and the student who is intent on improving his character should be on his watch against even this comparatively minor form of his great enemy. The steady effort to be patient with, kind to, all, will gradually eradicate from his character the fault of Anger.

Harsh Fault-Finding, Backbiting, Slander and *Abuse* are the opposites of Magnanimity. They proceed from the same source as Irreverence, etc.

The way to correct these faults is always to examine whether the defect for which we wish to condemn another is not present in ourselves. As Vidura says to Dhṛitarāṣhtra:

---

11 *Manusmriti*. iv, 153.
12 *Bhagavad-Gītā*, xvi. 21.
13 Ibid. 4.

राजन्सर्षपमात्राणि परछिद्राणि पश्यसि।
आत्मनो बिल्वमात्राणि पश्यन्नपि न पश्यसि॥

"Thou seest the holes of another, though small as the mustard-grain, O King!; thine own, that are large as the Bel-fruit, even seeing thou ignorest !"

Rudeness, Churlishness of bearing, a rough manner, are the faults which are the opposites of courtesy and consideration. They are exceedingly common in modern days, and are spreading in modern India. They are signs of a coarse and vulgar nature which – uncertain of its own power and of the respect of others—tries to assert itself by loudness and to force itself on the attention of others, and it is thus always a mark of weakness. The gentle courteous bearing of a man conscious of his own strength and position contrasts with the rough rude manner of a weak man, unfit for the position he is in and trying to cover his unfitness by self-assertion.

Crookedness, Unfairness, Deceit, Infidelity, Quarrelsomeness, Fickleness, Instability, are other common faults which appear in the relations between equals, and cause many troubles alike in family and social life. They all help to disintegrate families and nations, and men who have these vices are bad citizens, and sooner or later fall into well-deserved contempt and distrust.

Vindictiveness and *Revengefulness* are the opposite of the readiness to forgive, which we have seen is a part of magnanimity, and they perpetuate troubles, keeping them alive when they might die by forgetfulness. The wish to return an injury suffered by inflicting an injury in return is a sign of complete ignorance of the working of the law. A man who suffers an injury should think that he has inflicted an injury on another in the past, and that his own fault comes back to him in the injury now inflicted on himself. Thus he closes the account. But if he revenges himself now, he will in the future again suffer the equivalent of the revenge he takes on his enemy. For that enemy will not be likely to think that he has been justly punished, and will nurse revenge again, and so the chain of claim and counter-claim will continue endlessly. The only way to get rid of an enemy is to forgive him; revengefulness stores up trouble for the future, which will inevitably come to the revengeful person, and the injuries we suffer now are only our own revenge coming home to ourselves. No one can wound us unless our own past places a weapon in his hands. Let a student remember this when someone injures him; let him pay his debt like an honest man, and have done with it.

Intolerance is a vice which has caused immense destruction in the world, especially in modern times. Endless wars have been caused by men of one religion wishing to impose their faith on men of another creed, and torrents of human blood have been shed in the name of God. Persecutions stain the page of history with blood and tears, and we may see a striking example of national ruin caused by religious persecution in the case of Spain, once the greatest of Western Powers, whose decay dates from the days when she slew by thousands, the Jews and the Moors, and finally expelled the survivors because their faiths differed from her own.

Sectarianism, when it is bitter and quarrelsome, is a form of intolerance, and in modern India, this subtle enemy of religion is undermining the ancient noble toleration of Hinduism. Sectarian bigotry divides Hindu from Hindu, and blinds them, by magnifying unessential differences, to the essential unity in which they are rooted. As men lose the spirit of religion and cling chiefly to its forms, caring only for the external ceremony and not even understanding its meaning and the objects it is intended to bring about, they become more and more bigoted and intolerant, and split up into more and more numerous parties. Thus religion, which should bind men together, is changed by intolerant bigotry into a disintegrating force. The remarks which apply to religious intolerance in India apply with even greater force to social convention in India as well as elsewhere. In India, they have a special application because of the inseparable interblending of social customs with religious, so that the paltriest and most trifling customs, having their origin in some temporary need on some special occasion, rapidly assume a deeply religious and permanent importance.

The true Āryan must avoid intolerance and bigotry as he would avoid poison, and should remember that it is utterly alien from the spirit of his ancestral religion. He must look on all Hindu sects as members of his own family, and refuse to quarrel with or to antagonise any.

And he must look outside the pale of Hinduism, and see in the other religions that surround him rays of the same Spiritual Sun in which he himself is basking, and thus spread peace over India, and make possible for her a united national existence. Let his religious watchword be "Include," not "Exclude," since the Self is One.

VIRTUES AND VICES TOWARDS INFERIORS

TO COMPLETE THE outline of the virtues and vices evolved in human relations, we must consider those which arise in a man's relation to his inferiors, accordingly as he is ruled by the love-emotion or by the hate-emotion. The virtues in this case will come under the general name of *Benevolence*, the will to do good to those who are weaker than ourselves; the vices will come under the general name of *Pride*, the sentiment which causes a man to look down on others, and to do them injury, according to the activity of the hate-emotion in him.

Love showing itself to an inferior inevitably takes the form of Benevolence, and its commonest form is that of *Compassion* and *Pity*. Weakness, ignorance, folly, arouse in the man ruled by the love-emotion, the desire to help the person who is at such disadvantage, by bestowing on him strength, knowledge, wisdom. Compassion at once springs up in him, as by *Sympathy* he feels the weakness, ignorance, and folly as though they were his own, and thus becomes anxious to remove them, to raise the sufferer above them. From these virtues springs *Beneficence*, the active carrying out of the will to do good, the performance of actions expressive of the goodwill felt.

In the conduct of parents to their children we see these virtues brightly shown forth. The weakness of the child, its dependence and helplessness, awaken the tenderness of the parent, and he becomes filled with compassion and pity for the little creature that is so unable to protect and support itself. These virtues express themselves in softness of language, caressing gestures, encouraging looks and smiles, so that the child may lose the feeling of its own littleness and feebleness, and may in effect share and direct the strength and skill of its elders, and thus supply its own deficiencies. Compassion and pity seek, as does all love, to lessen the distance between itself and its object, to raise its object towards itself. It allays the apprehension which might arise in the inferior, in presence of strength greater than his own, by gracious aspect of *Kindliness*, expressing in every way that there is no reason for fear. Where it sees timidity and shrinking in the weak, it increases the outward manifestations of *Gentleness*, *Softness* and *Sweetness*, becoming the gentler as the object of compassion is the more fearful and hesitating.

The stronger, the older, those who are in any way superior, should always remember to practice these gentle virtues towards the weaker, the younger, the inferior in any way, and should especially bear in mind that their exercise is the more needed when the inferior shows any of the manifestations of fear, of the idea that the superior is a hostile power, likely to inflict injury on him. Power is so constantly used to oppress and to injure, that the first feeling of the inferior in the presence of his superior is apt to be one of fear, and it is necessary to remove this by a manifestation of love.

Compassion and Pity readily give rise to *Protection* of the weak, whenever they are threatened by those stronger than themselves, and in protecting them *Heroism* appears, the cheerful risking of oneself for the sake of a weaker. The Hero is the man who risks his life for the good of another who is in need of help, without grudging the cost. The name is most often given to the warrior who gives his life for his King and his country, or to the martyr who dies for his faith; but it is deserved equally by many, an unknown man and woman, who in ordinary human circumstances sacrifices life or health for others—the physician or nurse, who dies, worn out by strenuous exertions in aid of the plague-stricken; the mother, who rescues a child from death by ceaseless tendance, careless of her life and health, caring only to supply everything that the babe needs; the bread-winner, who becomes exhausted by excessive toil, sacrificing leisure, strength, health, that the weaker ones dependent on him may not feel the pinch of starvation. The heroic virtues—*Courage*, *Valour*, *Endurance*, etc.—have for the most part their root in Compassion and in a sense of duty to the weak, a sympathy with them in their sufferings and a desire to remove these sufferings; they are most readily evoked in presence of the inferior in need of help. In fact, when they appear in the relations to superiors and equals, it is always in connection with the *need* of these persons, and the man showing the heroic virtues has something to give of which they are in want. It may be a King who, though occupying the position of a superior to his soldiers individually, needs their help for the protection of his crown; or a brother who, normally equal, has a deficiency which his brother can supply at the moment, and so it still remains that the Hero is always the giver, and leaves in his debt those for whom he pours out his life or his possessions. Compassion, Protection, Heroism, are virtues that especially befit Kings and Rulers.

Liberality is a virtue, again, which is called out by the presence of inferiors, and the readiness to give, the virtue of *Charity*, is one which has been placed by Hinduism in the very first rank. दानम्, Gift, has always been an essential part of every sacrifice, and the feeding and supporting of true and learned Brāhmaṇas has been no less essential. By these rules, men were trained to sacrifice part of their wealth for the benefit of others, and thus, were led onwards to a true understanding and acceptance of the great Law of Sacrifice.

Manu says:

श्रद्धयेष्टं च पूर्तं च नित्यं कुर्यादतन्द्रितः ।
श्रद्धाकृते ह्यक्षये ते भवतः स्वागतैर्धनैः ॥
दानधर्मं निषेवेत नित्यमैष्टिकपौर्तिकम् ।
परितुष्टेन भावेन पात्रमासाद्य शक्तितः ॥
यत्किंचिदपि दातव्यं याचितेनानसूयया ।
उत्पत्स्यते हि तत्पात्रं यत्तारयति सर्वतः ॥[1]

"Let him diligently offer sacrifices and oblations with faith; these, if performed with faith and with rightly earned wealth, become unperishing.

"Let him always observe the duty of charity, connected with sacrifices and oblations, with a contented mind, having sought with diligence a worthy recipient.

"Something verily ought to be given ungrudgingly by him who has been asked, for a worthy recipient will surely arise who will save him from all (sins)."

The way in which charity should be done is very clearly laid down by Shrī Kṛiṣhṇa, who divides gifts, according to their nature, into sāttvic, rājasic and tāmasic.

1 *Manusmriti*. iv 226—228.

दातव्यमिति यद्दानं दीयतेऽनुपकारिणे।
देशे काले च पात्रे च तद्दानं सात्त्विकं स्मृतम्॥
यत्तु प्रत्युपकारार्थं फलमुद्दिश्य वा पुनः।
दीयते च परिक्लिष्टं तद्दानं राजसं स्मृतम्॥
अदेशकाले यद्दानमपात्रेभ्यश्च दीयते।
असत्कृतमवज्ञानं तत्तामसमुदाहृतम्॥[2]

"That gift given to one who does nothing in return, saying, 'It ought to be given,' at right place and time and to a worthy recipient, that gift is accounted sāttvic.

"That verily which is given for the sake of receiving in return; or again with a view to fruit, or grudgingly, that gift is accounted rājasic.

"That gift which is given at unfit place and time and to unworthy recipients, disrespectfully and contemptuously, that is declared tāmasic."

That charity should be done with courtesy and gentle kindliness is a rule on which much stress is laid. We often read in the Itihāsa, directions to show careful respect in the making of gifts; charity should ever be gracious, for even a trace of contempt or disrespect makes it, as above said, tāmasic.

The idea of showing to weakness the same courtesy that is extended to rank and superiority, a tender deference and consideration, comes out strongly in the following shloka:

चक्रिणो दशमीस्थस्य रोगिणो भारिणः स्त्रियाः।
स्नातकस्य च राज्ञश्च पन्था देयो वरस्यच॥[3]

2 *Bhagavad-Gītā*, xvii. 20—22.
3 *Manusmriti*, ii. 138.

"Way should be made for a man in a carriage, for one who is above ninety years old, for a sick person, for one who carries a burden, for a woman, a Snātaka, a king and a bridegroom."

Similarly we find, when directions are being laid down as to the giving of food to people in the due order of their position, preference over all is given to the weak:

सुवासिनीः कुमारीश्च रोगिणो गर्भिणीस्तथा।
अतिथिभ्योऽग्र एवैतान्भोजयेदविचारयन्।।[4]

"Let him, without making distinctions, feed newly-married women, young maidens, the sick, and pregnant women, even before his guests."

Another virtue which should be cultivated in relation to inferiors is what may, for lack of a better term, be called *Appreciativeness*, the full recognition of all that is best in them.

This recognition, generously expressed, has a most encouraging effect, and stimulates them to put out all their energies. The sense of weakness, of littleness, of inferiority, tends to paralyse, and many a man falls simply by lack of confidence in his own powers. A word of hearty appreciation gives the encouragement needed, and acts like sunshine on a flower, causing the whole nature to expand and glow.

Patience is also most necessary in all dealings with inferiors; lesser ability generally implies less quickness of understanding, less power to grasp or to perform, and the superior needs to practise patience in order not to confuse and bewilder the inferior. With children and servants this virtue has special opportunity for exercise, and its existence in the elders is peculiarly helpful and

4 Ibid. iii. 114.

peace-making in the family. Strength should be used to help and support weakness, not to crush and terrify it is a sign of a truly great and strong nature. Appreciativeness and Patience are specially needed in parents and teachers.

The vices that spring out of the hate-emotion to inferiors are of the nature of *Pride*, the sense of superiority in the separated Self, looking down on those below it, and desiring to still further lower them, in order to make its own superiority more marked. The character of a man filled with pride is graphically described by Shrī Kṛiṣhṇa:

इदमद्य मया लब्धमिमं प्राप्स्ये मनोरथम्।
इदमस्तीदमपि मे भविष्यति पुनर्धनम्॥
असौ मया हतः शत्रुर्हनिष्ये चापरानपि।
ईश्वरोऽहमहम्भोगी सिद्धोऽहं बलवान्सुखी॥
आढ्योऽभिजनवानस्मि कोऽन्योऽस्ति सदृशो मया।
यक्ष्ये दास्यामि मोदिष्ये.................... ॥[5]

"This to-day by me hath been obtained, that purpose I shall gain; this wealth is mine already and this also shall be mine in future.

"This enemy hath been slain by me, and these others I shall also slay. I am Īshvara, I am the enjoyer, I am perfect, powerful, happy.

"I am wealthy and well-born; what other is there that is like unto me? I will sacrifice, I will give, I will rejoice."

Such a man, looking down on his inferiors, seeking only his own gain and his own advantage, will see in them only persons to be used for his own purpose. To them he will show the vices of

---

5 *Bhagavad Gītā*. xvi. 13—16.

Scorn, *Contempt*, *Arrogance*, *Disdain*, expressing in words and actions his sense of the distance between himself and them. His own bearing will be marked by *Aggressiveness*, *Self-assertion*, *Overbearingness*, implanting dislike and hatred in those with whom he comes into contact, unless they are thoroughly dominated by the love-emotion.

If his inferiors possess anything which he desires, and he is able to deprive them of it without danger to himself, he may fall into robbery and murder; and he will use his superiority to oppress and enslave. The characters of many such men may be studied in history—tyrants, oppressors, causing widespread destruction and misery, and thus sowing in the breasts of the oppressed the seeds of evil passions which sprang up into a crop of revolt, bloodshed and anarchy. Manu sternly condemns the Kings that fail in the duty of protection:

अदंड्यान्दंडयन्राजा दंड्याश्चैवाप्यदंडयन् ।
अयशो महदाप्नोति नरकं चैवगच्छति ॥[6]

"The king that punishes the innocent and punishes not the criminal, he goeth into infamy and hell."

In smaller fashion these evils are reproduced in the family and in society, where the superiors show out the fruits of hate instead of love. The tyrannical father or master implants and fosters in his children and servants the vices of the oppressed, and creates the evils which he later endeavours in vain to destroy.

Hauteur, *Haughtiness*, *Reserve*, are subtler forms of this same emotion, and work much mischief when they appear between those between whom cordiality, affection and openness alone

6 *Manusmriti*, viii. 128.

should prevail. They should be very carefully guarded against by the student, when he comes to deal with those who are younger than he, or those towards whom nature or circumstances place him in the position of superior to inferior. He should ever remember that the duty of the superior is to bring the inferior up to his own level so far as is possible, and not to keep him inferior and constantly remind him of any distance that there may be between them. If he makes the mistake of following the latter course, the probable, nay the certain, result will be that he will drive the inferior either into a slavish cringing and timidity and nervousness, on the one hand, or rebellion, pride and contempt, on the other. But if he behaves otherwise, and treats his inferior as his equal, then the probability, almost the certainty, is that the inferior will readily see his superiority, and treat him with due respect and reverence. It is they who selflessly help others to rise that are honoured, not they who desire aggrandisement for themselves.

Let the student then remember in all his relations with his inferiors to cultivate sympathy and compassion and active beneficence. If in the family he shows these virtues to the younger and to the servants, in his later life in society and in the nation, these virtues will still mark his character, and he will become a true philanthropist, a benefactor of his community and of his country.

THE REACTION OF VIRTUES AND VICES ON EACH OTHER

IN order that a youth may understand how to improve his own character and meet the difficulties and temptations which surround him, it is important that he should know how the virtues and vices of people react on each other. By understanding this, he will know how to be on his watch against evil reactions, and how to promote the good both in himself and in others.

The general law is that an emotion and the virtue or the vice that is its permanent mood—when exhibited by one person to another, provokes in that other a similar emotion, virtue or vice. An exhibition of love calls out love in response; an exhibition of hate is answered by hate. Anger produces anger; irritation causes irritation; gentleness brings out gentleness; patience is responded to by patience. If the student will observe himself and his neighbours, he will soon discover for himself the reality of this law, and will see how the moods of people are affected by the moods they meet with in others. One ill-tempered man will set a whole company jangling; one sweet tempered man will keep everybody at peace.

This is the general law, working among average people who are equals, in whom the love emotion and the hate-emotion are both present and are about equally balanced. When the people are not equals, but one is inferior to the other, the emotion, virtue or vice shown by one will also produce in the other one similar in kind, but *corresponding* to the one first shown, not *identical* with it. Thus an exhibition of love to an inferior will produce in him love, but the nature of the love will be governed by this inferiority, and will be reverence, trust, serviceableness, and so on. Benevolence will be answered by gratitude, and pity by confidence. An exhibition of hate to an inferior will produce in him hate, but the nature of the hate, again, will be governed by his inferiority, and will be fear, deceit, treacherous revenge, and so on. Oppression will be met with sullenness, and cruelty with silent vindictiveness. The good will produce good, and the evil, according to the general law; but the particular nature of the good or evil shown will be governed by the relative positions of the individuals concerned.

When we come to study exceptional people, another law comes in. If an exceptionally good man is observed, one in whom the love-emotion is dominant, then it will be seen that he does not answer anger with anger, but that when anyone shows the vice of anger to him, he meets it with *the opposite virtue*, kindness; if a man shows him the vice of pride, he meets it with the opposite virtue, humility; if a man shows him the vice of irritation, he meets it with the opposite virtue, patience; and so on. The result is that the vice is checked, and very often the person who showed it is led, by the exhibition of the opposite virtue, to himself imitate that instead.

In the case of an exceptionally bad man, one who is dominated by the hate-emotion, there is but too often an exhibition of vice in answer to an exhibition of virtue. A man showing humility to such a one is met by pride; gentleness provokes insult; patience stimulates oppression.

We have thus two laws:

1. Among ordinary persons, emotions, virtues and vices provoke their own likenesses, or correspondences.
2. In persons who are definitely dominated by love or hate, emotions, virtues and vices provoke the appropriate subdivision of their own dominant emotion.

Let us consider instances.

Two ordinary men, equals, meet, and one, in a bad temper, speaks angrily; the other flares up in reply, answering angrily; the first retorts, yet more angrily; and so it goes on, each getting more and more angry, until there is a furious quarrel. How often have friends been parted by a quarrel beginning in the ill-temper of one.

Two other men meet, and one, in a bad temper, speaks angrily; the other answers softly; with a pleasant smile and friendly gesture; the anger of the first, finding no fuel, dies down, and the soft words and smile awaken an answering smile, the anger is gone, and the two walk off arm-in-arm.

A man in whom the hate-emotion predominates, superior to another, treats the latter with insolence and threat, trying to force him to yield to his will. The inferior meets this exhibition of evil emotion with fear, distrust and sullen submission, and in his heart springs up the desire for revenge, which he nourishes until an opportunity occurs to injure the superior. The latter, seeing the fear and sullen submission, shows yet more insolence and scorn, the sight of the fear increasing the original contempt for the inferiority of the other. This again leads to increased fear and distrust and more slavish submission, with growing longing for revenge, and thus the vicious cycle is repeated over and over again.

A superior man, in whom the love-emotion predominates, comes into contact with an inferior, in whom the very sight of his superiority arouses fear and distrust. The exhibition of these vices moves him to pity and compassion, and he answers the fear and distrust by increased kindness of manner and softness of language. The inferior thus met is soothed and encouraged, and his fear diminishes to slight timidity of approach; this in its turn disappears, and is replaced by trust and confidence in the goodwill of the superior. Thus in his heart, the love-emotion is aroused, and the seeds of virtue are implanted instead of those of vice, and the relation established is one which conduces to the happiness of each of the persons concerned.

The Itihāsa and Purāṇas have many instances of this interplay of emotions, of the effects of the exhibition of virtues and vices reacting on each other. Bhīma's scornful laughter over the blunders of Duryodhana awakens hatred and the desire for revenge in the bosom of the latter, and the hatred grows into one of the causes of the destructive war between the Pāṇḍavas and the Kurus. Kaushalyā's angry reproaches as to the treatment of Rāma are met by Dasharatha with gentle humility, and she is quickly moved to repentance and shows loving humility in return. Arjuna's fear at the sight of the Virāt-rūpa is allayed by Shrī Kṛishṇa's gentle words and re-assumption of His ordinary form. These stories are told for our instruction, that we may learn how we should meet and conquer evil, not by imitating it, but by exhibiting the opposite emotion. A fire is easily put out at the beginning, but when it has fuel thrown into it, it grows and increases, and at last destroys all with which it comes into contact.

The student will now understand the scientific nature of the command addressed to their followers by all the great Teachers, never to return evil with evil, but always with good. We can understand now why and how it has ever been said: Do unto others as you would they should do unto you.

यदन्यैर्विहितं नेच्छेदात्मनः कर्मपूरुषः ।
न तत्परेषु कुर्वीत जानन्नप्रियमात्मनः ।
यद्यदात्मनि चेच्छेत तत्परस्यापि चिन्तयेत् ॥[1]

This is the summary of the Science of Conduct, because the "others" are in very truth "you" yourself. Says Manu:

क्रुध्यन्तं न प्रतिक्रुध्येदाक्रुष्टः कुशलंवदेत् ।[2]

"Let him not be angry again with the angry man; being harshly addressed, let him speak softly."

The *Sāma-Veda* says:

सेतूंस्तर दुस्तरान् अक्रोधेन क्रोधं सत्येनानृतं ।[3]

"Cross the paths difficult to cross; (conquer) wrath with peace; untruth with truth."

Says the Buddha:

"Hatred ceases not by hatred at any time: hatred ceases by love."

And again:

"To the man that causelessly injures me, I will return the protection of my ungrudging love; the more evil comes from him, the more good shall flow from me."

1 *Mahābhārata*, Shanti Parva, lxxvi.
2 *Manusmriti*. vi. 48.
3 *Araṇya-gana, Arka-*. 2nd *Prapāthaka*.

And again:

"He who bears ill-will to those who bear ill-will can never become pure; but he who feels no ill-will pacifies those who hate.......Overcome anger by not being angered; overcome evil by good; overcome avarice by liberality; overcome falsehood by truth."

Says Lao-tze:

"To those who are good, I am good; and to those who are not good, I am also good; and thus all get to be good. To those who are sincere, I am sincere; and to those who are not sincere, I am also sincere; and thus all get to be sincere."

Says Jesus Christ:

"Love your enemies, bless them that curse you, do good to them that hate you, and pray for them which despitefully use you and persecute you."

Evil is only perpetuated when it is returned, the wrong emotion growing ever stronger as it is fed with fuel of its own nature; but as water poured on fire is love poured on hate. Happiness can only be gained as the fires of hatred are quenched, and this can only be done by love, generously and freely outpoured.

This is the general law, and, in the strictest sense, this is the last method of finally changing an evil nature into a good one. But, in dealing with limited times and spaces, it becomes the duty of those occupying special positions or offices in the community, or finding themselves in special situations created by the exceptionally evil, to apply the law of justice and punishment rather than that of charity. The Sovereign and the judge, representing the aspect of nature embodied in the law of equilibrium, find it their special duty to punish the evildoer and suppress the disturbances caused by crime, restoring the equilibrium of society. Apart from this special modification, the general law holds good.

Further, understanding the nature of virtues and vices, and their relations to and reactions upon each other, the student will now be in a position to cultivate deliberately the love emotion in his own nature, with the virtues which are its permanent moods, and he will also learn to awaken and stimulate these in others by exhibiting them in his own conduct.

In his superiors he will awaken benevolence, compassion, tenderness, by showing to them reverence, service, dutifulness and obedience; and if he meets a superior who shows any harshness or pride, he will check in himself the feeling of fear which springs up, and by showing a frank humility and a confidence in his goodwill, he will awaken the love-emotion, and will thus turn the harshness into kindness and the pride into compassion.

In his equals he will ever seek to arouse affection by showing it himself, to win them to kindness by showing kindness, to courtesy by showing courtesy, to uprightness by showing uprightness. When they show any of the vices of the hate-emotion to him, he will restrain the similar emotion that leaps up in himself in answer, and will deliberately show the opposite virtue that belongs to the love-emotion, and will oppose kindness to unkindness, courtesy to rudeness, uprightness to deceit. Thus he will not only avoid increasing the mischief caused by others; but in those others themselves, unless they be exceptionally evil, he will arouse right emotion and help them to improve.

In his inferiors he will try to plant the seeds of trust and confidence, encouraging them by his gentleness and patience, and eradicating all suspicion and fear. When he finds an inferior showing these vices, he will not allow himself to give way to scorn and contempt, but will increase his own gentleness and patience, and gradually lead the weaker into the love-relation with himself that will make their relations mutually pleasant.

If these principles ruled human relations in the family, the community, the nation, how changed would be the aspect of the world. How quickly would discord change to peace, storm to calm, misery to happiness. To use knowledge to guide action, so that right action may spring from right knowledge, should be the aim of every student of the Science of Ethics. Only thus can character be built; and India's sons become worthy of their motherland. The student of to-day is the citizen of tomorrow. May right instruction lead him to noble life.

"I am giving you complete union of hearts and minds, in which ill-feeling finds no place. Even as the cow is pleased with the new-born calf, so let one be pleased with another. Let the son follow his father and be of one mind with his mother.

Let the wife remain in peace with the husband and speak sweet words to him. Let not the brother bear malice towards brother or sister. Let all become harmonious with each other, and let all treat each other well."

INDEX

A

B

C

D

T

U
